God Made Only One of Me

Sally & Mike

A Triumphant Journey from Pain to Hope

Stay Strong & Courageous!
Thank You for being so Kind.
God Bless You,
Love Diane

Written by Diane Dike, Ph.D.

Foreword by Michael W. Smith

Second Chance
with Saving Grace, inc
Transforming Lives

Eagle, CO
Printed in the USA

GOD ONLY MADE ONE OF ME
By Diane Dike, Ph.D.
P.O. Box 673
Eagle, CO 81631

www.DianeDike.org
DianeDike@aol.com

ISBN 978-1-932738-46-9
Library of Congress Control Number: 2008925747

First Edition
Printed in the United States of America
Published by Second Chance with Saving Grace, Inc.
 Our mission is to bring hope and encouragement to the masses.
*Disclaimer-This memior contains facts and memories of the author. Some names were changed or left out

Original and Final Edit by Paul E. Dike
Cover Picture by Karen Peck, Edwards, Colorado
Cover, interior design support, and logo design by Jodi Grasso

DEDICATED

I dedicate this body of work to my devoted husband Paul and to God, praising Him for the grace He has given me to live this life. xxoo ✝

Gracie

To:

_____

From:

_____

Occasion:

_____

Date:

_____

Message:

_____

_____

_____

_____

TABLE OF CONTENTS

*Uttering a word is like striking
a note on the keyboard of
the imagination.*

— Ludwig Wittgenstein

ACKNOWLEDGMENTS

There is more hunger in the world
for love and appreciation than for bread.

—Mother Teresa

This book has taken a lifetime to compile. It's the result of much encouragement, prayer, and the contributions of many people.

First and foremost I must thank my dear husband, Paul. You are my knight in shining armor. You painstakingly made sense out of my erratic writing to bring forth the truth and understanding I so desired to share. You asked the tough questions and helped me get this story in written form, spending hours of your biking, hiking, and skiing time to help. I couldn't have completed this book without you. Jesus loves me through you and I am so thankful.

Mom and Dad: thank you for being a great example of never giving up. Mom, your battle with cancer and Dad, your fight against Parkinson's, encourage me to continue to fight my battles. You always give and do the very best you can. I appreciate you. I'm blessed and I thank God for you both. You taught me well. I love you.

My sisters: I cherish, pray for and love you. These are the days of our lives, thank you for sharing them with me.

Michael W. Smith: when I look back over some of the best times in my life, there you are in person or through your music. You have made my story so much more interesting! You introduced me to a wonderful Tennessee family that I treasure. Keep up the good work. Your music inspires me and has helped me through some of my darkest hours, even before I came to know you as a dear friend and brother.

Thank you, Pastor Ron Bos: in the midst of a pressure-filled ministry you were obedient. You turned your car around and gave me a message and intervened; otherwise, this book never would have been written.

Pastor Tommy Schneider: thank you for all the support you have given Paul and me over the years. Every hospital visit, prayer, and hug made a difference. To your lovely bride, Debbie: you didn't know that I was several months into this project when you shared a heartfelt prayer that I should write my story... I'd planned to stop. Thank you for being a vessel of revitalization; your prayers encouraged me to continue with this monumental project!

A very special thank you to Max Lucado, Denise Jones, Don and Laura Lyn Donahue, David Carr and Third Day, Andrea Roth-Moore, Millie Farthing, Rob Lohman, The Ride, Jan and Dave Lack, Kate Negri, Chrissy Wooley, Christ Community Church, Inwood Baptist Church, First Baptist Church of Winter Haven, Dody Davis, Mike Macaluso, IG Times-Patricia Kelly, Liz, Eric, and Taylor Kennedy, the Second Chance Board, The Vail Church (formally called Vail Bible) and Doug Lockwood. The support, friendship, and encouragement you offered during this project helped keep me afloat.

Karen Peck: you are wonderful, always willing to join me on a project or adventure. I'll never forget our day together doing the photo shoot from which the cover of this book came. You always make time for me. Bless you, and your wonderful family.

Debbie Brockett, Jewel Sample, Bob Armstrong, Jodi and Craig Grasso: your vision, friendship, support, and gracious editorial feedback have helped bring this project to reality. Your camaraderie has proven invaluable and means much to me professionally and personally. Jodi I couldn't have made it to the finish line without you. I love you!

Rich and Terry Wahl, Jo Ellen and Greg Nash, George and Carol MacKenzie: I appreciate your friendship now and especially when I was in Mexico. You have no idea what a comfort you were at such a difficult time!

I especially thank John David, Kirsten Webster and Calvary Chapel of the Vail Valley for the scripture cards made during John David's benefit concert; I plastered my hospital room walls with them. Knowing you cared helped me battle through the dark nights in Mexico, as did speaking those powerful scriptures out loud. Thank you for all the wonderful meals you delivered to our home while I convalesced from many health battles. Your assistance has buoyed my spiritual and physical strength over the years.

Gracie: you are my little treasure from Heaven. {Yes, I am talking to my dog. I do it every day.} We were made for each other. You work hard accomplishing your life-saving tasks for me daily. Thank you for being so obedient. You deserve much credit for keeping my blood circulating, alerting me, and improving the quality of my life, especially during all the hours of writing this story from my bed. Thank you for your service, unconditional love, and help. Sniff-sniff, snuggle!

Father, Son and Holy Spirit: You are what this is all about. You know how much I look forward to being with You in Heaven. Yet, I am here at this particular time and place, hoping I can make a difference for You. May You be glorified in this labor of love. May hearts see what You can do with a life that is surrendered to You no matter how broken or messed up it may be. Thank You for NOT giving up on me.

To all those I love and all those who love me: stay strong and courageous! You are an important part of my life and have helped make the tapestry of my story worth revealing. It would be impossible to name each of you, but you know who you are. Thank you! I celebrate living this life with you, hugs and kisses as Gracie wags her tail!

Get The Most Out Of This Book

To the reader, my new friend: I have prayed for you, thought of you, and looked forward to meeting you as I wrote this book. I would like to hear that you made it your own by writing in the margins, underlining or highlighting special thoughts as I do with my favorite books. I pray you will find encouragement and insight, comfort and consolation as the story resonates with your life. I don't think it's by accident that you have it in your hand, right now. I believe that what He did for me, He wants to do for you. I entrust you with some of my deepest hurts and greatest joys. Please don't skip the Prologue and Introduction they include important details. As Leo Buscaglia said, "Life is God's gift to you. The way you live your life is your gift to God. Make it a fantastic one."

I would like to thank the non-profit groups who work tirelessly to save discarded animals, help hurting people and work to find cures for rare diseases. Profits from the sale of this and our children's book series, *The Adventures of Gracie and Diane* will go to support these efforts and those wonderful organizations that reach out to the hurting of this world, including our non-profit, Second Chance with Saving Grace, Inc.

THANK YOU to all the wonderful people who patiently waited for this book and believed in it and me, including:

Mom and Dad	Jim and Barbie Allen
Joanne Provencher, my sister "Jo"	Chris and Nedra Bonta
Maureen Vynlecka, my Godmother	Carol and Doug Richards
	Jim and Susie Burns
Gene & Henrietta Brumbaugh	Marc Lemay

Janet Haley
Nancy Dunlap
Jo-Ann D'Agostino
The Billcheck's
Rick and Tina Jones
George F. Coolidge
Brenda Chafman
Heather Heminger
Rosa de Lourdes Garcia
Alan J. Nitchman
Steve Polstra
Denise L. Smith
Mrs. Kathryn Hill
Florrie Ellen Hicks
Anita Kingsley
"Pumkin" Barbra Smith
Rena and Gary Roth
Rachel Griffin
Lee and Ada Fowler
Joann Cottle
Pat Johnson
Joyce Quillen
Jane Richevine
Janie Pulford
Durk and Susie Price
Mary Anne Jones
Ron and Robin Leoppke
Rhonda and Bill Todd
Barbara and Paul Smith
PawsUpPetSupply.Com
Andi Saden-"The Carrot Lady"
Rick and Collen Gardner
Dick Blaire
Larry (who has gone home to be
with the Lord) and his wife
  Basille Blaesing
Jim Metzger Owner of the Vail
  Valley UPS Stores
Mark, Danielle and Aaron Lobe
Dan, Larau and Hannah
  Harbridge
Diane, Michael and Mario Bruns
Kristi Mullen
Eileen M. Wright
Christa Whitaker
Cindy Connors
Bill Doty and Doty's Farm &
  Garden Supply, Inc.
Jerry Ptak
Judith Snyder
Chris Meissner and Diane Faul
Charlotte Rosen and IG Ollie
Renee Krabbe
Donna Courtney
Jan, David Smith and Marty
Grace and Loren Kotz
Kelly and Peter Strople
Randall and Carrie Calvart
Jay Heinlein
Stephen Hultquist
Cindy Engles
Sherri Connell
Ellie Parsons
Cyle, Maranda, Melinda and Cary
My prayer group

Those I may have missed

Thank You! ❤

Stand strong and courageous!
Arms Outstretched,
Diane and Gracie

FOREWORD

*Seek first the Kingdom of God
and His righteousness and all these
things shall be added unto you.*

— Matthew 6:33

By Michael W. Smith

Infectious smile... eternal optimism... contagious joy... these are just some of the descriptions that come to mind when I think about my friend Diane. Her courage in the face of great obstacles has always challenged and encouraged me. But her unwavering faith in the God she serves is probably the greatest lesson of her life. I see in her the walk by faith that is tested and found true: trusting and waiting in the Lord; casting her cares on Him; the incredibly hard "filling up the sufferings of Christ" in her own body. But I don't remember a time that Diane has ever complained about an ache or pain or worse. She instead serves even harder, caring for her family (including Gracie), blessing all those around her and giving some killer massages! Her days on the road on a few of my tours provided many road-weary musicians some much-needed therapy, always bathed in prayer.

I am very thankful that God brought Diane into my life many years ago in Beaver Creek, Colorado, for "just a massage." What ensued has been a deep, warm

Backstage with my brother and my friend Michael

friendship that now includes Paul and, yes, Gracie. Her Service Dog's name could easily be her own: Diane lives in a state of grace that few do this side of Heaven. Enjoy getting to know this vibrant woman through the pages of this book.

Love you, Happy D!
Michael W. Smith

George Lucus Ranch, CA
Recording, Healing Rain

In the studio at the George Lucus
Ranch, CA

Cutting Michael's hair before the
Christmas party in his home in TN

In Michael's home in
Beaver Creek, CO

PROLOGUE

 *Nobody cares how much you know, until they
know how much you care.*
— Theodore Roosevelt

May of 1995 seems like a long time ago and yet like yesterday. My plan
was set: I would kill myself today.

*No more pain, suffering, disappointment, guilt, or shame. I wouldn't
have to fake it anymore. What would it matter and who would care if
tomorrow came and I wasn't there? God couldn't be mad at me for wanting
to end this painful life since He surely is as disappointed with me as I am
with myself. I will end it and get what I deserve. I called the poison control
800 number to be sure I had enough pills, afraid that I couldn't even kill
myself correctly.*

"Hello," I said, with a shaky voice and trembling hands. "I'm calling about my son. He just started taking amitriptyline, for depression,
and I was wondering how many pills it would take to kill a person?" My
voice trailed off; *just tell me so I can get this over with.*

The woman hesitated. "That's a very powerful and dangerous drug.
If you think your son is suicidal, you should take him to the hospital,
immediately."

"Yes, I understand, I don't think he is in danger right now. I just
wanted to know for precautionary reasons. I mean, is a week or a month's
supply dangerous? You know, if taken all at once... that way I can be sure
to keep the extra amount away from him," *trying to sound motherly.*

She started asking all sorts of questions as the beads of sweat began
to build on my forehead: "How old is your son; how long has he been
on the antidepressant; have you talked to the doctor about this?" She
knows! I slammed the phone down. The next thing I knew, I was being
whisked away to the psychiatric ward.

Completely humiliated I wondered, *"How had my life come to this?
On suicide watch with no privacy, even in the bathroom?* I was stripped of

essentials so I would not hurt myself. The other "inmates" were absorbed with their own hells, walking around with blank looks on their faces; some were talking to themselves. The wary eyes of the nurses carefully watched my every movement, often with a look of pity.

I wanted to shout, "*I'm not crazy!*" But in the deep recesses of my mind I wondered if indeed I was. I settled on to the edge of my pristine bed and sobbed a river of tears into a teddy bear that the staff mercifully allowed me to hold after hours of uncontrollable weeping.

It's not crazy to want to die, especially when you're as empty, sick, and tired as I am. Is it? I truly believed the world would be better off without me and that I wasted air every time I took a breath. I cursed the day I was born and begged God to put me out of my misery.

Through my puffy eyes I imagined this was the lowest my life could go, but I was wrong...

INTRODUCTION

Being unwanted, unloved, uncared for, forgotten by everybody, I think that is a much greater hunger, a much greater poverty than the person who has nothing to eat.

—Mother Teresa

As exciting and difficult as some of the pages of my life may be, the final chapter is not yet written. But so far, my story is filled with sadness and joy, despair and hope, defeat and victory—like your life, I suppose. Although I have brought trouble on myself through bad decisions, much of my pain has come from circumstances and events beyond my control. I share my story so you will know that you are not alone in the midst of your trial, bankruptcy, diagnosis, disappointment, or divorce... If you don't give up, good can come from your pain. Reflecting on my life has been difficult, yet if my story can encourage or help just one person, the endeavor will be worth it, and I will not have lived in vain.

I have a rare, incurable, life threatening blood disease that affects every fragment of my body. It's called cryoglobulinemia, and no one knows what causes it or how to cure it. It's painful! It's debilitating with symptoms much like multiple sclerosis, arthritis, diabetes, Chrohn's disease, cancer, and lupus. It has weakened my body, organs, and immune system so much that I have fallen prey to many other diseases, syndromes, and maladies that work daily to erode the quality of my life. I know that things could be worse, yet this knowledge does not always bring comfort.

Cryoglobulinemia attacked me in my early twenties, and I didn't handle it well. I was not prepared to face the fact that my life would never be the same as this silent killer began to travel throughout my body, tricking it into vicious cycles of attack. How would I ever come to terms with the fact that I was trapped in a body that no longer functioned "normally" as I suffered daily with the knowledge that my illness could take a limb, my heart, my sight, or my life without a moment's notice?

When diagnosed I was completely unprepared for the grief that assaulted me, and for the anger I felt toward everyone, especially myself. Living with this ticking time bomb has been challenging. It struck like an earthquake and revealed cracks in my foundation and marriage. My husband and I were not equipped to make the necessary repairs and my life spun out of control. As I lost my health, everything around me seemed to lose meaning. I pushed my husband, family, and friends away. Eventually, they gave up on me just as I had and I lost precious loved ones forever.

One day my throat tightened against the tears as I asked, "Why, Lord?" He answered, "My grace is sufficient for you. Focus on Me, not the circumstances and I will take you through." This divine reply comforted me, but fear still gripped and directed my behavior. I quickly realized I was being squeezed like a tube of toothpaste and I didn't like what was coming out, evidence of how little I trusted my Lord.

We all have challenges. Dealing with them can drain our emotional and dwindling physical bank accounts. Initially, I lived in denial. I decided that my disease wasn't who I was but simply something to get over. Much to my chagrin, I quickly discovered that my illness had everything to do with who I was. If I wanted to see tomorrow, I had to make drastic changes in the way I lived.

Daily, I feel like I have a fresh case of the flu with swollen glands, headaches, and exhaustion. My body aches, itches, swells, discolors, gets sores, and when I walk, it feels like sharp rocks or seashells are stabbing the bottoms of my feet. Because of systemic inflammation, I sleep on pegs that stick into my back trying to reset nerves that scream with pain. As I write this my left leg looks like it was beaten with a baseball bat (both feel like it). I've got embarrassing sores on my scalp and hematuria (blood in my urine). My vision is affected with black spots that make it hard to focus. I try to act as if I'm fine. Who wants to be around someone who is hurting or doesn't feel well most of the time?

I don't want to be left out but included and invited to join in activities with friends and family. However, there are days when I can't hide how I'm suffering. Consequently, I feel that I'm a terrible burden, and discouragement sets in when I must use my wheelchair, or when my husband has to carry me. As a result, I can feel depressed, unworthy and unnecessary—as though I don't matter or have anything to offer anyone and it's hard to see any purpose in living. I struggle daily with facing the truth about my predicament and real life sentence.

When one day at a time is too long, I have to take it one second at a time. I try to live each day as if it were my last. Still, year after year, living this way is difficult, draining, and peculiar. I continually read Jeremiah 29:11: "For I know the plans I have for you, says the Lord. They are plans for good and not for evil, to give you a future and a hope." These words of wisdom remind me that God indeed has a plan, even for my broken life. And so, I fight on.

I've looked death in the eye several times yet the Lord hasn't taken me home. I'm here, learning lessons like being thankful even for the pain that keeps me on my knees dependent on God. Every day I wake up, I choose to accept the day as a miracle, ready to see His glory in my challenge and the opportunity to show what He can do with a life surrendered to Him. I believe in miracles, because I am one.

The Purpose in Writing This Book

My purpose in writing this book isn't to wallow in the sorrows of my past or present challenges. Rather, it is to reflect a revolutionary HOPE that I found in a revolutionary man. The terrors of life can erode our courage and strength but they also offer lessons to be learned. By sharing both the terrors and the lessons authentically, I pray that you may realize that you are not alone. Victory and triumph are within your reach if you hold on—if you never give up! I'm here to tell you, You are close to breaking through to where dreams do come true! Do NOT give up!

One of the biggest blessings in my journey has been Gracie, my small Service Dog. She is a lighthouse in this rough and stormy sea, my unexpected life-saver, and gift from God. She's been trained to perform impor-tant and life sav-ing tasks. She improves the quality of my

Gracie

life by enhancing my circulation with her lifesaving heat and retrieving items when I am bound to my wheelchair or my hands are too tender to pick them up. She also alerts me before my disease is about to hit hard so I can make necessary changes to avert a disaster. Soon, you will learn how one prayer changed my life forever and that sometimes angels have fur on their wings.

Cardinal Mercia said, "We must not only give what we have; we must also give what we are." I've made this my motto for living. Here I offer you a part of what I am while I learn to live while I am dying. After all, we will all die and being ready may help us learn how to truly live.

A prayer for us:

Thank you; Lord, for allowing me the privilege of sharing my story honestly to encourage others to never give up. Give us the strength to be who You have created us to be and do what You have called us to do! You give and take away; we bless Your holy name in either case. For You are God, and we are not. Please bless each heart reading this now. Reveal Your truth that will set them free and renew their strength. For You are a true friend. And Father, if You are willing, please take this cup of suffering, not my will, but Yours be done, with the simple faith of a child I pray. Amen. ♥

"I am yours, save me." —Psalm 119:94

CHAPTER 1

KEEPER OF THE HAPPY

*The best way to cheer yourself up
is to try to cheer somebody else up.*

— Mark Twain

I Vowed To Make A Difference

I wanted to fix everyone and everything. I wanted everyone to be happy and I desperately wanted to be happy too. There is a secret to happiness that I've learned along my journey; through the pages of this book, I will share it with you. Are you in the midst of challenging circumstances? Have you wondered, "Is life worth living? Do I matter? Why me?" I invite you on an adventure to find hope. No matter what you are going through there is hope for you.

    I'll begin with a little background so we can get to know each other. My parents have been in love for almost fifty years. Mom's name is Joan Patricia (Nealon). She is a spunky Irish-Catholic who had a rough upbringing when her father abandoned the family just after she was born. Dad's name is Bernie Robert Provencher and he is a stoic French-Canadian-Catholic. He came into the world just as his eleven year-old sister was dying of leukemia.

    My parents are "salt of the earth" people with "old school" ways. They dedicated their lives to providing for their three chil-

It all began with a dance. On Oct. 1, 1960 my parent's got married.

My mom was about to turn 26 and dad was 29.

dren, Jacqueline Marie, Joanne Barbara, and me, Diane Joan. Dad says we four girls are his ticket to heaven.

Mom and Dad adore their five grandchildren. It's amazing that Mom changed diapers for nearly forty years. I am eternally grateful for the sacrifices my parents made and for the home they provided, often filled with the fresh aroma of apple pie, home cooked meals and chocolate chip cookies. They are good neighbors, always willing to help others change oil, fix fences, mow lawns, bake cakes, take in mail, and water flowers. They taught us the value of community service and the responsible use of natural resources by cutting coupons, shutting lights off, and never wasting water. Thriftiness and efficiency were paramount values in our home. My parents are hard working, well-thought-of people. As the years have marched on they can't keep up as well but their hearts of gold still shine through in their desire to do good, fulfill the rituals of their faith and help others. We are good friends now and I adore them yet, that was not always the case.

October 23, 1966

I interrupted the world on a cool Massachusetts afternoon October 23, 1966, causing my mother to miss her own birthday cake—I was an inconvenience right from the start. Dad warned Mom that she was going to have me on her birthday but they decided to throw the party anyway since big celebrations were a family tradition. After the meal, mother started feeling poorly, even as those in attendance anxiously awaited the cutting of the homemade flower covered marble cake. Dad said, "We better get going to the hospital or you are going to have that baby right here on the patio." They made it just in time and I dashed into the world, seven pounds fifteen ounces, a little after 4:00 p.m. Even then it seemed I had a burning sense of destiny; I had things to do, places to go, people to meet and nothing was going to hold me back.

Rascals

My sisters and I enjoyed entertaining others from an early age. We put on plays and organ recitals for my parents, guests, or just ourselves. Shirley Temple, Carol Burnett and Tim Conway were some of our favorite skit performers. We pretended to be news-women and frequently hid a tape recorder under the dinner table to record relatives gossiping or telling jokes. When we played it back for them, they would chuckle or cover their faces in embarrassment as Mom scolded us and then shared in the laughter. Joanne still has some of those tapes and we enjoy a hearty laugh even today.

When I was one

In our basement we set up a classroom and played school (Jackie was a good teacher and still is today). For some reason, Meryl Streep reminds me of her. She was book smart and five years of maturity ahead of me. Because of this and the fact that Joanne and I shared a bedroom, I was closer to Jo while growing up. I loved climbing the musky willow trees down by the river. And I could entertain myself for hours making mud pies, watching bugs, riding my banana seat bike, rolling in the autumn leaves and watching the March winds spin my colorful hand held pinwheel. No matter what, we always ran to meet the bell-ringing ice cream truck that traveled through our neighborhood. Sometimes Mom would allow us to enjoy an Italian ice for twenty-five cents on a hot afternoon. The smell of grape transports me back to that childhood memory.

No Family Is Perfect

No family is perfect or without conflicts and we are no exception. Our family operates at an emotionally charged frequency where a trivial situation often mutates into a full-fledged crisis. My mother often says, "Wouldn't it be nice if we could all get along." My father does everything he can to keep the peace and when his four girls do not get along, it is very important to him that everyone "get over it" and "be happy." He even buys Cheer detergent. He likes the idea of a "happy" basket of laun-

Easter Sunday Lowell, MA--me, Joanne and Jackie

dry. Yet, unhappiness, in spite of all we have been through, hovers over us even while we try to accept and love each other unconditionally.

I too want everyone to be happy. It seemed like an innate part of my nurturing personality so it was only natural that I took after my father and assumed his role as "keeper of the happy."

Feeling loved and good enough was all I ever really wanted but somehow that acceptance seemed to allude me most of my life. An oddball by nature, I didn't fit in. There was an eerie enemy that lingered doing anything he could to steal my joy and keep me from moving forward. My personality, upbringing, and circumstance seemed to intensify the prospect of trouble. In spite of that detail, I vowed to make a difference wherever I could. Rather than focusing on my problems, nagging doubts and fears, I focused on helping and reaching out to others. It seemed to take the spotlight off of my own inadequacies.

Misunderstood Love

My grandmother, Nana, frequently asked, "Are you for real?" She usually asked this after watching me perform some random act of kindness—like giving my favorite toy away or hugging a stranger. Her tone made me feel as though I did something wrong or that I was peculiar. No one in my family was "touchy feely" and they wondered where it came from in me. Often joking that the nurse must have switched me at birth. Even in kindergarten, I would chase the boys home from the bus stop to give them kisses. I never understood the chasing part of this ritual because they needed my love, didn't they?

I was helpful to anyone who needed it: new students, teachers, and the underdog. If you needed a friend, you could count on me. However, sometimes my helpfulness was misinterpreted. Throughout my school years my teachers often wrote on my report cards that I was a "busybody."

My parents didn't seem to understand my loving nature. One cold and rainy day Mom was over-stressed and tired. With my five-year-old eyes, I looked at her across the big front seat of our station wagon as we waited for my sisters to finish their organ lessons. The rain trickled down the big windows and the windshield wipers thumped, I thought, *Maybe Mom would feel better if I sat closer to her.* I moved her purse to the right of me and scooted across the seat, expecting her to reach down and wrap her gentle but strong arm around me to pull me in close and say, "What a good girl you are." Instead, she looked down and asked, "What are you doing? Are you a weirdo or something?" *How was I supposed to answer a question like that?* I quickly slid back across the seat and put her purse where I longed to be.

Jackie's 8th brithday Lowell, Joanne, Jackie and me

My sisters soon got into the station wagon and we pulled away. I brushed away the tears dribbling down my cheeks, feeling stupid and unlovable. Although my mother may have been preoccupied or responded in the only way she knew how because of her own rearing, it doesn't change the fact that my five-year-old mind and heart interpreted this incident as rejection. The seeds were planted and I began to translate people's dismissal or puzzlement of, or, about my love as rejection, leading to a lifetime battle with low self-worth.

I Want To Help Others Get Better

Childhood experiences mold us into who we are today. Learning to build our lives on a strong foundation that cannot be swayed by every unreliable emotion that we feel or how others treat us is key. I didn't always know this but now it helps me realize that even if rejected, loving and helping others is a vital part of being human and of my personality and it is okay! Challenging moments can build perseverance, character, and hope; we will get bitter or we will get better. I always seek to get better and I want to help others get better too.

It's a gift and a curse to be sensitive. The world can be so abrasive and overwhelming but then also bristle with colors and sensations that can be easily missed if not sensitive to them. It's a funny balance. Finding my place in this world has been a challenge. I frequently don't see things the way others do and because of this, I feel abnormal or left out of some secret knowledge that appears to come easily to others. A song called, *Place In This World,* written by Michael W. Smith asks the questions I've struggled with my entire life: "Where do I belong? How do I fit in? Is there a purpose and plan, a vision I can call my own? And among the millions, God, can you still hear me? Do I matter? Do You care? Show me! Help me!" These questions plagued my mind for many years as I desperately "roamed through the night."

I've concluded that God made me this way for a reason and it's okay to be me, even if I feel like a fish out of beautiful blue water. I've come to realize through scriptures in the Bible that I am "just passing through." C.S. Lewis said it this way, "If I find in myself a desire which no experience in this world can satisfy, the most probable explanation is that I was made for another world." Using my abilities, experiences, and gifts to benefit the world in the best way that I can is important and it's okay not to feel too comfortable in my earthly mantle. This spiritual truth comforts me now, but I didn't always possess this knowledge or have this depth of faith.

Camping: A Cool Slumber Party

On the weekends, our family frequently camped in a small camper on Cape Cod National Seashore. Around 1972, we upgraded from our travel trailer to an Airstream, the aerodynamic silver bullet you often

see beaming down the highway. It appeared mammoth to me. My sisters and I were given little cameras by the dealership when Dad bought the camper and those cameras documented much of our travels during our younger years.

Camping was like the coolest slumber party and I found great comfort in the closeness. The days and

Jackie and me by the Airstream in our driveway

nights were punctuated by a plethora of aromas that, when smelled today, return me instantly to childhood evenings around the campfire: smoke wafting from firewood, seared hot dogs and hamburgers, and marshmallows on the end of a stick. I remember, too, coconut sunscreen and moist salty sea air, the warm sand between my toes when my sisters and I marched down the trail to the ocean surf, loaded with buckets, shovels, strainers, and other tools essential to the construction of castles and finding treasures by the sea.

I recall that all our gear, especially the Airstream, was in mint condition. Dad repeated to us each trip, "Take care of your things. Have some respect for yourself!" If we didn't, he would say with a wrinkled face of disgust. "Sad, real sad, what a disgrace," while shaking his head. Mom would chime in whirling her clenched fist, "Smarten up! We brought you up better than that." Spankings were often the outcome of disappointing or disobeying my parents, but usually "the look" with eyes narrowed and blazing was enough! Maybe my parents were so irritable because they thought we were ungrateful or they were just tired. We learned vital lessons of self-respect, discipline and taking care of material things.

Unfortunately, I concluded that things were more important than I was. My parents took such pride and placed such importance in taking care of stuff and everything looking good on the outside... sometimes I wished they would have taken as much effort to learn how to care for me, the me inside. Now, I understand they did the best they knew how and the values they was trying to teach me but the means by which they tried to achieve this goal left me feeling less than good enough. I'd think, *Maybe they wanted a boy instead of a girl since they're always exasperated with me.*

Whenever something turned up broken or there was a quarrel, Dad automatically thought it was my mistake. When I was eleven, he reached to slap me in the face but instead hit the side of my head when I flinched. As the blood trickled down I felt terrible that I was constantly, in trouble. While my ear was ringing he said, "For crying out loud, can't you do anything right? Why are you always causing trouble? What's the matter with you?" Those words hurt as much as the blows. Joanne spoke up, "Dad she didn't do it." The grumble of thunder in the distance seemed to echo my inner turmoil and I went to the bathroom to check my ear. I thought, *one day I will run away far, far, away and he will not have to put up with me anymore.* When he realized he hurt me he felt bad. Apologizing he said, "I didn't mean to hit your ear but why do you have to be such a "pesty-pest" all the time?" (That's his nickname for me).

My First Holy Communion May 11, 1974, in Lowell, Massachusetts. From left to right-Mom and Dad are in the back, wih Jackie and Joanne behind me

Kindergarten

We traveled up and down the East Coast of America in the Airstream making family memories until 1976 when Dad took it to Florida to find us a new home. My parents finally sold the old girl in 1977. So ended a season in our lives of camping together as a family.

"Busy Body"

Watching my sisters go off to school with their books and lunch boxes in hand, I couldn't wait for it to be my turn. I wanted to be smart just like them. Finally, just before I turned five I started Kindergarten at Peter W. Reilly School in Lowell, Massachusetts. By first grade, schoolwork was a lot more difficult than I ever imagined it would be. I had trouble paying attention so following directions was nearly impossible. Besides being called a "busy body," some comments on my report card said, "Diane can't seem to sit still. She doesn't listen or get her work done. She doesn't seem to care." But that was not the case at all. Pleasing my teachers and parents was extremely important to me. Unfortunately, undiagnosed ADD (Attention Deficit Disorder) would complicate my efforts and I never measured up. I am a visual learner and do not do well with lengthy instructions. I struggled all the way through until my college years when I finally discovered my learning style and trained myself to manage it.

I was the self-proclaimed "Welcome Wagon," teachers and school personnel didn't have to ask for a volunteer because with a big smile I met each new student with: "Hi, my name is Diane. Is this your first day?" Then I would take them on an adventure showing them where the bathroom or lunchroom was and do whatever I could do to help. Offering gifts of kindness and compassion is my way of life. My radar is always on. I understand Winston Churchill's thoughts, "We make a living by what we get, but we make a life by what we give."

When I noticed beautiful flowers growing in the field I'd pick them for my mother: tangy yellow dandelions, crisp evergreen leaves, soft pink hibiscus and delicate purple lilacs. I was thankful when she carefully put them into a small vase with water and acted like she treasured them as she drank in the most wonderful smell and then kissed my brow. I felt happiest when I was able to share, but I often felt hurt when the receiver didn't appreciate the offering. A fellow student once asked me, "Why are you so friendly? I see you five times a day in this hallway and you smile and say 'Hi' every time." I replied, "I never thought about it, I guess because I want you to know you are important to me and I'm glad to see you each time." "Hmmm, That's just weird," he decided.

First Holy Communion.

Wanting A Special Friend

During the early years I imagined having a soft cuddly buddy. A tiny, rabbit smart like "Thumper" (from the movie *Bambi*) and small enough to fit concealed in my pocket. My special friend would offer words of wisdom so I could be and do things right. Maybe he could help me feel like I mattered and fit in. Maybe others would want to be my friend because of him. Most of all, I prayed for someone to rescue me from the shadows of fear and loneliness. Each night I'd pray for such a friend but to my dismay, when I awoke in the morning, I didn't find him. In my childlike faith I hung upside down looking under my bed and looked all around in case he was hiding. Then I'd contemplate, *how come God won't answer my prayer? I know that He can. Maybe He doesn't like me? Maybe I'm not good enough.*

CHAPTER 2

GROWING UP CAN BE HARD TO DO

God loves you tenderly. What He gives you is not to be kept under lock and key but to be shared.

—Mother Teresa

Painful Sundays

"God helps those who help themselves." I actually thought this phrase was in the Bible because my parents recited it to me so much during my childhood. I now know that it's not scripture, but Ben Franklin's motto. I thought it was my job to do everything, and if God had time after tending to His many responsibilities, maybe He could fit me into His schedule *if* I was good.

Far from an encounter with the divine, Sunday was often the most painful day of the week. It would start at the breakfast table and continue with the brutal drive to church. Mom shouted, "Bernie can't you drive a little faster we're going to be late." Dad would hit the gas and scare us all. "Watch where you are going you'll kill us all! Why are you parking way over here? Diane where's your envelope, get your coat on? Oh, for heaven's sake can't you people do anything right... Stop that crying or I'll give you something to cry about." Mom would threaten that she was never going any place with us again. Nothing was good enough. And after a full blown crisis just to get there, we would pile out of the car and walk into church as Mom spit into a tissue and rubbed the milk mustaches from our faces. Fear and frustration was heavy in air. After arriving, we put on our "church face" to greet the people inside. I often felt sick as my stomach twisted and turned. Nevertheless, I learned how to wear a "happy face" mask very early in life.

Each family member would go through the standard Catholic procedures, systematically dipping a finger into the Holy water, genuflecting while making the sign of the cross, kneeling, praying, and promptly sitting on the hard church pews. During the service, to break the tension, Jo and I would smirk or tease each other behind our dad's back when he was kneeling. Once Dad realized what we were doing, he would squeeze our arms until red streaks appeared and we were coerced into submission and tears. We had to sit up straight, kneel properly, sing, read, and do church just right; it was our duty. We were to be seen as perfect or get Dad's pinch. He saw the way we behaved as a direct reflection of his parenting skills and had no intention of being shamed.

Church was boring. From start to finish, it was stiff, cold and filled with a heavy musky fragrance. It wasn't sulfur (we know who smells like that) but a smoky mixture of bitter myrrh and frankincense. The preacher Joseph Parker once said, "Preach to the suffering and you will never lack a congregation. There is a broken heart in every pew." My tail did not endure the hard pew very

well so my mind did not absorb much of a message. I was always really glad when it was over. We could then get out of our uncomfortable dresses and back into our tree climbing gear. I reflected, *when I get older, I'm never going to church.*

Parental Discipline

The words "I love you" were never spoken in my family and spontaneous hugs were seldom given. Nonetheless, when Dad got home from work—needing a little quiet time before he tackled the paperwork that occupied him late into the evening—we would run to greet him, happy to see him for the first time that day. "Ta-da! Look what I made for you, Daddy!"

After he got cleaned up from his full day's work in the elements, Dad would turn on the easy listening radio station and lie down on the living room floor. Waiting patiently for Mom to call us for dinner while we climbed all over him. All he wanted was a moment's peace, but we three girls couldn't give it to him. Joanne and Jackie seemed to have more self-control and would lie still when he told them to. However, I lacked that restraint and often persisted by tickling his toes or measuring his big hands to my small ones, wondering in my heart, *Is he as happy to see me, as I am to see him?* "Daddy, I want to go to work with you tomorrow so we can be together all day. I miss you." After humming and talking constantly he finally would say, "You are such an itch" and head to the dinner table while I sat on his foot and hugged his leg for a ride. I wanted my daddy's affection and attention; unfortunately, I often sought it at inopportune times.

My dad was a Snap-On® tool salesman. Dad worked hard and taught me to do the same, always expecting the very best from me. Sometimes I interpreted his expectations as "needing to be perfect." When he compared me to others, I never seemed to measure up. Consequently, I felt like a failure. He thought this method would challenge me to better myself. I tried tirelessly to impress him, desperately needing to know that he was proud of me. Every evening, I trotted downstairs to the cellar where he worked in his office. I'd reach up on my tippy toes to give him a hug and kiss goodnight hoping I could do better tomorrow.

Dad's Mercy And Grace

I'll never forget in second grade when I received forgiveness from my dad when I didn't deserve it. I got caught cheating in a Valentine's Day contest in school. I was brought in front of my entire class and shamed; I hoped that was the end of it. Later, I was sitting on the swing in the back yard when mom called my name. I knew I was in trouble. She sent me to my room, "And you stay in there until your father gets home!" I trembled thinking the wooden paddle (minus the rubber ball and band), or a wooden spoon would be stinging my back side soon. When Dad got home, Mom took me into their room (forbidden ground) and I was certain that I was doomed. As Mom told Dad what I'd done, the room seemed so big and I felt so small. Tears welled up in my eyes and overflowed down my cheeks. Dad bent over and looked me in the eye. He asked, "Do you know what you did was wrong?"

"Yes, Daddy" as my lower lip quivered.

"Are you sorry?"

"Yes!"

"Are you going to do it again?"

"No. Daddy"

"Alright, I think you've learned your lesson."

Wow! I received mercy and grace when I deserved punishment. I never forgot this important lesson. He even gave me a hug and patted my back. I walked out one thankful little girl! I never did that offense again and I never forgot my daddy's mercy. This is a time when dad lived out the scripture verse in Ephesians 6:4: "Don't keep scolding and nagging your children, making them angry and resentful. Rather, bring them up with the loving discipline of which the Lord Himself approves, with suggestions and godly advice."

Family Gatherings

Family gatherings with decorations, streamers and noisemakers for birthdays and holidays were fun. Members of the extended family brought their grumpy or cheery personalities and gifts. It was a lively group and there was never a dull moment. I liked hanging out with my relatives even though I didn't always feel like I belonged. Dad usually handled the grill, sometimes charring the hot dogs and hamburgers, out of fear that if they were undercooked we would get sick. Mom tended to big bowls of chips, deviled eggs, and coolers full of soda pops and beer. There was storytelling, gossiping, laughing, drinking and arguing, all of which transformed these occasions into notable memories. And just before dark, my cousins and I would get in one last game of "hide and go seek."

Nana and me, August 9, 1986 Winter Haven, FL

I closely observed past generations; watching and learning from how they trotted their laps and passed the baton. Regrettably, Dad's parents died before I was born. The only grandparent I knew growing up was Nana, my mother's mom. I giggle recalling the time she bought me funny underwear with the days of the week printed on them. It never felt right to wear Saturday on Tuesday. I cherished my Nana.

In September of 1992, Nana was fighting cancer, and the doctors didn't know if she would pull through; Mom, Dad and I rushed to her bedside, making the trip from Florida to Massachusetts, but made it just after she passed. Looking at her so small and frail squeezed all the air out of my lungs and I thought I would pass out in my fears and tears. She was the first person I'd seen right after they died and with a shaky voice I gently touched her cool ing hand, leaned in and whispered, "I love you Nana. I'll see you on the other side."

I led the funeral mass in song and upon my mother's request sang, *On Eagles Wings*, by Michael Joncas. They put my sentiments, "You will never walk alone..." on Nana's gravestone. I picked this saying because Nana and her son, Bob, Mom's only and youngest brother, were so close. She never walked alone here on earth because of him, and I know that she will never walk alone in Heaven.

Dear Lord,

Thank you for the memories of childhood. May mercy, grace and peace wash over our recollections. Help us use them to get better. May we each learn what you would have us learn from our past to become the people you want us to be. May we run our lap with fearless determination to pass the baton of faith, hope and love on to the next generation with bold confidence and strength that can only come from You. Help us to continue to grow and change for the better and to realize you are taking care of us no mater what. I love you. Amen

The home Nana and my Mother grew up in Lowell, MA
Joanne, Jackie, Nana, me and Mom

CHAPTER 3

Florida or Bust!

One of the greatest diseases
is to be nobody to anybody.

—Mother Teresa

The Summer Of 1976

As I squinted out the car window at the unending swamp and large moss laden oak trees, the warm sun adorned my cheeks. I considered, *Wow, we are actually going to live here.* I remembered the trips we made to Florida in the Airstream and how often my father spoke of moving here, but I couldn't believe that it was actually happening.

Dad was tired of the snow and long cold winters in Massachusetts and dreamed of retiring in Florida one day. He wanted to be close to his girls when that time came. These and other reasons led him to live in the legendary Airstream for six months and find us a new place to call home. When he gave us the "all clear" sign, we packed up and drove down to Winter Haven, Florida, in the summer of 1976.

As we entered central Florida, Mom, Nana, my two sisters, and I rode down streets lined with perky palm trees and ominous cypress trees. Dad found a red brick, single-family home with a screened-in pool in a delightful neighborhood. We were in a state and a city where we knew no one. Uncle Bob and Aunt Barbara assured me before we left that it was going to be great. I wondered, *what will my new school be like? Will the other students like me? Will I have any neighborhood friends to play with? What will winter and Christmas be like*

Our last night in our Lowell, MA home-1976 Joanne, Jackie, Mom and me

without snow to sled on or to make snowmen with? How will we celebrate birth-days without the rest of the family? I had lots of questions and concerns but I was ready to embrace the adventure and possibilities a fresh new start could offer a ten year old.

Plaid Skirts And Knee High Socks

With my new home came a new school. I was very nervous about attend-ing a private Catholic school that was bound to be very different from the public school I attended in Lowell. For starters, they had a dress code

that allowed only blue, white, or yel-low shirts, plaid skirts and knee socks and uniform blue book bags. As I stepped through the classroom door the first day, I expected classmates to introduce themselves but no one did.

My heart beat like I just finished running a 50 yard dash. I gathered my courage and walked up to the girl closest to me. She had golden hair and big blue eyes. I held out my hand and said in my northern accent, "Hi, my name is Diane, what's yours?" The girl looked at me as if I were an alien from outer space and walked away laughing. This drained what little confidence I had right out of me. It appeared my worst dreams were com-

September 1977, age eleven.

ing true. I didn't fit in and I felt as ugly, rejected and unwanted as the ugly duckling in the childhood fable.

One Of My Least Favorite Things

Going to school quickly became one of my least favorite things. As a matter of fact, it topped the list of things I loathed to do. Spending hours on end indoors, feeling inadequate and without friends, made me sad. And when the teacher wasn't looking, the boy who sat behind me kicked me, wrote on my shirt, pulled my hair and took my things. When I shared with my Mom that I didn't like or want to go to school she tried to relieve my distress by pinning different medals with saints' pictures on them to my undershirt. She insisted that they would protect and help me: I didn't notice any improvements.

I was continuously teased about the way I talked. I asked questions like, "Wherz tha wata bubbla?" (which means "where is the water fountain") and, "Could I have a soda pop?" Upon hearing my northern accent, kids howled in laughter and gestured to each other how odd I was. I enjoyed hearing people laugh, but this was a different kind of laugh, I could feel the mean spirited edge of it. They were laughing at me instead of with me. I was convinced that something must be wrong with me and that *if* I was only prettier, smarter, cooler, and not such a weirdo, maybe I could fit in.

Unlike the medals pinned to my undershirt, my sister Jo, came to my rescue. Before school, during lunch, and after school, I shadowed her everywhere she went. I didn't feel so alone when I was with her. One time her classmates asked, "Why is your sister always hanging around?" Looking sympathetically in my direction she replied, "She is having a little trouble making friends." In sixth grade Jo graduated from my school to join my sister Jackie at the Catholic high school. I was lost without my "Saint Jo."

A Simple Surgery?

Little did I know that something more traumatic than Jo moving on to a different school was on the horizon and that it would lead me face to face with the dark cloud of depression. During fifth and sixth grade I was plagued by strep throat and colds. After scores of antibiotics and other prescriptions, my glands remained swollen and my tonsils infected so the doctor chose to remove them.

After the tonsillectomy, the nurses took me to the bathroom even though they were instructed not to move me. In the process, I fell off the toilet and hit my head. The nurses rushed to my aid and, to their surprise, discovered that I had stopped breathing. They got me back to the bed and administered CPR, resuscitating me just as my mother walked into the room. I remember opening my eyes and looking up to a black balloon that was attached to my mouth and that a nurse was still squeezing. I don't remember much after that other than throwing up large amounts of blood. I woke up to see both my parents sitting aghast in chairs at the foot of my bed. They were obviously alarmed by my predicament. Memories like these remind me of how much my parents cared, how thankful I am for them, and what they were willing to go through for me.

Three days later, when I got home from the hospital, I realized that I didn't receive a card or a phone call from anyone at school. This caused me to conclude that I was of no consequence to anyone outside my family and an overwhelming feeling of despair and gloom enveloped me. Dad was at work and my sisters were in school. Mom was at the store and I remember sitting alone, staring out the bedroom window as a storm cloud swallowed up the sun. Tears suddenly streamed down my face. Something inside of me broke.

Later, when everyone got home, no one seemed to notice my melancholy. I couldn't talk because of the surgery, but even if I could, I didn't feel safe expressing my feelings to my family. After all, how does an eleven-year-old child put depression into words? I felt a sinking feeling in my stomach yet couldn't put my finger on why. I berated myself, *what do I have to be sad about? I don't have to go to school. I can eat as much ice cream as I want . . . Snap out of it!*

Don't Cry Out Loud

Deep inside of me a void began to grow. In this vacuum my soul yearned to cry out but didn't know how. Isolation set in and I felt no one understood me, that no one wanted to, or had the time to. While in a room full of people, I felt lonely. My internal struggle was compounded by the fact that my dad had pounded in my mind that I was not to be a "jellyfish" and to "have some backbone." He conditioned me to believe that stoicism is the embodiment of strength. It was important to my father that I learn to travel through life with a "stiff upper lip" and calm exterior no matter what kind of strife, internal or otherwise, that I was dealing with (just like he did). He didn't want me to cause any ripples in our superficial calm.

Feeling the weight of the world on my shoulders, my theme song became *Don't Cry Out Loud*. Melissa Manchester sang of learning to keep emotions inside and hiding your feelings. This was what I set out to do. I scolded myself, *get over it, what's the matter with me, how can you be so weak?* Of course, the reality of my situation was that I had begun a life or death battle with mental illness in the form of depression.

The challenge with depression is that it is not just a "mind over matter situation." It can be as chemically oriented as diabetes, but is often not given the respect it deserves. I desperately wanted to be perfect and to please others and often mistook their indifference towards me. This added to the message that continually played in my head that I was not good enough for the love of others. These thoughts began to permeate my soul and I didn't know what to do with them. Again, how does an eleven-year-old express such thoughts, especially to a family that prizes the virtues of stoicism and emotional fortitude; my only option was to suffer in silence behind my "happy face."

Seventh Grade

In seventh grade, I finally began to make friends. In fact, I actually had a best friend named Angela and we created a secret language that only we were able to understand. Unlike myself, Angela was tough. Our friendship sparked a confidence that led me to be active in sports. I played softball, basketball, roller skated, swam in our pool daily, tap-danced, and performed ballet, jazz, and acrobatics. I was no longer one of the last kids picked for a team in gym class. Participation in sports became my saving grace, not only because it occupied my thoughts and time, but also because of the positive endorphins it released.

My fellow classmates recognized that I was a permanent fixture at school so there was a semblance of acceptance. My northern accent faded but at the same time a southern one crept in. Now, it was my northern relatives who teased me about sounding like a Southern Belle. That didn't appear to be so bad since the Southern Belles were beautiful girls that walked around at Cypress Gardens (the local amusement park) in their "Gone with the Wind" dresses.

Our local community theater was putting on the production, "The Velveteen Rabbit." I tried out and to my delight was awarded the part of an alphabet block. (Amazingly, Joanne took a picture of the blocks on stage and they spell my current last name—DIKE—what are the chances of that?) I enjoyed entertaining others and the play allowed me to do so within a community. More important, at the cast swim party celebrating the last show, the coach of the city swim team invited me to try out

I was a toy block in "The Velveteen Rabbit" in the 7th grade, 1979. I am the "I" and the "E" The blocks spell my last name today!

Preparing for the backstroke race in the Rowdy Gaines swimming pool. Thirteen years old.

for the team. I was flabbergasted that he selected me out of all the others in the pool that day. The next day I tried out and succeeded in making it on the city swim team. Things were looking-good.

Public School

At the end of seventh grade I convinced my parents to let me attend the public school. I was able to meet a wide variety of kids, and friends were much easier to make. However, there were still a few sour grapes in the bunch. Every once in a while a "Kick Me" sign seemed to be attached to my back. Kids can be so mean for no reason at all, and bullies inflict a sadness that is hard to forget.

One bully in particular, Mike, terrorized me daily on the school bus. He was cruel and called me names like: stupid, ugly, buckteeth, fat lip, pimple face, seaweed hair, and toothpick. He also took pleasure in making fun of my clothes; nothing was off limits. I felt inferior, scared, and lonely. I thought I was who he said I was. When his barrages pressed me against the side of the bus in fear, I asked myself over and over, *what had I done to deserve this? Why does he hate me? What is wrong with me? Why am I so unlikable?*

In search of a solution, I confided in my mother. She was angry about it but did not really understand the depth of my despair. She replied, "Tell that boy, 'Your clothes are clean, bought and paid for and guaranteed to wear!'" She also offered, "'Sticks and stones will break your bones but words will never hurt you.'" When I gave the bully these replies it only increased the intensity of his assaults and I learned that words can hurt, they can break your heart.

Fighting Back With Forgiveness

I didn't know how to fight back, so I internalized all that hurt. When I used love and helpfulness, confusion sometimes replaced the anger in his eyes but most of the time it only increased his attacks. I didn't know then that bullies usually act the way they do because they feel inferior or because they were picked on at one time. When others joined in I felt powerless to the offenses. I felt like I was floating in a pool of piranhas during a feeding frenzy all the way to my stop.

For a long time I lived in fear and was tortured by the memories of his enraged shouting and fists coming toward my face. Yet, the embarrassing and excruciating experiences chiseled into my heart and mind how devastating words, actions and deeds can be making me more aware of the importance of compassion. It motivated me to never cause anyone to have to feel this way.

Years later I was working in a flower shop in the mall and recognized my antagonist going by. He was in a wheelchair. I stepped out of the shop to ask his friends if he was Mike ____. His friends said, "Yes," with a questioning look. I knelt next to Mike's wheelchair and looked him in the eye. "Hi Mike, remember me," putting my hand to my chest, Diane?" He acknowledged slightly. "How are you," I asked? With a raspy whisper he said, "Okay." It was scary looking into those eyes again but I felt such compassion for him. "Listen, I run this flower shop. Would you like to hang out with me sometime? I could use the help and company. I'm going to give you my phone number, and if you need me, I want you to know, I'm here." I reached out gently touching his hand that was stuck to his chair. Tears weld up in our eyes and I could see his heart had changed since I knew him. My throat tightened to see this nineteen year old who used to be so strong and ready to take on the world was now confined to this chair. "It's okay; I forgive you," I whispered. Mike signed. "Thank you," he whispered.

As the group turned to leave, I held one person back and asked, "What happened?" He told me Mike had a deadly car accident and was now a quadriplegic. Paralyzed from the neck down, this was his first day out in months. My jaw fell down as I gathered my thoughts. I offered, "Here is my number. Please do not hesitate to call me if I can come over and move his arms and legs... anything." His friend nodded gratefully before re-joining the group. I watched them for a moment, then thanked the Lord for this opportunity to see my former bully again. Though I could do nothing to take away the pain of his accident, I offered something that was healing for both of us—forgiveness. The Bible says, "Be kind to one another, tenderhearted, forgiving one another, even as God in Christ forgave you" (Ephesians 4:32).

Back To School

To avoid the bus bullies, I began to ride my bike or walk everywhere that I went. Athletics played a more crucial role in my life and not showing my feelings or crying out loud were woven with the "No pain, no gain" mentality. As Tom Hanks yelled in the 1992 movie, *A League of Their Own,* "There's no crying in baseball!" I got tougher and learned to push through the pain of lifting weights, and swimming longer, harder, and faster; I found sanctuary in my athletic ability, working out, and helping the younger swimmers.

I attended Winter Haven High School where friends and activities surrounded me. Yet, somehow I still felt unworthy of friendship and struggled to see my accomplishments, or my worth. A discordant sound track repeated in my head all my faults, failures, and mistakes. My feelings of failure were compounded by my academic struggles. Math was particularly difficult for me and seemed as foreign as my French class. As hard as I tried, I just couldn't "get it." The principles that seemed to come so easily to the other students eluded me as I'd stand at the blackboard in front of the class unable to complete or compute my problem.

I'd experienced digestion problems throughout my early years. Every day my stomach gave me troubles, sometimes bloating out until it felt like it might pop. Even so, I pressed on and did my best not to let this discomfort distract me from my daily activities. On top of my stomach problems, I started experiencing joint pain. The gnawing pain made sleeping difficult and sleepless nights became sleepless weeks. I began to feel physically exhausted and easily overwhelmed.

In desperation, I cried out, "Dear God, help me!!"

CHAPTER 4

Sports Was My Life

*Blessed is the one who perseveres under trial,
because when they have stood the test, they will
receive the crown of life that God has promised to
those who love him.*

—James 1:12

Boot Camp Regime

To deal with my increasing physical discomfort, I focused on working harder. Success in my sporting and working endeavors was paramount to my identity and self-esteem. In particular, success in the pool kept me afloat with an outlet to experience the joys of accomplishment and acceptance. Participation in sports was life changing.

When I was unable to sleep at night I thought, *if I just did more, it would help me sleep better* and I would resolve to do better the next day. I followed a "boot-camp" regime that included at least thirty pull-ups, fifty push-ups, one hundred sit-ups, and up to a five-mile run several times a week. I also swam up to five hours a day training with the swim team, giving lessons, and teaching water exercise classes. Every minute of the day was planned. Meanwhile, I continued taking tap, ballet, jazz and acrobatics at a dance studio. I could take some classes for free if I helped to teach them so I began assisting the teacher and continued babysitting in the evenings and on weekends.

I was dedicated, obsessive and I wanted to be successful. I wanted to feel good and sports gave me a taste of confidence. I remember standing on the side of the pool in the cold December wind thinking, *what am I doing? It's cold. I'm tired. I should go home and rest!* In the face of these thoughts, I jumped into the cold blue water and felt the surge of triumph that occurred when I was able to ignore my pain and finish what I set out to do. I would swim one lap after another and when working out in the pool did not occupy enough of my time, I joined the track team to run and throw the shot put and the discus. The ability and joy of participating in sports was my life, my cover and my identity.

Life-Guarding

I passed the grueling tests to become an "advanced lifeguard" for the Polk County Recreation Department; it was a big accomplishment. I saved several children and adults from drowning and dealt with emergency situations for the three years I worked there. It's ironic that my mother saved my father from drowning when she was pregnant with me. Swimming and saving others came naturally, seeing anyone sad or left out was unacceptable.

Every hour that I life-guarded at the Rowdy Gaines Pool or the local lakes, I took fifteen minute breaks to cut hair or massage heads, necks, and shoulders. I would stroll over in my slaphappy flip-flops and work for food, a milk shake, or even a dinner date, so thankful to be needed. Judging by the line that formed for my services, it seemed that I had the gift to alleviate headaches and sore muscles, as well as giving quality haircuts. Focusing on others helped alleviate my own physical and emotional discomfort and I found myself living up to Elisabeth Elliot's words,

> When I am in need of refreshment, it isn't easy to think of the needs of others. But I have found that, instead of praying for my own comfort and satisfaction, I ask the Lord to enable me to give to others, an amazing thing often happens-I find my own needs wonderfully met. Refreshment comes in ways I would never have thought of, both for others, and then, incidentally, for myself. (Elliot, Gateway To Joy, 2005)

Whether I was swimming competitively, working out in the gym, teaching dance classes or instructing, I was always sore. I could handle it during the day, but at night the absence of distractions made it nearly impossible to sleep. This proclivity for pain didn't alarm me at first since I reasoned that without such pain, there could be no gain, in athletics or in life. I learned to push through.

Walking The Plank

Laying awake most of the night, even after trying diversions like listening to music, drinking warm milk, doing homework, and stretching, got really old. I'd try to sleep in the pool on a float, begging Mom to rub my back, to let me stay up to watch a movie with her, anything to help me sleep but she usually told me, "Just go to go to bed and close your eyes." After a long day she was tired, didn't want to be bothered and needed some time to herself. It didn't matter what I did. I couldn't get comfortable. I had an uncontrollable urge to rock my feet back and forth, like windshield wipers in a rainstorm. My anxiety about not sleeping and being too tired for the next day's activities would drag on, hour after hour. When I finally got to sleep, it was time to get up for another day. I never felt rested. My body was committing high treason and my mind was walking the plank. The ravens were circling while I was pirated by the mystery of what my body was trying to tell me, yet I didn't know how to listen.

Jobs, Car Accidents, and A Catch 22

Just before earning my life-guarding job I was offered a job at Elaine Powers, a local, ladies only exercise club, and was trained to teach exercise classes and to counsel woman on fitness. At the same time, I started my own cleaning business. This heavy workload was made more difficult when I began to experience episodes of hypoglycemia. Without warning, even after finishing a meal, I would suddenly get shaky and clammy, and at times, have to lie down, or worse, pass out. Carrying snacks with me at all times became imperative because the episodes became daily and sometimes hourly. I am sorry to say that I used processed, high glycemic index snacks to pull myself out.

Tap, Jazz, Acrobatics, and Ballet Senior Year dance photo

This caused a roller coaster effect because the blood sugar would swing up rescuing me from bottoming out only to bring me crashing down again. This scenario wreaked havoc on my already fatigued system.

As a passenger, I sustained injuries in two car accidents. I hyper-extended my spinal cord, suffered whiplash, and received a knee and slight head injury. These smash-ups exacerbated my already inflamed condition; fibromyalgia was diagnosed. Massages were the only thing that offered relief, so I started getting them every Friday. I appreciated their therapeutic value so much that the masseuse trained me to give them as well. Where it used to be a hobby on my life guarding breaks, massaging now became a significant and skilled gift I offered others.

The addition of daily physical pain to my already challenged emotional state threatened to disrupt the delicate balance I struggled to maintain. Regardless of what I did, I couldn't win and, even worse, my life had become a deadly "Catch 22." To combat my depression, I needed to engage in as many activities as possible, but such engagement left my body in such a painful state that even sleep was not attainable. As a result, the physical pain and lack of sleep I experienced set me up for bouts with depression turning my attention inward, turning up the volume of those self-destructive tapes that played inside my head. I was like a gerbil running in its exercise wheel as I tried to cope with my life: the harder I tried, the faster I went nowhere. I desperately needed a break or, at least, a different way of dealing with life. It became obvious to me that what I was doing wasn't working, and something needed to change.

Is something missing in my life? In response to this question, I started buying items like kitchen bowls, towels, pans and pot holders so I would be ready to purchase my very own home someday, grasping for purpose and meaning and focus. I wanted to move out of my parents' home and make something worthwhile of myself. I was

State Swim meet Gainesville, FL-Freestyle Relay Team

so driven, so determined. I hid the items under my bed and dreamed of a white picket fence, big picture windows, and being independent one day in a safe home where I could finally find rest, where I could finally sleep.

Unhealthy Infatuation

One day, I noticed that my coach seemed really down so I asked him what was wrong. He told me that his long-term relationship was over. Coincidently, I'd just broken up with my boyfriend. Our association grew into more of a friendship and we encouraged each other until one night, our eyes met from across the table at a lifeguard pizza party. For the first time, we saw each other as kind of equals and we noticed a spark. When I dropped him off at the pool, he got out and started to walk away and then, just like in the movies, he turned and looked back over his shoulder at me. With no words spoken, he came to my window, leaned in, and kissed me. Wow, I felt special. I knew my coach was twice my age but his attention was like a drug. I was hooked. *How could something that felt so right, be so wrong?*

Our relationship flourished with daily contact including hugging, kissing, eating together, and flirtatious games. I became his special helper during meetings and classes. When I entered his office and his face lit up it delighted me. I'd never experienced this kind of excitement before and it made me feel alive. Suddenly, I started breaking all of my swimming records and qualified for the Junior Olympics in the butterfly stroke. Then he told me if I lost a little weight, I could probably swim even faster. My body had a layer of fat from too many carbohydrates, milk shakes, and chocolate chip cookies, (which unbeknownst to me, increased the occurrence of my hypoglycemia). The weight dropped off easily enough because I hungered more for his attention than for food. The relationship was thrilling and stimulating. We were having a great time.

Disappointment

The euphoria collapsed one night when he was supposed to join me at one of my dance recitals but never showed up. I felt like a balloon someone had let the air out of, limp and lifeless. When I went to see why he had not come, I found him walking around the lake trying to figure things out. Later he said, "Di, I'm really sorry. I don't want to hurt you. I'm scared, you're so young, what am I doing? You're like a drug I can't get enough of, I love you." It was the first time I heard those words and whatever disappointment or apprehension I felt about this unhealthy infatuation completely vanished. My balloon was filled up, made all new, and we were back on track.

The next month, we made plans to watch the fireworks on the Fourth of July, but when he didn't show up at work and I couldn't get hold of him, I went to his place where he always left the door open and had told me I was welcomed anytime. When I went in I found he was sleeping, so I took a shower, did his dishes, cleaned up, and then checked in on him again. Since he was still sleeping, I started to write him a note because I had to get back to work. *"I'm looking forward to watching the fireworks with you. See you later! Love, Diane."* Just then, his bedroom door opened. The man I'd grown to love stood dejectedly against the doorjamb. His eyes

Summer of 1983

encompassed a mixture of love, fear, and sadness. It scared and startled me all at once. Without saying a word, with his lips pierced and nostrils flared he turned and closed the door. I'll never forget that moment, when my candle was snuffed out. My posture slumped as I walked out the door, leaving the note on the table feeling stupid, ugly, and foolish... Somehow still hoping he'd show up; I sat on the diving board at the pool and watched the fireworks alone not understanding what I'd done wrong.

Our Secret Relationship

There was a good reason for this last encounter. Apparently, my mother and father talked to my coach's boss about their suspicions of our "secret" relationship. My coach was fired and told not to have any further contact with me. My parents must have read my diary and I was furious. At the time, I didn't realize they were saving me from what could have been a complete catastrophe. Instead, I felt betrayed and grew even more alienated from them. In my mind, they were responsible for ending the one relationship that provided the affection I so desperately needed. "Why? We didn't do anything wrong," I shouted! I felt rejected by my coach, betrayed by my parents, and worthless—again. I wanted to run away but had nowhere to go.

After he left and moved to Orlando, it was difficult for the team to find a new coach and I felt responsible. On our awards night, I was given special recognition for my improvements, but the cloud of shame and disappointment I felt over the entire situation overshadowed the joy of achievement. My coach was a fixture at the pool for so long it just didn't seem right that he wasn't there anymore. I got his new phone number from another lifeguard and mustered up the courage to call him from a pay phone at the pool. As the phone rang my heart ached and my stomach fluttered with hope. *Would he be happy to hear from me? Would he hang up when he realized it was me? Was I still lovable to him?*

I looked across the white water reflecting the puffy clouds above as the sun sank behind the building and a little wind blew a ripple across the surface of the still swim lanes. I remembered the first time he saw me swimming and invited me to join the swim team. I reminisced about swim meets, helping him teach lifeguard classes, working together daily, and all the hours and years here at this pool. Would it ever feel like home again?

My thoughts were interrupted when he answered the phone. He was happy to hear from me and missed me, too. For a moment, I felt better knowing I was not alone in my sorrow and that he still seemed to care about me. I called a few more times until finally a woman answered who he said was his cleaning lady. That was it; I was the fool? I had to face the fact that he was gone, gone forever from my life. I never spoke to him again.

CHAPTER 5

FINDING FAITH

*So faith comes from hearing, that is,
hearing the Good News about Christ.*
—Romans 10:17 NLT

Like a ship without a rudder, I fought to get my life on track after the scandalous relationship with my coach. Growing up religious made being good and going to Heaven my focus, especially in times of trouble. With a crucifix above my bed, routine prayer every night, church every Sunday and holy day of obligation, and participation in all the sacraments, I hoped I was doing enough and being good enough to earn my way to Heaven. Yet, I wasn't sure.

Peripheral vision permits us to notice our surroundings even while our eyes are focused on our objective. In my peripheral vision I noticed something. Knowing about God but not really knowing him wasn't enough. Who was this man who chose to die for my sins, whom people died brutal deaths to stand for, macho fishermen dropped their nets for, tax collectors walked away from their greed for, and zealots gave everything up for? A hunger to know the answer to this question began to distract me from my routine.

Hunger And Thirst

There was a terrible void I relentlessly sought to fill. Nothing satisfied the hunger and thirst in my soul until I experienced an authentic encounter with Jesus Christ at an Evangelical Church. The pastor talked about sin and I came to realize that unconfessed sin was one of the greatest barriers to happiness and a relationship with my maker. I learned that if I confessed my sins to Jesus, He would be faithful and just to forgive and cleanse me from all unrighteousness. Jesus is not only my Savior, but also my friend whom I can go to directly to find solace. He loves me despite my imperfections and proclivity to sin and will always be there to support and guide me if I accept the gift of salvation He bought for me by dying on the cross. Wow, that's the kind of friend I really needed!

The pastor called it "getting saved" and "born again." He said, "The Bible says, 'Unless you are born again you can't enter the Kingdom of Heaven.'" I wanted to be sure I was going to Heaven so I listened carefully to his teaching. I also realized I'd tried to live my life by my own determination and that covering up my true self and feelings caused my walk of faith to be as stiff and cold as a frozen wet rag. I wondered, what have I been doing all these years?

The service also made me realize that I had to figure out what I believed, not through second-hand information, but from the primary source of truth, the Bible. I searched the scriptures, what Jesus did on the cross was enough, even in my best efforts, I could never be good enough, do enough, or hope enough. His pain became my gain. He is the only ticket to get to Heaven. Salvation was a gift freely given that Jesus paid the ultimate price for with His life. I was trying to buy something that He'd already bought. Could I give Him any less than my life?

When I heard the invitation to ask Christ into my heart as my personal Savior, I didn't just walk down to the alter, I ran. I asked Him to forgive me of my sins, wash me clean, and help me to become more like Him so I could live a life that was pleasing to Him and could be happy and whole. I thought of the parable of the talents where one man buried them, one man did little, and one man did a lot. God was very happy with the one who did a lot. I wanted to be that faithful one!

Walking With Jesus

I dedicated my life to the Lord and repented of my sins. The song I was singing was "I Surrender All" and I did. Deciding to live for Jesus caused the emptiness in my soul to evaporate. He said, "I am the way, the truth, and the life, no man comes to the Father but through Me." I fell into His loving arms realizing that what I had been seeking for all these years was my newfound faith and a personal relationship with my maker!

After I learned about the Christian radio station, I prayed for God to give me a desire to listen to and enjoy Christian music and programs. Dr. James Dobson, Robert Schuller, Pat Robertson, and many others became mentors for me. Their radio programs, words of wisdom, 800 numbers, and ministries helped me work through many challenges as

High school senior picture.

I figured out my faith. I received letters of encouragement and booklets that helped me on this most important journey. Because of the support they offered and the example they set at such a critical time in my life, I am motivated to reach out to others as they find their way to Christ.

With a voracious appetite for reading the Bible, visiting different churches and participating in Bible studies. I grew in devotion, knowledge and love. This didn't go over well with my Catholic parents. They accused me of losing my faith and didn't understand my quest at all. Hurtful things were said and it was a difficult time. But I was desperate for the assurance that I was "right" with God and that somehow, to Him, I was good enough.

It Is Well With My Soul

Even though things at home were tough, for the first time in my life I felt okay with me, and ran everywhere I went with my new outlook on life. As this new life blossomed within me, I realized that I had friends who cared for me. I had the best "Sweet Sixteen" birthday party at the roller skating rink followed by a pizza party. A secret garden of peace and confidence bloomed vibrantly in my life and I thought, *it is well with my soul,* and thanked God for His amazing grace! My life didn't become perfect, but I was optimistic that my best days were just ahead.

During the 10th and 11th grade when I was a cheerleader, I'd self medicated with alcohol off and on to deal with the depression. It started when I was thirteen. I drank gin right out of the bottle until I blacked out and later threw up after making a scene in the middle of a busy street trying to get myself run over. I'd been numbing my pain off and on ever since but I made the choice to stop drinking, or doing anything that would take away from the health of my body because I looked forward to having children someday! If I made a bad choice for my body and did anything to hurt my future baby, I would never forgive myself. With big plans, dreams and hopes, I did my best to make good choices and take care of this temple that I had invited the Lord to live in. I even enjoyed a grueling summer P.E. course daily for two summers in a row, not because I needed the credits but because I enjoyed the discipline and militaristic regimen the hard core football coaches put us through.

My final year of high school was a victorious one. I was voted co-captain of the high school swim team and vice-president of an early release work program. I still enjoyed visiting other churches, but to please my parents, I studied the history of my Catholic upbringing and rooted myself deeply in our church. I also sang and disc jockeyed with a young Catholic group called "Sonrise." I helped lead the singing at Mass, weddings, and funerals and performed concerts at the church and local prisons.

I finished high school being awarded a trophy for "Most Improved Swimmer," a medal for being a Junior Olympic qualifier, and earned the "Miss Personality Award" in dance. I finished three years in cotillion and attended all three high school proms. One of my teachers must have recommended me for *Who's Who Among American High School Students* because in 1984 I was awarded an honorable mention. Even though I still struggled with insomnia and muscular pain, these were some of my best years.

CHAPTER 6

LIFE'S ROLLER COASTER

*Facts are facts and will not
disappear on account of your likes.*
—Jawaharlal Nehru

Life and love are like a roller coaster ride. They are fun but also tiring and scary with huffing and puffing, ups and downs with fears and tears, giggles, and screams. There are sharp turns, jerky movements, upset stomachs, great views, and dark tunnels. Life and love can be an edge-of-your-seat thrill with flashing lights and heart stopping possibilities. My ride has transported me to places I never dreamed I would go. Some would say, "Expect nothing and you won't be disappointed." But I say, "Love much, laugh often, and forgive bunches. Reach for the moon and you may get a star. Hate what people choose to do but love them no matter what. Pray! Never give up! Take the punches as they come, get back up and dust yourself off. Reach out to help as much as you can, and enjoy the ride!"

Saying Good-Bye To Bill

My family was about to enter a difficult season just before I graduated. Joanne's fiancé, Keith, introduced Jackie to his best friend, Bill. They all went camping together and things seemed to be going well. Jackie was attending Flagler College in St. Augustine, Florida. She was almost finished and often came home on the weekends to see Bill: she was in love. They discussed marriage and it was the happiest I'd ever seen my sister.

Jackie and Bill

I returned home after work Thursday around 9:00 p.m. to find my family and Keith sitting in the family room looking down at the carpet in silence. My knees felt weak as panic settled into my pounding heart. "What's wrong?" I asked. Jackie had talked to Bill earlier that day and they made plans to spend the weekend together. She may have been the last person he spoke with. Bill shot himself in the head in his parent's bedroom. He was dead at twenty-five. Jackie was devastated and everyone was clearly shocked. Dazed, I sank to the floor with questions no one had the answers to.

Bill's death was another traumatic brush with mental illness and the impact it can have on all involved. It was devastating to see the pain the demon of depression inflicted on so many people through the suffering of one person. At the grave side, Jackie, Bill's family, and two women sat in the special chairs in front with the casket. A young man was with them and stood behind alone because there were no more chairs to sit in. Without thinking, I reached out and held his hand through the entire service.

A New Friend

Later I found out that the young man's name was Walter "Scott" Harper III. Bill was like a brother to him, and Bill's younger brother, John, was Scott's best friend. Their mothers were life-long friends so the children all grew up together.

Scott wailed in anguish as he and John embraced after the funeral. It was extremely moving. I could sense a corporal sadness. Nearly everyone was weeping or wiping away the tears they could no longer contain. I was thankful that I followed my heart when I reached for this stranger's hand. I prayed that this simple gesture comforted Scott and helped him know that he was not alone in his grief.

We caught up with each other about a month later and a wonderful friendship blossomed. He became my best friend and we fell in love. He no longer needed the antidepressants he was taking and forgave his mom for divorcing and moving him away from his stepfather, three stepbrothers, and home in Orlando. The love that grew between Scott and me was the one good thing that came out of all that was so bad, broken, and sad. The entire family felt some healing because of this turn of events. We adored each other and knew that we always would. We were each other's treasure in a scary, broken world.

Life was good in spite of my challenges. I was thankful for my faith and Scott. I rode the roller coaster of life like a seasoned veteran, taking

Scott and me on a date, August 17, 1984.

the ups and downs, enjoying the view and trying to see the good in all life had to offer. Others often commented positively on my ever-present smile, athleticism, and good disposition. I maintained my post as "Keeper of the Happy" with proficiency.

Facing The Future

My savings account multiplied from the various jobs I worked throughout my childhood and when Scott told me he needed a new car—equipped with an air conditioner—I used most of it to buy him the one he wanted. He was happy so I was happy, much like the tree in Shel Silverstein's children's book, *The Giving Tree* (Silverstein, 1964) that gave all it had to the boy it loved.

He was a year older and had already graduated but took me to my senior prom. For the remainder of my senior year we were high school sweethearts. We had heard from others that our closeness could disintegrate because of regrets over not experiencing the single life after high school; still, Scott and I decided to face the future and its challenges together. I couldn't imagine my life without him and didn't want to. Before long, he went shopping with his mother for a wedding ring. We wanted to keep our relationship pure and looked forward to consecrating our vows as each other's first sexual partner. Everything seemed perfect.

Rolling Up The Hill

My parents were against our getting married, partly because Joanne had recently returned home after a disastrous three-month marriage with Keith, and Jackie was having troubles as well. My parents' were distressed that Scott and I often enjoyed fellowship at other churches and the fights about the issue escalated. Regardless of what distinguishes our faith walk, I thought the unifying purpose of our faith was the person of Jesus Christ and on that we could agree. Trying to express my faith, I suggested to my parents that God probably enjoys variety and that the various styles of worship allow our unique personalities to shine. We are like diamonds in the rough and as we grow in relationship with Him we shine brighter and brighter with a unique brilliance that glorifies Him. It's not a matter of the name on the door of a church but a matter of the heart.

Still, my parents did not understand me or my way of thinking. They were distraught with the whole situation thinking I'd lost my faith, not realizing I had actually found it. They told me acrimoniously with a frown that, "I was a disgrace" and how disappointed they were in me and with me. I struggled with balancing "honor thy father and mother" and the command, "To seek God first over everything."

My Wedding Day, August 9, 1986

Matrimony

One thing was for certain: I was intent on marrying Scott sooner, not later. My parents told me that if I decided to get married before I graduated from college, I would be responsible for paying for my college education. Therefore, Scott and I developed a plan for getting married and putting us both through college: I would go to school first and work, while he just worked. Then he would attend college and not work after I completed my undergraduate schooling.

I asked Mom and Dad to walk me down the aisle. It was one of the few occasions I saw my Father cry.

*Dad, me and
Mom right before
we left their
home for the
church in the
wedding limo*

This plan made sense because we wouldn't get too far in debt and we thought that I could handle school and work at the same time better than he could.

When my parents realized we were serious about getting married, they decided to throw us the best wedding possible. Scott had to go through classes to become a Catholic and on August 9, 1986, two starry-eyed youngsters wed and promised to be friends forever, for better or for worse, and in sickness and in health. We entered into our marriage with absolute commitment. We enjoyed a traditional wedding ceremony and my parents spared no expense to ensure that it was a once-in-a-lifetime event including a band, videographer, photographer, sit-down dinner and dance. Our favorite love songs were sung during the service and reception among the refreshing pink roses, babies breath and perky pink carnation floral arrangements I'd created along with the boutonnieres, corsages, and even my bridal bouquet.

You And Me Against The World

At the reception, I told a touching story and dedicated "You and Me Against the World" (by Helen Reddy) to Scott and his mom; it was their song through his challenging childhood. They called me out midway through the chorus, and, as we huddled in tears, she told us, "Now it's the two of you," and passed the "torch" to me. There wasn't a dry eye to be found, even in the camera people and servers. Karen told me, "It's every mother's dream to be honored like that, but it never happens. You made it happen for me. It's something I'll never forget."

To honor my parents, Scott and I went to the Catholic Church and got very busy. I was a Eucharistic minister and continued to lead the

Mass worship accompanied by the organist. The priest bought me a twelve-string guitar as a thank you gift for my years of dedication to the children and the church. After a couple of formal lessons I taught myself to play. My goal was to play *El Shaddai* like Amy Grant. I thought this would show my appreciation for his gift. When this happened, God was glorified and the priest was visibly moved. On that occasion and several others he teased, with his strong Irish accent, "I thought I was in the Baptist church for a moment," while the congregation expressed a

Two Starry-eyed youngsters

nervous laugh. I often pushed the envelope, but he seemed to appreciate my originality and sincerity of heart for praising the Lord.

Cries In The Night

Scott and I now lived in the duplex I rented and carefully decorated with all the things I'd stored under my bed for his Christmas present nine months before we married. Our neighbors were a wonderful older couple with whom we exchanged desserts and friendly conversation. Not long after we wed, in the darkness of night, I heard a disturbing sound through the walls. It began softly, but got louder until it sounded like someone was in terrible torment. I feared someone may have broken in and could be hurting them. I woke Scott to hear the unrest. He walked around the house; everything seemed to be in order. We prayed for them, thinking they must have gotten some terrible news.

After hearing the wailing each night, we decided to get to the bottom of this troubling situation. Larry was coming out the door toward ours and we met in the middle. In tears, he told us that his wife suffered from a mental illness called manic depression; she was overwhelmingly depressed. He shared with us that it was worse than ever and that she was slipping away. They had tried everything; even shock treatment and she only seemed to get worse. He apologized for the disturbance and wanted to assure us he was not hurting her; the hurt was coming from within her mind.

I was heart-broken for both of them. She was always a down-to-earth, wonderful lady; someone you enjoyed sharing a cup of milk and homemade cookies with. She and Larry fit together like puzzle pieces and I never heard one utter a cross word to the other.

Ultimately, with the help of his adult children, Larry made the excruciating decision to put the love of his life into a hospital where they gave her strong sedative medications to relieve her intense misery. He was afraid she might do something to hurt herself. He was devoted to her and refused to abandon her, spending his days watching for a spark that would indicate that his fun-loving best friend had returned.

They were very active in their Baptist church and Larry cherished the support he found there. The only time he left his wife's side was to come home to sleep or go to church. A month later, at the end of a worship service, Larry slumped over in his pew; his broken heart had given out and he died.

This was my second encounter with the demons of mental illness in others. I had no idea that this was a taste of things to come, or how intimately I would come to know how devastating such a disease could be.

Teamwork

While Scott worked at the organ and piano store in the Winter Haven Mall, I managed the flower shop, worked as a substitute teacher, waitress, bartender, exercise instructor, house sitter, babysitter, and any other job I could fit into my schedule. I also attended Polk Community College in Winter Haven, and then Warner Southern College, a Christian college in Lake Wales, Florida. I enrolled in Warner Southern to pursue my Bachelor of Arts degree in physical education, recreation and health, with a minor in theology. Throughout primary school, most teachers and guidance counselors didn't think I was college material. One teacher even mentioned her thoughts in front of all of my peers in class one day. Consequently, I was not certain that I was, either. But I had goals, and failure was not an option.

I was the only female in the physical education program. It was great since I always wanted a brother and now I had a bunch of them who looked out for me. I completed my course work at Warner in record time—in the middle of the public school system's year—with honors and applied with male candidates for the only physical education position available in the Polk County school system. It would be a long drive and a long shot, but I called the principal every day, or stopped in to remind him that I was the best candidate for the position. I was relentless because the moment I began my career, Scott could quit his job and start school. Finally, the principal came to see my point of view and hired me! I worked hard and valued the opportunity to teach; I found my calling. Life was good and everything was on schedule.

Yearning For A Child

There is nothing fun about the menstrual cycle. The pain and discomfort associated with my menses intensified during this time and I was diagnosed with endometriosis. My doctor performed a laparoscopy on March 12, 1991, burning the nerves at the base of my spine so they would not register the pain any more. However, within a year, the nerves grew new networks and the pain returned. The doctor suggested the best option was to get pregnant  so that is what I set out to do. When I went a few months without a period, I was excited and prepared to have a child in our new home that my parents helped us build, just two streets down from them.

Children are a gift, a miracle, a way to touch the future, and a holy calling. I took preparing for them very seriously. A baby's crib, white rocking chair, and changing table were quickly added to a nursery room where I painted a border with blue bears and pink bunnies for Scott Jr. or KD, for Katherine Diane. I often awoke in the middle of the night only to find myself wandering into the nursery to contemplate the future. I relished the opportunity to dream about what he would be when he grew up, or the first word our precious princess would say . . . I longed to whisper lullabies in my angel's sleepy ears. While rocking in the chair I wrote love letters, sharing my hopes and dreams and was amazed by the adoration, anticipation, and love I already felt for our unborn baby.

As I glided along in my ideal world, I was jostled by a fever, became ill, and passed a mass followed by a very painful period. Yearning for motherhood did not bring it to pass this time. In my lament, I reached for Scott's affection but he was preoccupied. To deal with the grief, I focused on helping him finish his schoolwork—introducing him to my principal who hired him—and on loving my students. In the early morning of our marriage, I had no clue that circumstances were brewing that would test every value Scott and I shared.

CHAPTER 7

An Incurable
Diagnosis...

You will have trials and tribulations
but be of good cheer for I have overcome the world.

—Jesus

At the age of twenty-three my life would change forever. I tried to put on a calm exterior to live through the jolt and disbelief of the words INCURABLE, LIFE THREATENING and CHRONIC. All three together sounded much like the other dreaded word, CANCER which I was half expecting. Unlike most cancers, with this diagnosis there was no treatment plan to follow and beat it. In a New York minute life would never be the same, not the way I saw myself, not the way I dealt with my world, and not the way others would come to see me. It's a staggering punch in the gut yet you stand there and take it with hardly a flinch. Your body goes numb, your hands go clammy and cold, and you see the doctor's mouth moving but can't make out his words. You can handle no further information as your thoughts race out of control. And then, you're all wrung out like clothing in the final spin cycle of your washer machine. You can't think of what to ask or say even if you had the strength to.

Mysterious Symptoms

Let me crack open the door a little further so you can look in and see what was happening at this time in my life. I transferred from teaching Physical Education outside to teaching inside and became a Special Education teacher. My students were three to six year olds who were abused, autistic, deaf, blind, had Down syndrome, or suffered from cocaine exposure, and other disabilities. Like a sponge that couldn't soak in enough education, I attended classes at Florida Southern

College (FSC) and the University of South Florida (USF) in pursuit of my master's degree in behavior disorders. The opportunity to expand my philosophy of teaching and discipline helped me stay focused on goals. I'd begun swimming several days a week again and was the track coach at my old Junior High School, leading the girls to their first championship in over twenty years. I was making a living shaping young lives with love even as I helped them and there families deal with horrifying personal tragedies. My Mother-in-law, Karen, helped me make our beautiful new home was just right and when Scott graduated, he began teaching second grade at the school where I worked. I loved that we were together. Our strategy for the "good life" was working out great. But...

Just after my birthday and before a sinus surgery for chronic sinus infections and allergies in 1990, I developed a terrible pain in my left hip. By Friday night my foot began to ache deeply and I noticed two red spots on the arch. On Sunday morning, I stepped out of bed and fell to the floor, unable to walk. I crawled to the bathroom and realized my foot was completely swollen, red, and hot to the touch. Scott rushed me to the emergency room. After several hours of restless waiting, the doctor said I must have banged my foot without realizing it and called it a hematoma. He prescribed ice, no work for three days, a prescription for the pain, and some crutches. He told me to "return if the symptoms persisted or go to my primary physician."

AIDS Scare

It didn't get better. In fact, later we found out that the ice was the worst thing I could use. After the sinus surgery when I hoped my health troubles would finally get behind me; each week a new joint or area of my body became inflamed, swollen, got hives, rashes, red spots and/or did not operate properly. My primary care physician didn't know what to make of it. He tested me for AIDS since I was exposed to many health risks through my students. After anxiously waiting, I was thankful the test came back negative. Still, I was in and out of the hospital every few weeks for observation of various strange flare-ups. Many specialists were sent to my room to inspect my medical anomaly. They thought it could be lupus, leukemia, or rheumatoid arthritis. They couldn't understand why the manifestations jumped all over my body. In the midst of an ordinary activity, sharp pains, fevers, chills, sweats, and profound fatigue would strike, leaving me helplessly vomiting or with bloody

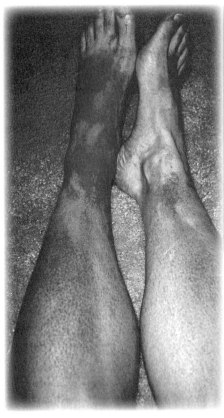

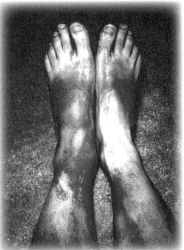

The blood disease and vasculitis (inflamed blood vessels)Like being hit with a hammer, pricked with needles as a million bugs crawl under my skin. My skin turns black, red and blue. It's very painful. It can take days or weeks to re-cuperate from an attack like this. Other symtoms include: dizzyness, nausea, vision problems, exhaustion

diarrhea. My menses magnified the problem so much that these painful episodes often confined me to my bed for several days.

Physicians ordered progressively more sophisticated and expensive blood tests without finding the answer. I was diagnosed with irritable bowel syndrome (IBS), systemic inflammation, and many other problematic conditions. Nothing was off limits to the disturbing antics of this mysterious disease. I continued to visit doctors and hospitals with little relief and no accurate diagnosis.

The intensity and frequency of my attacks increased to a dangerous level, even as I tried to push through. Many things exacerbated my condition including: panty hose, high-heeled or pointy toed shoes, tight clothing, medications, stress of any sort, temperature changes, air conditioning or drafts, driving, sitting or standing with my feet hanging down, and even just thinking about something upsetting. Blood vessels would burst like fire works on the Fourth of July. The escaped blood would leak through the superficial layers of my skin and make a bloody mess or bruise me as though I were hit repeatedly with a baseball bat, or come through the skin as sores. My extremities itched, tingled and burned like a million bugs were crawling under my skin. A simple ride in the car for a movie date often turned into an emergency room visit followed by days in the hospital to recuperate and get further uncomfortable testing.

One time my feet and legs turned so black, red, green, and blue that a doctor who specialized in amputations showed up at my hospital room door. He said my physician asked him to stop in for a consultation. He'd never seen anything like it. He felt a good pulse in the heel of my foot so he opted not to remove my legs. He declared, "Keep me posted" and instructed the nurses to call him immediately if they found any sign of gangrene from the sores that had broken through the skin.

Slipping Away

My health and active way of life were slipping away. However, I couldn't accept that I was sick; getting sick didn't fit into my plans! I was determined to push through the pain of this challenge. When the flare-ups came, I rested the best that I could, utilized crutches, elevated my feet, and reduced stress. If these steps failed, back to the hospital I went. With this happening on the outside of my body, I could only imagine the damage being done internally as my body tried to filter and process the toxic by products of these relentless attacks.

The knowledge that I could lose both of my legs was unsettling and contributed to my poor handling of my situation. I don't think I can accurately describe my mental state at this time. When the attacks came, all I could do was helplessly watch as my body deteriorated before my very eyes. I was filled with so much fear, anguish, and anger, that any healthful mechanism for dealing with my situation escaped me. My internal turmoil was exacerbated by my futile trips to the hospital where they offered me little in the way of explanation or relief.

One visit to the hospital was especially poignant. As the specialists scratched their heads in dismay with the multiple symptoms that would come and then go as quickly as they came including all mentioned already and the fever, stiff neck, blinding and severe headaches, disturbances in memory, mood, and sleep, persistent fatigue and aching problems. Especially disconcerting was the fact that this mystery disease appeared to be progressive, damaging, and debilitating, and if not treated soon could be fatal. After weeks feeling like I had a perpetual flu they diagnosed chronic fatigue syndrome, a Lyme disease phenomenon, arthritis, and vasculitis on my tattered being. Working, socializing, shopping, and performing daily chores like house cleaning were excruciating and the gnawing pain of fibromyalgia was worse than ever. I felt as though I had a thousand pound ball tethered to me, and no matter how hard I tried to kick it away, it held on and threatened to keep me from realizing my dreams. I was sick and tired of being sick and tired!

A Good Doctor

I was finally sent to Dr. Charlie Becknall, a dermatologist, on February 10, 1993. I told him about the trouble I was having taking all the medications; how the steroids didn't seem to work, and how the NSAID's anti-inflammatory medications were tearing up my stomach and even seemed to increase the vasculitis. I showed him the ulcerated sores, the large bruises, the swollen joints, and he noticed the lupus-like coloration on my face. I told him about my difficulty sleeping and the gnawing pain I experienced all the time in my connective tissue, joints, muscles, head, and stomach. I also shared the sadness I was experiencing from being unable to keep up with my daily routines, sports, and responsibilities. Appalled and puzzled that I'd suffered for over two years with no answers, Dr. Becknall concluded that biopsies from my inflamed foot and leg were necessary. He gently told me that the procedure would leave a scar and that the cut would be the size of a dime and an inch deep. This didn't sound fun, but I desperately wanted him to tell me what was wrong and fix it so I could get over "it" and on with my life!

I lived in denial for as long as possible, but my body was breaking down and my needs were becoming so complex that I felt like I was letting down my husband, family, friends, my employer, and students. As if God were crying with me, raindrops rolled down the large window as I spoke with Dr. Becknall. I couldn't hold back any longer, and as he stuck the needle into my leg and then my foot to numb the area, the tears began to sting my eyes and roll down my cheeks. He said nothing to interrupt me. He reached for my hand and told me that he realized how hard this must be and that he would do everything in his power to help me find the underlying cause of this mystery. I tried to keep a stiff upper lip to make my father proud but it quivered uncontrollably.

He explained further that there was no question that something was wrong with my immune system, and that it could be leukemia, lupus, or some other complex condition. He wanted me to be prepared for such a diagnosis, but he didn't want to speculate further until the tests came back. He scheduled a return visit for a week later so he could review the results. I wobbled out of his office washed out by the tidal wave of sorrow that had finally crashed ashore, but was thankful for his gentle and caring spirit. I was hopeful that we would finally discover the underlying cause of my mysterious symptoms.

The Not Knowing

The revolving merry-go-round of misery continued and that week of waiting was as grueling as all the others before. It was difficult for me to calm my imaginative mind, especially since I didn't know what type of sentence I would receive from the test results. The site of the biopsy seemed to be getting infected as I tried to give over control of my situation to God. After all, He was the center of my life, wasn't He? Or, had I gotten so caught up in my goals and the troubles of my world that I lost my genuine relationship with Him? Without realizing it, God had become secondary in my life and the need to find out what demon was plaguing me became my focus. I wanted to know so I could expel it, beat it, and move on with what life I had left. It was the "not knowing" that seemed the hardest. I literally felt the storm of disease rocking the foundation of my world. Just like the fisherman named Peter in the Bible, I let the pelting rain and wrenching winds of life distract me. When Peter was focused on Jesus he walked on water. When the storm captured his attention, he sank. I was sinking.

I returned to the doctor's office only to be let down again: the biopsies and tests were inconclusive. The doctor asked me if I would be willing to go to the University of South Florida (USF) in Tampa to see a group of experts who might be able to shed light on this medical anomaly. I promptly complied.

The Diagnosis

I went to the USF medical campus for more tests and heard nothing for a month. Finally, I got a letter with an invitation to return. The University was hosting a dermatology conference on Tuesday, May 11, 1993, with some of the world's leading physicians in the field of rare and difficult to diagnose diseases attending. For my part, I had to keep a journal of my symptoms that they would read as they poked and prodded. I lay on the cold hard metal examining table in an open hospital gown, while one doctor after another looked me over and examined my body, my diary and my file. My symptoms got worse before their eyes as I lay there in the chilly air-conditioned room. Some of the doctors had good bedside manners while many did not; I felt like a piece of meat under inspection. In the end, the group ordered a specialized blood test.

I was sent home to wait again. Scott was busy with his new career and responsibilities when the blood test they ordered finally revealed what was wrong. Almost three years after those little spots first appeared on the arch of my foot, the doctors concluded that I suffered from a rare, incurable blood disease called CRYOGLOBULINEMIA. It's a painful autoimmune blood disorder. They also confirmed: vasculitis, purpura and Raynaud's phenomenon. I was told to minimize all exposure to the cold and avoid standing, sitting, or ANYTHING that seemed to inflame the potentially dangerous and painful symptoms. They were educated on the strange things that increased my symptoms and outbreaks by reading my journals of torment.

As far as they knew, I was one the youngest patients ever to be diagnosed with this disease. They took pictures of my legs and I signed a release form so they could publish them in medical journals and text-books. They confided that I was not a good candidate for studies because of the other health variables that I experienced. They explained, "The best you can do is keep the 'flare-ups' to a minimum in order to prevent further damage to your blood vessels and organs. It's a life-threatening disease that you must mitigate well to stay alive." My immune system was compromised. They seemed to think this blood disease was a pre-cursor to a form of leukemia, lymphoma, or a type of cancer. I would need regular blood testing every three to six months to monitor the pro-gression of the disease and it's affects on my body.

Since the illness is rare and few people are acquainted with it, I have included photographs of flare-ups and I invite you to visit our web site, www.DianeDike.org for more information.

Treating The Incurable

I had to try and figure out what this disease was and breaking down the word to its linguistic components was helpful: cryo=cold; globu=clot; nemia=blood. The first line of treatment is staying warm or my blood turns to a deadly jello like consistency. Using mittens just to open the refrigerator is of utmost importance and a necessary preventative mea-sure. Keeping warm seems simple enough, but it's not as easy as one might think. For instance, I lived in warm, sunny Florida, which would seem like a good place to reside for someone with this condition. Well, try going into a grocery store, restaurant, or anywhere the air conditioner runs after sweating or being out in the heat. I needed to wear full mountain ski gear to make it through a grocery, eating, or shopping experience safely.

Have you ever seen anyone in a grocery store in Florida with full ski gear on? People give looks of judgment, whisper to one another, and say hurtful, insensitive things. I began to think it easier just to stay home. When I did go out I tried to ignore my symptoms and paid the consequences.

The illness is unpredictable. Kidney damage can be serious and result in failure. Death usually occurs from heart disease, infection, or brain hemorrhage. Because of the thickness of the blood, stroke, blood clots, and blood clots in the eye leading to blindness can occur. Vasculitis of the arteries can result in blockage, leading to damaged organs like the skin, heart, kidneys, and lungs. Ulcerated sores can lead to gangrene because of a profound lack of blood flow, especially in the extremities. The vessels shut down as if a tourniquet were applied. Neuropathy often results because of the damage caused to the nerves by constant inflammation. (See Appendix B for additional medical information)

My Response To Cryoglobulinemia

The diagnosis did nothing to boost my self-image and the statistics were not pretty. People with chronic localized pain have a 55% increased chance of getting cancer and/or dying early. Those who suffer with overall body pain have a 105% higher chance of getting cancer and/or dying early. Beating this "thing" was my only option; I was unwilling to accept any other.

I finally knew what plagued me. The only problem with this knowledge was the fact that even the world's experts concurred, without much hope, that there is NO cure. I wanted to ask the doctors so many questions: *"What do you mean? This is it? I just have to live with it? How do I live with a painful disease and its many companions that attack like terrorists without warning? What am I supposed to do, sit around and hope they don't? And if they do, I am supposed to lay down while they ruin my life?"*

I was further distressed by the knowledge that this disease was not confined to one part of my body; that it emanated from my very bone marrow and spread throughout the rest of my body by way of my circulatory system which explained the intense and deep pain. I began to take hold of the fact that if I didn't make some drastic changes, I wouldn't have a life worth living. My body had turned on me and my way of life was gone, gone forever.

Spiritual Strong Tower?

Jesus is the same yesterday, today and tomorrow and by His stripes I am healed. I was ready to see and experience my healing. I desired to be a spiritual strong tower but my personal relationship with Jesus had been distracted by the details of life. I'd gotten too tired to pray. Now I deliberated where would I find the strength to carry on. I saw glimpses of God's glory in the smiling faces of my severely handicapped students. I reasoned that if they could make it through the day with all their challenges, so could I. I felt a deeper connection with them as we learned to deal with our handicaps together.

Even so, I still faltered and fell into a vat of self-destruction that threatened to destroy me. I felt so lost. The decisive factor came when they told me that I should not, even if I were able to, have children. I was devastated. This news squashed any glimmer of hope I had. How would I break this news to Scott? I tried to lean on the scripture, "Though I am surrounded by troubles, you will bring me safely through them... The Lord will work out His plans for my life" (Psalm 138:7-8).

But all I could feel beneath each step was sinking sand. I shut the door to my precious little nursery and couldn't bare to opened it again.

CHAPTER 8

DOWNWARD SPIRAL

 Until one has loved an animal, a part of one's soul remains unawakened.

—Anatole France

Love In Any Language

Only the love of God can meet our needs. No person can fill the God shaped hole in our souls, especially when we face crushing challenges. However, one of my joys at this stage of my life was my very first pet, a miniature dachshund named, Millie. She was nine pounds of unconditional love just what I needed. I bought her right after we moved into our new home and we developed a profound relationship. With approval from my principal, I took her to my pre-kindergarten special needs classroom. It was a great experience for the children and became weekly therapy for us all. She shared pure love and even seemed to sense my children's special needs. They were able to play with her ears, snuggle her close and love her. She never displayed a ounce of aggression. I will never forget the excitement of Sherika, my blind student, when Millie touched her cheek with her cool wet nose and lavished her with kisses. This otherwise detached student laughed with every part of her being. Millie brought much joy to our classroom and everyday lessons came to life with her as a tail-wagging example. Some students had only been around scary dogs but Millie showed them a love and joy they may never have had the opportunity to experience. Daily they ran with joy off the bus to our classroom to be greeted by Millie.

I also took Millie to hospitals and nursing homes on the weekends. She cheered up the residents we visited and enjoyed an enthusiastic response from patients and staff alike. I think she brought back childhood memories of simpler and happier times for my elderly friends. Cheering up people who were sad, sick, disabled, or lonely came so easy for Millie. George Eliot said, "Animals are such agreeable friends—they ask no questions, they pass no criticisms." I could see how her loving

Millie in the classroom. Her tail is wagging but she is not happy that the rabbit is in her usual spot.

presence could heal where words had no effect. "Love is a language which the blind can see and the deaf can hear," exclaimed Donald E. Wildman.

The Millie Degree

My experiences with Millie helped direct my higher education. After the children spent time with her, I witnessed many behavioral, social, emotional, cognitive, and psychological improvements. The benefits were obvious from the start of the project. I was excited about the results and improvements we were seeing. I realized that children have many feelings, anxieties, and thoughts they can't put into words, and that animals don't need verbal communication to interact or connect with a person at an intimate level. I hypothesized that inter-species contact and interaction had therapeutic benefits that could be investigated in a study in which Millie would be the animal and my special education children would be the subjects.

Obtaining My Doctorate

The desire to get my Ph.D. by the age of thirty caused me to investigate the possibilities. I decided to apply and was accepted by Walden University and began my doctoral work on my birthday in 1992. The work load was intense but, before long, I submitted a dissertation proposal entitled: *Alternative Therapeutic Interventions Utilizing Animal Therapy with Three to Six Year Old Special Needs Children.* I felt truly blessed to be able to combine my love for children and animals, not only in the pursuit of my personal educational goals, but also in the attempt to help all children who struggled to understand their own feelings, the world around them, and how to better deal with it's challenges. (I had no way of knowing just how important and relative this work would be to me personally).

I began formal observations of my students interacting with Millie. In three months I compiled over 200 pages of notes. My average day during these years went from 5:00 a.m. to after midnight. It was hard work going to school and working full time while dealing with major health problems. My insomnia actually allowed me to accomplish much of this work. Quite frankly, the work gave my mind something else to focus on instead of my intense physical pain, and when the flare-ups caused me to be still, I worked even harder on my studies from bed until I couldn't hold my head up anymore. My school and work load challenged me. Nevertheless, I was focused and determined to live a fulfilling life even as I lived in a denial of the seriousness of my condition.

The Beginning Of The End

My failing health became more difficult to manage with each passing month and I became increasingly obsessive about everything being in its place at home. I've heard from others who suffer from chronic illness that this obsession is a common behavior. Since we have no control over what is happening to our bodies, we become obsessed about the things we can control; no matter how trivial or inconsequential they may appear to others. The slightest thing could send me into a meltdown of tears. The insanity of my impossible schedule caught up to me again.

I remember staining the kitchen sink when I cleaned some brushes with paint solvent. I almost had a nervous breakdown, thinking how stupid and worthless I was for ruining our kitchen sink. I could hear my father's words, "For crying out loud, can't you do anything right? Why are you always causing trouble? What's the matter with you," resounding in my head? Scott looked on in bewilderment, ignorant of what to say or do about this overreaction to an otherwise inconsequential event. I thought to myself, *I'm not the girl you married, how very disappointed you must be.*

I was slipping into a tub of despair and self-destruction. My greatest hopes and dreams seemed to be washing out from around me. I felt like less of a woman and so unattractive. The thought that having a child was no longer an option magnified my feelings of failure. My oldest sister Jackie was having one child right after the other so I relished the opportunity to give them all the love they would allow. But this also reminded me that my dream of having children was unattainable now.

As I shut the door of the nursery my heart broke into a million pieces. It was a mess I was unequipped to clean up.

Permission To Destroy My Life

In our seventh year of marriage, I started pushing Scott away, telling him that he got more than he bargained for and that he deserved better. Like trying to save *Old Yeller* in the Disney movie, I kicked dirt and threw rocks his way in an attempt to make him flee from imminent danger. I told him I didn't love him and that he would be better off without me: this was a terrible lie. It wasn't Scott I didn't love, but my double-crossing body and mind.

Despite my best intentions, I was unaware that I was sliding down a slippery road of destruction. All I knew was that I desperately needed a change; at least something to distract myself from my physical pain and mental anguish. I felt trapped, claustrophobic, and needed a reality break so I became reckless. In my view, our future seemed pathetic, and if I were lucky, I would soon die and be put out of my misery. Somewhere along the journey I swam into the harbor of hopelessness.

In all my plans, I never planned for this. We had no strategy to hold our relationship together during the desperate circumstances and overwhelming possibilities. We turned against each other when what we really needed to do was turn to God. Our relationship was wearing down and I was becoming numb. I felt like I was chained to a sinking rock in the middle of an angry ocean, while crashing waves quickly put distance between me and everything that mattered. When Scott noticed the severity of our situation, I couldn't even grab the life preserver he desperately threw my way. Without notice I swung wildly from despair to acceptance, to disbelief and back again. And then, I was gone!

Bad Decisions

I was stuck in dysfunction junction. My physical condition conspired with its mental counterpart to put me in constant "fight or flight." In nature, when an animal faces a threatening situation, its instinct is to choose one of these responses as a coping mechanism. However, it is perhaps one of the cruelest tricks that I chose both, simultaneously: I fought all those who only wanted to help and sought flight from my situation and myself. To be honest, I checked out, and became devoid of emotion. I was desperate to feel alive and free; I ran, believing I was doing Scott a favor. I made decisions for him that were not mine to make. When I think back, I can still see the fear on Scott's face that pleaded for me to come back to my senses.

Chapter 8: *Downward Spiral*

During the worst of the storm I made one last ditch effort to stop the tempest. Withering like a plant without water, I went to the new priest at our church. After visiting for fifteen minutes, he concluded, "Sounds as though you have done everything that you could do. You and Scott just are not in love anymore." On the one hand, this seemed like a very strange comment from a priest. On the other hand, it was exactly what I needed to hear since, in my deranged state of mind, the priest's words gave me permission to destroy my life and that is exactly what I set out to do.

Join The Navy?

As I found it increasingly more difficult to manage my work load and health, I took a leave of absence from my teaching position with the idea of focusing on completing my dissertation work and researched going into the Navy as a psychologist. I was desperate for a solution to my over-whelming need to run. When I told Scott of my idea to join the Navy, he was incensed. He argued that they would never take me with my health problems. The anger at that thought swelled inside of me. I rebelled, *who is he to try and control me, tell me what I can and can't do?* Scott also reminded me that he wouldn't think of moving and that being married, while living separately, would be no marriage at all. One foggy night, I packed my bag and walked out the door. In a frantic frenzy of push and pull Scott assured me that he would find someone new. He would not be alone. In 1993, I hoped the Navy would be my new home.

The Navy sent me to Norfolk, Virginia. I went to the medical hospital and toured a submarine and an aircraft carrier. My recruiter believed that I could begin my Naval career as a Lieutenant Commander because of my education and experience. I would work in the counseling psychology program. All I had to do was pass the physical, complete officer training school, and report for duty. I never mentioned my health problems and they never looked at my legs. All seemed to be in place. However, at this point I had not completed my Ph.D. They told me to call when I graduated and then they would move forward with the enlistment.

No Place To Call Home

This delay presented a difficult problem because I still needed to complete my observations of Millie with my students to conclude my dissertation. Even though I had taken a leave of absence from my teaching position, I still had access to the students but no longer had daily access to Millie. After our separation, Millie lived with Scott because I had no place to call home. When I still had the house key, I went there periodically when Scott was at work to get something to wear and to see Millie. When it was time for me to leave and put her into the kitchen, she would whimper, wail, and cry like never before. I would too. Nothing made any sense and as I stumbled away, I would look in the rearview mirror with tears streaming down my face thinking *I want to stay,* and would hit the brake. Then I would think, *no, I want to go* and would press my foot on the accelerator I would do this repeatedly and concluded, *I'm so stupid. What is wrong with me?* I would then sink my face into my hands until I couldn't weep anymore.

With no place to live and on leave from my teaching position with the school system and the College, my only income was the two hundred dollars a week I made doing public relations work for seven locally owned McDonald's restaurants. It was all I had to hold on to and it gave me hope to carry on, a purpose, and a meal to eat when I was working. I'd worked hard for them for several years creating outstanding programs for customers, students and employees.

One day my friend and boss called me in for a meeting. "You have a lot going on in your life right now," she mentioned. "Seems you are a little distracted. Why don't you take a break..." her voice continued as my mind drifted... *I'm replaceable. I've never been let go from a job in my life. No one wants or needs me...* A cold sweat came over me and before I knew it I lost my only job. When she was done, I mustered the last of my strength and dignity to get up and walk out of her office. In the foyer the employees looked at me as if they knew about the plan to let me go. It was an emotional crawl to my car and when I got there a breeze could have toppled me. I collapsed... like a robot I started the car, put it into gear, and started to drive. To where, I had no idea. My mind whispered, *what am I going to do now?*

Homeless

Homeless and with no income, I slept on couches, floors, or in my car. After I walked out on Scott it felt like I didn't have a friend in the world. I pondered selling my blood, like the desperate character in the movie, *The Pursuit of Happiness,* but no one wanted or needed my blood. It wasn't any good, just like me.

I wanted to go home to Scott so many times, but reasoned that it wouldn't be fair to him. I was so bewildered, ashamed, and lost. *Won't someone save me?* I thought. To complicate my issues, I went on drinking binges to numb the pain and looked for love in all the wrong places. My father's words resonated in my brain, "You are a disgrace. You look like the last rose of summer," and I knew it was true. I did things that took me far away from the things of God. I thought He'd abandoned me and I couldn't blame Him.

My greatest fears were coming true. I was angry with myself, with God, and with the winds of adversity that were chasing me. I didn't know what to do with my perceived failures and disappointments. My unacknowledged anger turned inward to mix with my low serotonin levels and became clinical depression. I was like a zombie in one of those horror movies, walking around aimlessly, lost, and dead. Some days I could barely motivate myself to wash my face, never mind find my next meal. Where I was once so full of promise, I was now full of dread, waiting, even hoping, for the pain to end. When I did make time for God it was to beg him, "Please, let death come quickly and put me out of my misery."

I mustered up enough courage to call an old friend. My heart pounded in my chest and moisture built up in my hands as the phone jingled once, twice, then she picked up. "Hi, Bethany, It's Diane. How are you?"

"What do you want?" she demanded. "Why are you calling me?"

"I've been missing you and wondered how you are and if we could get together?"

"Sorry Diane, there is no place for you in my life anymore. It would be best if you didn't call me ever again? Goodbye."

The dial tone persisted as my trembling hands hung up the dirty pay phone. I hadn't done anything to her personally, but with raised eyebrows and a scratch to my head I thought, she must hate me for leaving Scott. *What did I expect? I'm a loser and so stupid.*

Despair

On the plank of despair I walked, and walked, and walked until after 2 a.m., submerged in my ocean of failure. I leaned against a tree on a dark deserted street and let out a cry into the night. It sounded familiar; it was the same agonizing sound I heard our neighbor Larry's manic-depressive wife make years ago. Heaving sobs burst from me as I slide down the lonely tree into the dirt. I was far from being strong and courageous, or committed and loyal, as guilt and shame plunged me to what I thought was rock bottom. In the emptiness I cried, *"Please, someone, put me out of my misery."*

CHAPTER 9

THE DEMON OF DIVORCE

Love knows not its own depth until the hour of separation.

—Kahil Gibran

A Psychiatrist. A broken heart. Self-sabotage. Lost and miles from the next exit. What do all these have in common? Answer: My life while battling the demons of divorce and depression.

I went to a psychiatrist for the first time. I answered her questions, filling her in on my life story: the downward spiral of my health; my lack of interest in the things most important to me; how I hurt all over and felt like giving up; and even my decision to abandon my plans to join the Navy. The counselor asked about my upbringing, and my relationship with my parents. As she dredged up the past, I couldn't stop the dirge. She prescribed an antidepressant and I thought, "Great, that's all I need, another prescription." Then I thought, "Who cares, what's another medication? Maybe my freedom lies in the benefit I will get from this 'happy' pill!" However, I'd avoided drugs all my life to try and stay healthy. Now I was instructed to take them to get healthy. Nothing made sense to me and I was aware that the drug's side effects of dry mouth, irritability, and constipation (just to name a few) could cause more unwanted problems. I couldn't help but think that since the drugs prescribed to relieve my physical suffering had failed so wretchedly, anything prescribed to assuage my mental anguish would fail as well, just like it did for Larry's wife. I was like a wild animal cornered in a cage without any good options.

Sometimes I was too tired to cry and other times, I couldn't stop. Eager for relief from my mental and physical suffering, I started on the free samples of the antidepressant the psychiatrist prescribed. What else could I do?

Even though Scott and I were separated, I invited him to join me for an appointment. He agreed to come with me even though he didn't feel he needed to be there; after all, I was the one with the problem. My psychiatrist saw Scott separately. I do not know what was said, but we never had another appointment together. At this point I felt he hated me. I hated myself, too. I was lost and miles from home.

Overwhelmed And Abandoned

Have you ever felt abandoned... abandoned by God? Have circumstances overwhelmed you so much that you thought dying would be better than living? That was me.

Like a pilot in a fog relying on failing instruments, fear caused me to run away from everything that meant anything to me. Consequently, I lost it all. At last, Scott divorced me. As we walked into the county courthouse to sign the papers that would end our union, I tried to swallow the lump swelling in my throat. With tears running down my cheeks, I reached out to hold his hand. In a flash, I remembered our times together: Bill's funeral, ten Christmases, beach trips, my senior prom; planning our future, building our first home, laying sod in our first yard, working on projects around the house, squirting each other with the hose on hot summers days, birthdays, anniversaries, family gatherings... Our relationship ended as it began: me reaching out to hold his hand.

A Living Death

My heartbreaking divorce pushed me deeper into a turbulent ocean of despair. I was drowning in self-hate because I believed the lie Satan screamed in my ear: "If you hadn't been such a selfish, terrible person, none of this would have happened!" Instead of trusting God by using the armor He offers all who truly surrender to His will and acknowledging His sovereignty in all things, I tried to make it on my own and failed miserably. I now begged God for death and cursed the day that I was born.

Divorce is a living death. You lose the person with whom you became united but he is not really gone. He continues to live his life apart from yours even as he continues to live within your soul. He's there, but you can't reach him. The ink on the divorce paperwork was still drying when I began to reach out to Scott for reconciliation. My hope was that if I got my act together by getting a place, paying my bills, and showing some normalcy, maybe we could reunite and be better than before.

It was a new school year and I got a job at the high school I graduated from and saved all the money I could. Then, I rented a little place of my own and fixed it up with the few pieces of furniture from our house that Scott allowed me to have. I bought four loaves of bread for $1.00 at the day old bread store down the street each week and thought, *things are looking up.*

I called Scott on a Saturday morning and a young woman answered the phone. My heart stopped and I thought I'd dialed the wrong number but soon found out that, Scott met someone. They were engaged. I'd truly lost him. This wave washed over me and when it receded I had nothing left... *I can't do anything right.* The Devil whispered with glee, "Yes, you see, you do deserve every bad thing that happens to you, now you have lost it all. You have nothing! You are nothing."

We Needed Each Other

Monday came around and I made myself get out of bed to go to work. I was teaching older, special needs students in a self-contained room because some of them were considered too dangerous to mingle with regular students. Many of them were victims or perpetrators of violent crime. Several of the students had assaulted police officers, and others lived in drug-infested neighborhoods with poor or sick parents addicted to drugs. Others had been molested, tormented, or neglected most of their lives. Their case files and profile notes were daunting. The students were much larger than I and new students sometimes tried to intimidate me; one student threw a desk from across the room in a fit of rage on his first day. Despite the possibility of classroom violence, I was not frightened because I felt it was my calling to love the unlovable. I understood. We made a connection, and we needed each other to get through another painful day. I thought to myself, "If they can get up and come to school every day, then so can I." I didn't want to let them down.

I was too humiliated to let anyone know the extent of how desperate my life had become. I wore a mask even as I felt totally broken; sick in my mind, body, and soul. Hating myself made it increasingly more difficult to effectively reach out to others. It was like Clare Boothe Luce said, "There are no hopeless situations; there are only people who have grown hopeless about them." I was hopeless and thought this was the worst time of my life. However, I still hadn't hit the bottom yet.

Tormented

As time dragged on, sleep came infrequently and when it did, it often left me soaking from night sweats as nightmares and chasing dreams tormented me. I couldn't reconcile my divorce, the diagnosis of a rare and incurable disease, the abusive boyfriend I had gotten mixed up with, failure to reach my doctoral goals, my deteriorating energy and physical ability, poor choices, and the dark cloud of depression that offered no reprieve. I loved children, but had none of my own. It broke my heart to send my students home to dysfunctional and abusive homes. The lack of sleep and chronic pain mixed with my disappointments and self-hate to become a mountain that seemed insurmountable. All I knew was that I didn't want to live this way anymore and killing myself seemed like the only answer. Just the idea of it gave me a sense of relief that my torment would soon end.

I left my apartment and walked the streets in the middle of the night, hoping for a drive-by shooting, or for an alligator to drag me into the swampy lake. Neither of these scenarios occurred so I made a plan to kill myself. With a matter of fact attitude I thought, *I will jump out of my condo window. No, that could be messy. What if it doesn't work and I break myself and have to live with that shame. Maybe I'll take a bottle of my pain medication and antidepressants and gently go to sleep.* Not waking up seemed like the best alternative. Ironically, I was still taking the antidepressant when I became suicidal. (Later, it became obvious that prescription medication was not the answer for me. I am one of those for whom antidepressants and other medications seem to have the opposite of the desired effect. The often intolerable side effects only added to my laundry list of symptoms). I rationalized; *surely, the Lord would not send me to hell when I'd already been through it here on earth. He would have mercy on my soul, wouldn't He?*

Mercy Came A Runnin'

As the end of the school year approached, I took one of my desperation walks and composed my farewell note to my parents. The Lord's mercy came in a way very different from what I'd prayed for. As I went to cross a side street, a car pulled in front of me and stopped. It was my pastor, Ron Bos, from New Hope Church where I had attended off and on for the past six months. He got out of his car and said that he was driving home when he saw me, and that the Lord sent him back to stop me. He proclaimed, "Whatever you are going to do, the Lord says, 'don't do it!' Diane, what's going on?" After a very long talk and a promise that I wouldn't do what I was planning, he allowed me to walk home on my own with a plan that he and his wife would pick me up later.

They kept their word and brought me to their home for dinner. They insisted that I stay for as long as I needed but I wound up staying at the Sheffield's home, a family from church that I'd known and loved for a long time. God met me where I was. He met me through a man willing to take the time to turn around and be obedient to the Holy Spirit. My church and new church family helped motivate me to pull it together, if not for myself, then for them. But would that be enough?

I Needed God

The Book of Job is a timeless depiction of suffering. In Chapter five verse seven, he said as sure as sparks fly upward we would have troubles. The sparks were flying as I searched to find my way through the war zone. How did Job make it through the horrendous trials he experienced? He made it through by keeping his eyes on God. He got God's perspective when he could, and when he didn't understand, he trusted God regardless of what his wife, friends, or personal fears said. I wanted to walk toward healing and peace no matter my circumstances. I didn't need religion: I needed God, a fresh touch from the Holy Spirit and the saving grace of Jesus.

The church rallied around me and I went every time the doors were open. To this day, I don't know if the people of that church have any idea how much they helped me. I was ashamed, lost, and a dirty sinner yet they welcomed me with open arms. I rarely made it through a service without bursting into tears. Through these people God was able to reach in and touch my broken heart. They prayed for me and helped inject me with the knowledge that only God could handle the mess that I'd made of my life, and that no matter what, Jesus' arms were outstretched waiting for me to return to Him. I continued teaching and read all I could about how to live a victorious Christian life.

Pastor Bos taught me, "You've encountered the thief who comes to steal, kill and destroy (John 10:10), the one who's determined to keep you a failure, to defeat you on every front. The only way you'll bring him down, the only way you'll extinguish those fiery arrows that will impale you on the stake of continuous defeat until you're consumed in its flames of destruction, is through the Word of the Lord Jesus Christ. It's truth, and it alone, can sanctify you, give you strength for the battle—set you apart for victory. You must learn to bring every rebellious thought captive to the obedience of Christ. You're in the war zone. It's a real battle." The Bible says, "If you say there's no hope, you're listening to the father of lies." (John 8:44) I wanted the abundant, affective Spirit-filled life but I had to stop listening to the lies and change the tapes that recited my faults and failures.

There's a cleansing sacredness in tears shed before the Lord. Washington Irving penned, "They are not the mark of weakness, but of power. They speak more eloquently than ten thousand tongues. They are messengers of overwhelming grief... and unspeakable love." Grief changed my perspective on life. Grief felt like death until I could come to appreciate that afflictions could help me grow as a person of faith and show what is deep inside of me. Grief can be a gift. Like squeezing a tube of toothpaste, God was allowing me to see exactly what I was made of, to be broken and emptied out and then filled with Him. And the loss, was teaching me what was really precious and important. I would never take for granted the blessings; if I was ever able to have them back again. Kay Arthur wrote in *As Silver Refined*, "You may think there's no recovery from your failure. But, my friend, if you have God, you have a future—and it's not a dismal one." God helped me understand I could recover from my failures. But would my mind truly believe this and let my heart truly heal?

The Betrayal Of My Mind

The Sheffield's and other church members made themselves available to me night and day and faithfully prayed for me. Even with their efforts, the blazing furnace of trouble engulfed me and I was losing my fight with depression. Tylenol PM and antidepressants numbed my mind but even when I slept, I never felt rested. I was not completely obedient and failed to sever ties with the abusive boyfriend and paid dearly for that. During cycles of breaking up and getting back together he confirmed my feelings of worthlessness and that I deserved all of my difficulty. He was a funeral director and told me, "I could put you in the crematory and no one will ever know." Because I was physically, mentally and emotionally exhausted, the enemy was winning this war. Wouldn't it have been nice if I'd realized like Dr. Phil McGraw often says, "It is better to be healthy alone than sick with someone else."

My thoughts were so toxic and I was so weak that I let my boyfriend, shame, and continuous failure sidetrack me from going to church again. My strength to believe in a future wavered. I couldn't get past the idea that the world would be a better place if I were not in it. I was confused and tossed to and fro in my stormy messed up mind. My friend Dayla was very concerned and she took me to the hospital emergency room where they committed me to the "funny farm;" and there wasn't anything "funny" about it.

I was put on suicide watch and couldn't even go to the bathroom by myself. A large black man was assigned to watch my every move to prevent me from doing harm to myself. Then, all hell broke loose. Everything caught up to me again and I cried a river of tears long into the night, wondering how I'd made such a mess of my life. The ward was cold, sterile, and lonely. The attending staff took pity on me and gave me a soft brown bear to hold. I still had enough presence of mind to feel like a genuine nut case and the staff's kind act made me feel even more pitiful. Yet, I held that bear tightly anyway. After days of walking around like a zombie one minute and a basket case the next, I was diagnosed bipolar/manic depressive with rapid cycling and suicidal ideation, along with obsessive-compulsive disorder. This helped to explain the continuous mental gymnastics I'd put up with over the years. There answer? Increase medications.

The new drugs mixed with my emotional turmoil. It was like riding a broken elevator; I went up and down in rapid succession going nowhere fast. I was sure this was it. Who would want to be my friend knowing this dirty little secret? *I will have to keep it top secret. I must never let anyone know how broken I really am. It's not safe. I am an oddball, worthless, a waste and I deserve every bad thing that has happened. I guess I will never find my place in this world because I really do not matter to anyone or anything. Everyone would be better off if I was dead.*

Is There A Better Way?

I detested and blamed myself as I reviewed my long list of mistakes over and over again. My well being was based on my circumstances, which caused my roller coaster to gain terrific highs and to plummet to horrific lows. There may be no cure for what I've been diagnosed with but I wondered if there was a different way, a better way to live and deal with it?

The better way is to think as Philippians 4:8-9 directs, "Summing it all up, friends, I'd say you'll do best by filling your minds and meditating on things true, noble, reputable, authentic, compelling, gracious—the best, not the worst; the beautiful, not the ugly; things to praise, not things to curse. Put into practice what you learned from me, what you heard and saw and realized. Do that, and God, who makes everything work together, will work you into His most excellent harmonies." (The Message Bible)

Once again, Pastor Bos and his wife Vicky found me. They talked their way into the secured floor and I was able to visit with them. I was so ashamed and couldn't look at them. But they took my face into their hands and told me not to let any labels the doctors pinned on me overshadow who I am in Christ. "Who isn't bipolar? You are not a mistake. He can heal you. God chose you to go through these trials, He trusts you with it because He knows you will be faithful and fruitful. Soon He will flow through you like no one else. Power will flow from your broken place. In each broken place a gift is waiting for you to open so you can renew your strength. It's never too late. You've got to trust in the Lord with all you heart. Do not lean on your own understanding and He will be your guard. Diane, you've got to forgive yourself. God will help you cast all your cares away. He has paid the price for your sins so rely only on Him!"

Despite my shame, our few stolen moments helped me. In prayer they asked God to fill my mind with His thoughts, to make me living proof that He can liberate anyone from mental, physical, and spiritual prison, and to increase my faith in His powerful Word. He commanded my problems to bend the knee to the authority of Christ and had me repeat after him, "Nothing is bigger or more powerful than God! Nothing! He loves me! He loves me." Ron left me with this final scripture of power to stir me up, "I am the Lord God of all mankind. Is anything too hard for me?" Jeremiah 32:27.

"You're going to make it Diane. Do you believe?"

"Yes, Yes I do!" With what little time was left, Pastor Bos and Vicky hugged me goodbye and goodnight. I thought, I'm going to make it.

Or would I?

CHAPTER 10

A SONG RETURNED TO MY HEART

The pain you suffer now
is meant to put you in touch with the place where
you most need healing, your very heart.

—Henri Nouwen

Alone

There is one thing we all have in common. We know what it feels like to hurt. I knew hurt and hopelessness first hand through field trips of my own failure, weakness, and mistakes. Isolated in my own world of hurt I thought that I was all alone. I was estranged from my parents because of their disappointment and anger with me over my divorce and my unacceptable behavior. Yet, they came to the hospital and were visibly distraught. I was sorry for all the heartache I caused and was causing them. When I was released my parents brought me back to my apartment. They were afraid to leave me so they graciously invited me to move back home. I don't remember much from the days right after getting out of the hospital except that I was riding through a dark and rough part of my roller coaster ride.

Grow Up!

With no joy, stripped of everything, and feeling pathetic, I made the decision to grow up. It was summertime so school was out. I had just over two months to get my act together before school resumed. Hurting all over, as though my very bones were broken, I asked, *who will rescue me from this body of death?* During my study in the Word I discovered that the Apostle Paul asked the same question and concluded, "Thanks be to God—Jesus Christ the Lord... There is now no condemnation for those who are in Christ Jesus, because through

Christ Jesus the law of the Spirit of life set me free from the law of sin and death." (Romans 7:24-25; 8:1-2). Feasting on the meat of God's Word like never before, I asked Him to help me put into practice the lessons I'd learned and to help me grow up!

Reading the parable of the Sower facilitated my understanding of the process of growing up and the mystery of the kingdom of God. It taught me what I needed to do, and what to be on guard against. Jesus warns His disciples in Luke chapter eight, that His Word is received in four ways. For some it falls by the wayside and is snatched up by the evil one as soon as it enters their fluttering heart. The next group receives it with great joy, but falls away during a time of temptation and tribulation because they accepted it superficially. The next group hears His Word, yet the cares and troubles of this world keep them entangled making it impossible for them to bring spiritual fruit to maturity. But of the ones who listen and hear the Word with authentic and contrite hearts, they become strong and courageous, and grow up to bear much fruit no matter the circumstances. By remaining rooted in His word and nourished by fellowship and prayer, His truth began to sink into my head, but had a ways to go to really get into my hyper heart. I needed a spiritual breakthrough so I committed to seeking Him first no matter what and reminded myself moment to moment that, "Nothing is bigger or more powerful than God. He can do anything! He loves me. He loves me!"

A Song Kept Me Going

It was now or never. I had no television and chose to listen to the uplifting and encouraging Christian radio station continuously as I tried to reprogram my stinkin' thinkin'. This helped me to become sensitive to the Spirit's leading and to hear His voice above all the mental static and things that tried to take my attention. It was time to get real!

One evening, as I prepared to move back home with my parents, I felt so sad as I looked in my kitchen cabinets and thought, *that is exactly how I feel, empty.* Then, as if God himself gently reached His hand to my chin and lifted my face skyward, a song came on the radio that pierced my heart and brought me to my knees. The kitchen was all aglow and He was with me. As the tears soaked my shirt, I repented and extended my hands upwards, rededicating my life to Him. I implored, "Father, please forgive me! I have done so much wrong... against You, myself, my family and friends. I'm so lost. Daddy, wont You help me..." As I lay prostrate on the floor, He lifted me into His brilliant love and delivered me from my burden of shame. My circumstances were bleak yet He told me:

I know there are times your dreams turn to dust,
You wonder as you cry why it has to hurt so much.
Give Me all your sadness,
Someday you will know the reason why
With a child-like heart simply put your hope in Me.

Chorus: Take my hand and walk where I lead
Keep your eyes on Me alone
Don't you say why were the old days better
Just because you're scared of the unknown
Take My hand and walk

Don't live in the past 'cause yesterday's gone
Wishing memories would last you're afraid to carry on
You don't know what's comin'
But you know the one who holds tomorrow
I will be your guide, take you through the night
If you keep your eyes on Me.

Take My hand and walk where I lead
Keep your eyes on Me alone
Don't you say why were the old days better
Just because you're scared of the unknown
Take my hand and walk where I lead
You will never be alone
Faith is to be sure of what you hope for
And the evidence of things unseen

So take my hand and walk
Just like a child holding daddy's hand
Don't let go of mine
You know you can't stand on your own.

Take My Hand -Used with permission
by Jean-Luc Lajoie and Yves Lajoie

This song became our song, God's and mine. It was the start of a true love affair and the spiritual breakthrough I desperately needed. It always seemed to come on the radio just when I needed it most. It helped me make it and gave me hope that something good was coming, that I was not alone, and that God had a purpose for my existence even though I messed up in so many areas. I wept. I leapt. And I danced with thankfulness because it is true—He is God and nothing is bigger or more powerful than He is! Nothing! This song brought this message home to me and made it real. I didn't know who sang it, but because of it, I was able to hold on.

I made the decision to fix my eyes and mind on the promises of God. I became new. "Therefore, if anyone is in Christ, he is a new creation; the old has gone, the new has come!" (2 Corinthians 5:17) Old things in my life had passed away. The Lord promised I could have peace, protection, health, wholeness, provision... I made the choice to leave behind old behavior, old words, old thinking, old labels, and I embraced forgiveness and the new life I had by faith. It was another huge step forward into the life of blessing the Lord had in store for me. I said, *"Father God, thank you! Your Word is true and your promises will be fulfilled in my life. I'm trying to grasp that now and the love you have for me. I'm holding your hand, Daddy, don't let go. Please don't let go! Thank you, in Jesus' Name. Amen!"*

Coming Out Of The "Shadow Of Death"

Pastor Bos gave me the entire King James Version of the Bible on tape. He said, "Second Timothy 3:16 says, 'All scripture is God-breathed useful for teaching, rebuking, correcting and training in righteousness, so that the man of God may be thoroughly equipped for every good work.' So listen and let the Word change your life." I followed his advice and started listening to it day and night. The incredible started to happen as I began to pray and to spend time with God: In this place of refuge, the song in my heart grew stronger. I desired to read, study, and obey the Word again; to honor God with a fresh chorus of praise and I began to thank Him for who He is, what He had done, and what He was going to do in my life. As the twenty-third Psalm says, "Yea, though I walk through the valley of the shadow of death? I will fear NO evil for You are with me..." And he truly was. I was still me, odd and unique, but my perspective and understanding changed leading to a peace and inner assurance.

God was with me, whether I knew it or not, throughout my many struggles and would continue to be there no matter the circumstances because He loves me. The truth that the all-knowing, all-powerful, Creator of the Universe cared about me was hard to grasped but he had now given me the eyes to see. He knows my name; it's written on His heart, and He wants to be my friend. It's like when I was the class "welcome wagon" and all I wanted to do was reach out my hand to love and help the new student, God wanted to do the same with me. Why had that been so hard for me to accept?

It's an awesome privilege and honor to be cared for so much by God. Tommy Walker penned, "He knows my every thought and sees each tear that falls and hears me when I call." At a time when I thought I would never smile again, grasping this truth renewed my strength and my relationship with the Lord. It helped me realize why He created me: to love me, to be my friend and to be Lord of my life. I starved my fear by feeding my faith with the Word of God. The truth began to sink in and the next time the enemy tried to tell me that I was alone, that no one cared, or that I was too stupid, weird, or worthless, I fought him off with the word of God and songs of praise like, *Friend of God*, by Phillips, Craig and Dean. "God Almighty, Lord of Glory, You have called me friend." I'd been in the trenches and learned who God is, what I was made of, and what I was capable of. Then, I laid it all down at the cross accepting Him as my friend.

Serious Changes

It wasn't going to be easy. There are no shortcuts. Defining myself by what I did, not who God made me, had to stop. I could never do enough, be enough, or change enough to earn my way to Heaven and to happiness. But every time I felt overwhelmed, I would sing and I would pray. These became my weapons of warfare. I'd pray through-out the day, talking to Him like I would a friend, *"Father, thank You for being my friend, for loving me, for being faithful; help me be a better friend to You and replace the old tapes with new ones from You. In Jesus name, Amen!"*

I made serious changes. I got back on track to finish my doctoral work by beginning a new dissertation because I no longer had access to Millie. It broke my heart to abandon the hundreds of hours of work I invested in the "Millie Dissertation." The title for my second dissertation became something I knew much about: "A Study of Adolescent Depression, Suicide, Self-Esteem and Family Strengths in Special Educations Female Students Compared with Regular Education Female Students." All the while I continued teaching at the college and for the county school system where I got the approval to work with the students

PH.D. Graduation from Walden University at Indiana State -1996

Mom, me, Chrissy (my God-child) and Dad—we all drove up from Florida to Indiana for my graduation.

to gather data for my research. I worked really hard and couldn't have completed my work without the help of my friend, David Skaer, Ph.D., a psychologist I periodically invited to speak to my Psychology class at Polk Community College. I finally completed the study and achieved my goal. I GRADUATED, obtaining my doctoral degree before the age of thirty. The pressure was finally off—I did it! It was a milestone that commemorated my recovery. The ceremony was a low-key affair yet, a huge step forward.

Holding On

Moving back in with my parents almost ten years after my marriage to Scott, and living two streets down from the home we'd built together that he now shared with his new wife and child was difficult to say the least. Yet, my new understanding of God's providence and sovereignty radically changed how I interpreted my life. Instead of running from my fears, pain, or confusion I allowed them to be the prescription for my healing. I needed reconstructive surgery of the heart and mind and only God could deftly wield the scalpel that would cut away what needed to be removed from my muddied, dysfunctional mind. Such spiritual surgery could only be performed if I received God's love and acted in obedience on a moment-to-moment basis, rather than just when it was convenient or lined up with what I thought was best for my life. I was ready to let God be God in my life.

I adopted a warrior mentality. I had a reason to get up in the morning since my priorities now lined up with God's. God's Word changed my entire perspective. I used to think that God was too busy to concern himself with the mundane details of a wretched sinner like me. I now knew that on the contrary, God wanted to be Lord of my life and cared about every little detail. I had hope for the first time in a long time. I had hope that it was not too late, that I could be happy and I could be all He created me to be.

I don't know what you are facing in your life today but I know this: there is a way through it, and if you ask the Lord, He will show you. The past with its terrible sin and guilt is over, dead, and buried. Wake up to your new freedom and live the abundant life that God has for you; Jesus died so you could live. It's a gift of grace that we do nothing to earn. If you surrender all to Him, He can make a message out of your mess. Cling to the promise, *"He has not despised or disdained the suffering of the afflicted one; He has not hidden His face from him but has listened to his cry for help"* (Psalm 22:24). He heard my desperate cry for help and He hears yours, too. Reach to Him because He loves you. God made only one of me, and He made only one of YOU! You have nothing to lose and everything to gain.

Beginning The Healing Process

Christ was never more real than during the healing process when I was digging deeper; He was my guiding light. I had been to the door of death—death of the soul, spirit, and body—but was inexplicably spared from the fatal outcome I once sought. I could not get back all that I had lost, but just like my earthly father showed me mercy and forgiveness so many years ago when I deserved punishment, my Heavenly Father showed me the same. I could sense His presence, not only because of the knowledge that His holy Word promises that He will never leave me or forsake me was sinking into my heart, but also because I finally realized that living with Jesus is a daily process, not a one time event. Just as I can't live on yesterday's food for my physical body, I can't live on yesterday's soul food; I need a fresh supply each and every day in order to thrive. Renewing my mind on a daily basis helped me walk in love for others and myself. After all, you can't give what you don't have.

As in the Lord's Prayer, God gives me "my daily bread" each day when I come to Him. I make the choice daily to lay down my life and follow Him. As a result of my decision to change my lifestyle, doors opened, allowing some of my biggest "failures" to become my biggest assets for helping and encouraging others. Instead of getting bitter, which can rot a person from within, I got better as He softened my edges and molded me into the shape He crafted for me before the foundations of the earth. I learned a life without failures is a life without risk. Abraham Lincoln emphasized the need to keep trying when he said, "I am not concerned that you have failed. I am concerned that you arise." I put my fears to rest and focused on being sure I never quit trying.

I learned to comfort those in the way that I was comforted. With a kinder, gentler demeanor—filled with the fruits of the spirit, love, joy, peace, long suffering, compassion—I tried to do nothing out of selfish ambition or vain conceit, but in humility considering others better than myself (Philippians 2:3). I went from having a false hope, to having no hope, to having real hope. That final turnaround came when I began to praise and give thanks to God even in the midst of my turmoil. Everything was stripped away until all I had was Jesus. Listening to the Word, reading it constantly, as well as praying it, was the key that unlocked my door of strength to live triumphantly in this painful life.

The War Zone

This world is a war zone! We are all fighting battles of one sort or another. Living for Christ is not for wimps. God's Word says, "We wrestle not against flesh and blood, but against principalities, against powers, against the rulers of the darkness of this age, against spiritual hosts of wickedness in the Heavenly places. Therefore take up the whole armor of God, that you may be able to withstand in the evil day" (Ephesians

6: 11-13). I tried just about everything else but only His powerful Words of truth gave me the strength to endure; only He satisfies!

When you get to the place where the Lord is all you have, you are in the best position to discover that He is all you need. My true self was exposed; what I was made of, my strengths and weaknesses. I got radical about obeying God and dealing with whatever was in me that was not of Him. Gloria Gaither said, "We may run, walk, stumble, drive, or fly, but let us never lose sight of the reason for the journey, or miss a chance to see a rainbow on the way." I did all of the above and was now ready to enjoy my rainbow.

My Reality Check

Making excuses for my failures and broken dreams had to stop. I had a memorial service for how life used to be and accepted the truth of my condition, the consequences of my decisions, and moved on to the purpose and plan God created me for. I had to learn how to dream new dreams; look at all I could do, what was right and what was good.

Even though my head agreed with Jack Nicholson's character in "A Few Good Men" who said, "You can't handle the truth," I finally recognized the need to face my demons. I said, "Lord, if you can do anything with this broken vessel, do it. Help me face my personal problems and get better. I surrender my life to You, again. I'm sorry for not trusting You. Jesus, take control and let Your will be done." I had to forgive the doctors, friends, family, and especially myself. I made a conscious choice to do good daily and to pray for those who hurt me as well as ask for forgiveness from those I hurt. I stayed in fellowship with others realizing that to remain closed up and cut off from others as I suffered alone in my agony was not the answer.

Choosing to obey God, even if it doesn't always feel good physically, emotionally, or mentally means more than anything else in the world. Following Him even when I don't "feel" like it, and testifying of His wonders and mercy whether He heals me or not, is my mission. I truly believe that when I wake in the morning a miracle has occurred. I believe in miracles because I am one.

Like in my friend John David Webster's song *Miracle*, I see Him in everything around me and it takes my breath away. There is no way to explain it. He moved my mountains, awakened me, and stilled my weary soul.

Angel Belle
Dreams Do Come True

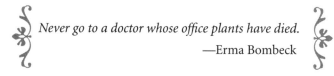

Never go to a doctor whose office plants have died.
—Erma Bombeck

My family visited Cypress Gardens, "The water ski capital of the world," on one of our trips to Florida before we made the Sunshine State our home. I remember seeing the "Southern Belles" sitting in various places throughout the park so that people could get their pictures taken with them. After we moved to Winter Haven, Florida, just down the street from the Gardens, I dreamed of becoming a Southern Belle and skiing there, but never made time for it.

Yet, while in my "comeback mode," the Lord granted me this opportunity. I was asked to be the star attraction of a song and laser show and performed before thousands nightly.

After teaching all day at the high school and coaching the swim team, I arrived at the gardens and transformed into Angel Belle Diane, complete with angel wings and a dress that lit up the night. It was, indeed, a dream come true! I had the opportunity to meet most of the skiers and soon started training to become one, too.

Entertaining At Any Cost

My favorite water ski trick was called the human tow. I jumped on Corky the Clown's back as he skied by the platform. We then circled the show ring while I climbed to the front of him, wrapped my legs around his waist, took the ski rope into my hands, and stretched out while the boat pulled us around. Just when I pulled the rope in and returned it to Corky, he would dump me to the side and I would swim to shore. I also aspired to become the first female (men were already performing this feat) to hang-glide into the show-ring. I trained at Wallaby Ranch, the first full-time, aero-tow hang gliding flight park in the world and was having the time of my life. But I soon found out that the variable weather and temperature changes would not allow me to ever ski or hang-glide in

Bare-footing lifting right foot

the show because of the flare-ups in my condition such exposure triggered. Consequently, I focused on my singing performances.

Doing good and encouraging others has always been cathartic for me. Enjoying photo shoots, autograph signings, "meet and greets," and inviting children up to dance and sing along during the show was great.

However, this joy came at a price since standing in the cool night air often led to flare-ups of my various maladies. I was exhausted at the end of each day, but was determined to push through the pain because of the joy I experienced entertaining. I believed that being on

Getting ready to hang-glide, Wallaby Ranch, 1996.

With "Flutter" at Cypress Gardens. My friend Diane from Russia is Flutter. Before the show, I shared my testimony with her, we hugged in tears and she gave her life to Jesus.

stage was a vital part of my calling and desire to bring joy, happiness, and love to as many people as I could. Hearing the crowd sing along each night refreshed and encouraged me to continue on. I figured if I died now, I would die very happy, doing what I loved. When that first season came to a close, I vowed to return for the following season so I could continue to live my dream.

Dr. D. Ministries

Meanwhile, I started Dr. D. Ministries, a nonprofit organization dedicated to bringing the love of Jesus to the ends of the earth. I visited prisons and nursing homes where I sang, preached, and testified. Ministry

work also brought me to many local churches where I sang at services or fellowship dinners. Since I still felt a special affiliation with suffering children, I contacted all the schools in our county to see if there were children I could help. I would then drop off care baskets at their doorsteps with scripture verses and my card if they needed further assistance. I especially enjoyed going to local hospitals where I visited the sick, both young and old. I knew first hand that hospitals could be sterile, void of fun, and lonely. My hope for those who suffered was that they knew that I cared, that they were not alone, and that Jesus loved them.

In the studio recording, Because You Asked Me Too

People I sang to from the stage as Angel Belle Diane and on my speaking engagements often asked for a recording of my music. I decided to make an album and called it, *Because You Asked Me To*. It was recorded in a studio in Bartow, Florida where I recorded eight songs. The studio technicians encouraged me when they said they had never worked with an artist able to record all their songs on the first take.

Five hundred copies went quickly as thank you gifts to the many people who made financial contributions for my outreach work. On a trip to North Carolina with the Fellowship of Christian Athletes, I met Scotty Smith who was the pastor of the church Amy Grant and Michael W. Smith attended. He said he would give one of my tapes to Amy since it was her rendition of *El Shaddai* that inspired me to learn to play the twelve-string guitar. A producer, James Kennedy, in Orlando, Florida was given a tape by one of the teens from that week. He called to see about producing my next recording. Everything checked out and we moved forward with, *Walk by Faith*. We spent the next twelve months working on the music and lyrics as my anticipation of great things ahead grew.

Autographing my first recording at a Christian Athlete Event

Nineteen ninety-six was a very busy and rewarding year in my life. It was filled with contentment, peace, and fulfillment because of my deep and personal relationship with the Lord. Answering the call on my life and learning to mitigate my diseases the best I could by using health products, studying the scriptures, staying in fellowship, praying, and eating better while taking few prescription drugs. Hang gliding at the ranch when the weather permitted and helping out part-time to pay for my flights was fun. Life was not easy when memories of failures tried to haunt me but change was coming my way again: I could feel it in my bones as I moved forward in faith with my life and yearned for a different place to call home.

CHAPTER 12

ROCKY MOUNTAIN HIGH

*Continuous effort—not strength or
intelligence—is the key to unlocking our potential.*
—Winston Churchill

Wherever We Go

The neat thing about God is He is with us wherever we go. Do you feel close to Him watching the sunset on the sea, in the Rocky Mountains, by a stream, in a meadow filled with wild flowers, in front of the old rugged cross, or in the chapel? He speaks to us there and everywhere. He'll do and He'll use whatever He wants to tell us, "He loves us." While humming some of the song, *Rocky Mountain High* by John Denver, I knew where I wanted to go... in quiet solitude. Seeking His grace in each new step while basking in the serenity of a clear blue mountain lake.

Go West!

When life is not what we truly want it to be, it doesn't take long to find someone to blame. Blaming myself was easy but in the end life's inconveniences and troubles are merely the occasion for our true self to come out and an opportunity to trust in God. When I put my trust in the Lord, everything works out much better! That doesn't mean everything that happens is good, but it does mean that if I trust in Him, He can bring good from bad situations. Tom Hanks declared as Forest Gump in the movie *Forest Gump*, "My Mama always said, 'Life is like a box of chocolates; you never know what you're gonna get.'" It's our choice to make the best of whatever life offers and trust the One who offers it to us. Nothing can happen that doesn't first go through His screen of love and that gives me peace.

There were many reasons why I was ready to move to Colorado. I always wanted to experience the West. I thought the fresh air and rustic atmosphere would do me good, and I truly felt the Lord was telling me

Rock climbing straight up Horse-Tooth Rock, in Fort Collins, Colorado. Wow! What a majestic view! (It dropped straight down... going down was harder than going up)

to go for it! I longed for the quiet of the forest and the streams as well as the serenity of the clear blue skies and couldn't wait to climb majestic mountains. The door to experience the West opened up when I got the chance to visit Vail, Colorado. It was beautiful! The seed was planted and I yearned to investigate all it had to offer.

Heading back to Florida on a flight out of Denver, I knew it wouldn't be long before I made the West my home. I spent the next three months preparing for the move. I eased out of all my part-time commitments and transitioned out of my teaching position. Many of the preparations fell right into place: I sold my car and that took care of the remaining amount of debt from credit cards and school loans; I finished the season as Angel Belle Diane; I put notice in where I was teaching water exercise classes and found a replacement for my swimming coach position.

Signing My Death Certificate

In the fall of 1997 my doctors at the Shands Cancer Hospital in Gainesville insisted that I was crazy to move to a cold climate because exposure to the cold was the worst thing for someone with cryoglobulinemia. Dad drove me there and concurred with the doctors who were concerned over the sores I had on my legs for over two years that wouldn't heal. The doctors were also concerned about the lymphocytes and nucleated red blood cells they discovered on this visit. They said this indicated a lymphoproliferative disorder and that I should come back every three to six months for follow-up testing to keep an eye out for numerous problems that could develop. One doctor even believed that "I might as well sign my death certificate" if I moved to Colorado. To that I said, "I'd rather die living then die dying."

On the one hand, I was afraid to go against the doctors' recommendations and was apprehensive about pulling up my roots and planting them in unknown territory. After all, it was pretty safe living at home with Mom and Dad. On the other hand, I couldn't help but wonder, *do I reach for nothing out of fear, that in doing so I could jeopardize what health I still have? Was adventure and happiness going to become an elusive goal because I was afraid of everything?* Would I someday wonder, "what if" and regret staying in my safety zone?

Discouragement. Who hasn't been seized by its relentless grasp? In the past it all but assassinated my hope, eroded my faith, and vaporized my courage. For so long it seemed that every time I reached for the next rung on the ladder of happiness, it broke and I fell face first in the dirt. Despite these concerns, I had a burning desire for a different life, a different set of circumstances, and was determined to leave behind my survivor mentality, which at times discouraged me from reaching too high because of the disappointment it invariably brought.

No way! I wasn't going to give up. I had come too far and grown too much to live that way. I felt the Holy Spirit leading me to Colorado and by now had learned that not following the Spirit only led to heartache and pain. I had dreams of a different life. I dreamt of having children, of being healthy, and of traveling the country and the world beyond. I began to think that maybe, just maybe, there was still time for the life I always dreamed of. Maybe I would have a miraculous healing.

In spite of everyone's opposition I prepared to go to Colorado. Ironically, John Denver died in a plane crash that very month. Yet, I didn't interpret this as a bad omen. I knew, deep in my heart that this was what the Lord was leading me to do.

Starting Over... Again!

Starting over at any age is not easy. However, in November of 1997, it seemed as though the Lord was on my side as I landed jobs with Vail Mountain, the Vail Athletic Club teaching exercise classes, and another at the Vail Cascade Club in the spa. I also secured a teaching position at Colorado Mountain College in the psychology department. I felt triumphant that I had followed my heart instead of my fears. Even though I left behind the opportunity to finish a second musical recording, I was truly *walking by faith!*

I stayed with a friend until I could find a more permanent place to live and performed massage therapy again. I tried to upgrade my knowledge and ability by reading about diverse massage techniques and attending classes at a local school. I received my certificate and God blessed me in a short time with a fair number of wonderful clients. I utilized techniques to keep my own blood flowing—to minimize flare-ups in my legs—as I treated clients to the most wonderful healing touch I could muster. People always asked me, "How do you do it?" I could only say, "It's the Lord's strength. I cannot do this on my own."

Making Good Decisions

Even though I believed I was doing God's will, things didn't come easy. The few friends I made in Vail thought I should go back home to warm Central Florida. But I walked on, even in the cold, learning how to manage my disease in a new climate. I was encouraged because the sores I had on my legs for the previous two years were finally healing. Furthermore, I wasn't afraid of dying. I was afraid of running out of time to enjoy living. I trusted that God would show me the way. I cried a lot, and felt lonely and

Stronger and more courageous!

sometimes scared. The difference was that I got into every Bible study I could find, stayed in prayer, and kept my eyes on Jesus because of my circumstances, not despite them. Given that, I was confident that I was making the best decisions I could.

I joined Vail Bible Church (now called, The Vail Church) and that decision redirected my life for the good in many ways. Cheri, the secretary, became my prayer warrior. She and many other Christians lifted me up in prayer and invited me to gatherings. A new friend introduced me to a man I was able to rent a room from and then she invited me to a dinner party. Going to that dinner party changed my life forever.

CHAPTER 13

MY KNIGHT IN SHINING ARMOR

*Love is extravagant in the price it is willing to pay,
the time it is willing to give, the hardships it is
willing to endure, and the strength it is willing to
spend. Love never thinks in terms of "how little," but
always in terms of "how much."
Love gives, love knows, and love lasts.*

—Joni Eareckson Tada

During this part of my adventure I enjoyed lying in the grass and warm sunshine by the Colorado River. One day, I found myself praying for a tall, dark, handsome man to come along and sweep me off my feet. The good Lord sent Paul. Renee Zellweger said to Tom Cruise in the 1996 hit movie, *Jerry Maguire*, "You had me at hello." Paul had me at hello, too.

My "Second Chance" at real love!

At a dinner party, I noticed a few guys talking to each other and, one in particular looked familiar. He looked a little like Michael Douglas to me. His name was Paul Dike. We hit it off and before I knew it, we planned a date. The next day when I met him for our date the first thing that came to mind was, "Wow, this is going to be good!" We skied, worked out and showered at a health club, and went to the Avalanche's professional hockey game in Denver. It was quite a first date and confirmed in my mind that this guy knew how to enjoy the adventures of life. Paul's vivacious personality and ability to speak intelligently on a wide variety of subjects helped win me over. On the way home from the hockey game, the psychologist in me asked him, "What kind of relationship do you have with your mother?" He responded, "I think she is the most awesome woman I know."

I concluded, "Yup, he's a keeper!"

Living

After our first date, we saw each other almost every day. Trekking down the hill on which I lived to catch the bus that would take me to Paul's office at the base of Vail Mountain, bundled up in so many layers of clothing that I could hardly move, Paul said—in the most romantic way possible—that I looked like the "Michelin Man" from the tire commercial. Waddling along, I thought, *what am I thinking exposing myself to freezing temperatures even breathing the cold air?* My Florida doctor's words, "You might as well sign your death certificate . . . " reverberated in my head. Even so, I didn't feel like I was dying, but instead, felt like I was living.

Just as I'd desired to join the water ski world in Florida, I soon got caught up in the skiing world in Colorado. Skiing is more than just a hobby for guys like Paul. Every decision he made was in one way or another connected to the next ski adventure. Paul would change plans if it started to snow. A late dinner date would get cancelled or a trip to Denver postponed if Paul thought the next day was going to be a "powder day." While riding the bus to go meet Paul one day, I overheard a young man say, "There are no friends on a powder day." Would this apply to me, the girlfriend? I decided to investigate this proposition.

Several days later it began to snow around two in the afternoon, and by six in the evening it was a "white out." Paul called me to see if we could eat earlier and I asked why. He replied, "Tomorrow's going to be a 'sick' powder day and I need to get to bed early."

"What's early?"

"Eight o'clock. I want to be at work by three tomorrow morning."

"Well, I am not feeling too good so I'll take a rain check."

"That's great. I mean, I am sorry that you don't feel good but it would be good for you to go to bed early, too."

"I'll see you sometime tomorrow. Have a good time skiing." I forestalled

The next morning I took the 8:00 bus and was at Paul's office by 8:15. I walked into virtual pandemonium. Music blared from the warehouse he supervised, and when I walked by the locker room to get to Paul's office, I saw at least ten guys scrambling to get their ski gear on. Several of them glanced at me, wondering what I was doing here so early (I usually arrived at his office around noon to have lunch with Paul in the restaurant upstairs). When Paul saw me in the door way, he stopped buckling his boots and stammered, "Ahhh, hi honey. What are you doing here? I mean, I thought we would have lunch together in a couple of hours."

"I thought I would come in early to enjoy the fresh snow."

"Well, I was just getting ready to leave, but maybe I could wait until you got ready and we could go up together."

"No, that's alright. I will meet you at Two Elk (one of Vail Mountain's many restaurants) at 11:30 for lunch."

"That will be great. I'll see you there." With this being said, Paul stood up and led his pack of "powder hounds" out of the warehouse and upstairs to catch the first chair lift.

I sat behind Paul's desk and pondered how much my life had changed since I moved to Colorado. I realized I was where I was supposed to be. I'd even prayed for a tall, dark, handsome man to enter into my life. I believe that Paul was God's answer to my prayer. I felt safe with Paul and even found myself expecting happiness. Rather than waiting for the rug to be pulled out from under me, I found myself looking toward the future. In God's will, I knew that good things were coming my way. With faith, I knew my best days were just ahead.

My First Private Powder Day

After putting on my heated boots and placing hand warmers in my gloves, pants, and shirt, I left Paul's office to experience my first power day. I felt victorious even trying to ski on a day like today, but Paul had equipped me with all the necessary gear. More importantly, I was able to ski because of the amenities Paul enjoyed through his job, including storing all my gear in his warm office. This was vital because trudging through snow in your ski clothes while carrying all your gear is actually quite a workout and can make you sweat. Then, sitting on the chair lift as it whisks you up the hill chills you instantly. I cannot tolerate such drastic temperature changes and it could be deadly. Through Paul I had gotten to know many of the managers and chefs at the mountain restaurants and could go to them if I had problems on the hill. I chose the warmer days to ski and knew that I could always come off the ski mountain and wait for Paul in his warm office.

I was excited to ski today because Paul had obtained a pair of "powder skis" for me to use from one of his connections. Skiing in powder is difficult when you first starting out but I was told that these wider skis would make it easier. Three chair lift rides later I chose a steep run and enjoyed Vail Mountain's best. The snow flowed over my knees and into my ski-mask-covered face on each turn. The fat skis made me feel much more comfortable, like water skiing, and I floated through the snow. This was my very first private powder day! Endorphins and adrenaline flowed through my body and I felt like the athlete I once was. I raised my arms in victory to the Lord and gave praise for the glorious day and the legs that allowed me to ride like the wind. I sang out one of my favorite scripture verses, Isaiah 40:31: "They that wait upon the Lord will renew their strength. They will mount up on wings as an eagle." I thought, *I'm living proof that it is true.*

Our engagement picture taken on top of Vail Mountain, on a warm, sunny day in 1998

After six more runs I realized it was past noon. To the restaurant I rushed where I was supposed to meet Paul. I walked in and exclaimed, *there he is!* He stood up with a look of concern and said, "Are you all right? You are thirty-five minutes late and I was worried sick about you." I replied, "I am so sorry honey, but I was having so much fun skiing that I lost track of time. And besides, you know what they say."

"What is that?"

"There are no friends on a powder day!"

Paul raised his arms in celebration and let out a yell. For the first time in many years that song of a victorious life, including hope and love, returned to my heart and I had someone to share it with.

Love Extravagantly

Since our first date on January 15, 1998, Paul treated me like a princess. He talked much about seeing Alaska so I worked out a surprise trip there for us and planned to unveil it to him on Valentine's Day. During a weekend getaway to Denver and then a romantic dinner at the base of Beaver Creek Mountain I would reveal my surprise. However, neither of us knew that God had a far greater surprise for us that day than we could have imagined.

Paul worked for Vail Resorts on Vail Mountain. I often joined him during the day to help him and to enjoy lunch together. We were so happy.

CHAPTER 14

VALENTINE'S DAY

Love is a symbol of eternity. It wipes out all sense of time, destroying all memory of a beginning and all fear of an end.

—Author Unknown

Valentine's Day came and I sang to Paul a song I'd written earlier while riding a chair lift with him on Vail Mountain. *You Can Count On Me* touched Paul's heart. This macho mountain man couldn't hold back the tears that burst out his eyes and we hugged for a long time. He exclaimed, "No one has ever done that for me." I was glad that my song was received so warmly. We then went to lunch at "Abos," in Boulder, Colorado. He wanted to show me his favorite pizza place whose pie he said was worth the 100-mile bike ride he often made from Fort Collins where he attended Colorado State University. While sprinkling some seasoning on the pizza, the top fell off, dumping a large quantity of garlic. We scraped the excess off, but Paul still experienced an upset stomach later that day. However, I don't think it was just the garlic on the pizza that upset his stomach.

A Friend In The Diamond Business

We left Boulder and headed towards Denver to jump on interstate 70, which would return us to Beaver Creek for our dinner date. On the way we saw a big sign for Shanes, a diamond and jewelry store known for the slogan, "You've got a friend in the diamond business." Paul knew that I had a diamond I wanted to reset and, since it was our first Valentine's Day together, suggested that we stop by to visit our purported "friend." I readily complied.

We entered the store to witness cupid's handiwork: countless couples strolled arm-in-arm peering into the many jewelry cases with longing eyes and looks of expectancy. Paul said hesitantly, "Do you think most of these couples are shopping for engagement or wedding rings?" I nonchalantly replied, "I suppose so. I mean, is there a better way to spend Valentine's Day? Oh look I like this one." Suddenly, Paul didn't look too stout and said, "I've got to go to the bathroom. That garlic isn't settling very well."

Paul returned to find me in deep conversation with a saleswoman. We were looking intently at the band that I had selected to hold my diamond. I asked him, "What do you think of this one?" Still looking a little green in the gills, Paul mumbled something inaudibly. The saleswoman and I looked at each other and continued our search; yet, I always came back to the first one that caught my eye. She then said to Paul, "I believe it is your turn sir." Paul responded, "I don't feel too well" then turned and walked away. I explained with a nervous smile that "Paul is a little out of his element in a jewelry store. I'm sure he will be fine."

Paul had been gone for ten minutes and I began to worry a little feeling badly about first messing up his pizza, and now his day. Finally, I could see Paul across the store and the saleswoman said, "Oh, there he is." Paul strutted towards us, looking much more self-assured. When he reached me, he reached for my hand, stared lovingly into my eyes and popped the question, "Diane, will you marry me?"

I almost fainted. We came to the store on a whim and here, the man that I had prayed for asked the question that I thought I would never want to hear again. We'd been dating for less than a month. The saleswoman gazed longingly at me, and with tears running down both our faces I nodded and said, "Yes, I would be honored." We both shouted, "Wow!" With a giggle and a cry, he picked me up and twirled me around.

It was now 4:00 p.m. and our dinner reservation was for seven. It's a two-hour drive from Denver to Beaver Creek so we didn't have much time to spare. We still had the matter of my stone that needed to be set in what Paul and I agreed would be my engagement ring. The saleswoman said that it would be a couple of days before we could pick up the ring. Both of us were disappointed to hear this and prepared to exit the store. A man walked up to us with hand extended and declared, "This is the first proposal we have had in the store. We are honored that you chose to share this day with us. Your ring will be ready in thirty minutes." I guess we did have a friend in the diamond business.

Formal Proposal

We raced home to clean up before going to the restaurant. After being seated, I couldn't wait any longer to unveil my Valentine surprise. He opened his card and other little gifts until there was just one envelope left; in it were the tickets to a seven-day Alaskan cruise to be taken in May for his birthday. When he opened the envelope and saw a brochure filled with pictures of whales and glaciers, his eyes grew as big as saucers. Then, Paul swung around, dropped one knee next to me, he handed me a perfectly wrapped little box. I could feel the eyes of the entire restaurant burning on me.

As I opened the little box, Paul—as if to be sure the answer was still the same and to make his proposal formal—asked, "Diane, will you marry me?" I exclaimed, "Yes!" But some of the crowd didn't hear me and shouted, "What did she say?" Through my tears and fears I shouted, "YES! I said, YES!" And the crowd cheered all the louder. Paul slipped the ring on my finger and we hugged for a long time.

A few polariods of Paul actually proposing to me in the resturant on Beaver Creek Mountain. This was the second "for real" time.

Notifying Our Parents

Paul told me that he had never brought a girl home to have dinner with his parents. Furthermore, he asserted that he'd always told them that the first girl he did bring home would be the one he would marry. After we finished the main course, Paul said he had a phone call to make.

Our toasting glasses on Nana's doily

It must have been around 11 p.m. East Coast time as we huddled together in the hall-way, waiting for someone to pick up at the other end. Finally, we heard, "Hello?" Paul said, "Mom, guess who's coming for dinner?"

"What, who is this?" she questioned.

Paul reiterated, "Mom, guess who's coming for dinner?"

"Paul is that you, what? Oh Rod, get up, Paul?" Paul's dad got on the phone and Paul declared, "I would like you to say hi to my fiancé." To which I said, "Hi Mom, Hi Dad. Guess I'll be seeing you for dinner soon." It was a heartwarming conversation.

We enjoyed our desserts, compliments of the restaurant, and relished our astonishing day. We left the restaurant to the cheers of our fellow diners and restaurant staff as well.

Not For Rent

Once engaged, Paul and I attended to the necessary details to merge our lives into one. At the time, Paul lived with two good friends in a house one of them owned, while I was homeless again since the guy I rented a room from told me after he found out that I was engaged that I was no longer welcomed. Paul moved me out in the middle of the night and brought all of my stuff to his house.

Paul suggested that we get a place together but I replied, "I am not for rent!"

"What do you mean you're not for rent? I want to rent a house, not you."

"If we live together before we are married, in essence, you are renting me. Did you mean it when you proposed to me?" Even though I believed that I was in the Lord's will by being here in Colorado, and that Paul was an important part of His plan for me, I was not willing to contradicted His Word. I had done this before and it led to much of my pain and unhappiness. I slipped the engagement ring off my finger and said, "You can have this back if you didn't mean it. Starting our life out in any other way than God's way is only going to lead to mediocrity. And that is not good enough for me. If we compromise, sin could destroy our chances at real happiness and what a waste that would be."

Paul looked as though he had just seen a ghost. The color drained from his face and his shoulders slumped as he looked like he was about to grab the ring. Then, he mumbled, "What's it going to take? I wasn't prepared to marry you immediately but I do not want to risk losing you by hemming and hawing. I suppose we could elope. Don't people get married on cruise ships?"

"Yes, they do," I said, "and I think that would be great. However, I only want to do it that way if it is truly what you want to do. Don't do it just to please me. It's your special day and life, too."

The next day I went to have lunch with Paul at the restaurant upstairs from his office. He said that after sleeping on it, he didn't want to elope because it would hurt his family that had waited many years for him to wed. He wanted to include them as much as possible but was willing to set the earliest possible date. Over lunch we decided that a Colorado wedding—especially on such short notice—would be difficult for both our families to attend. Paul's family was spread across the northeast while my immediate family was in Florida and the rest in Massachusetts. My father was embroiled in a crisis at his business. He recently discovered that one of his entrusted employees had been embezzling money from him for many years. My family's energy and finances were drained and being devoted to surviving this crisis. Paul decided that the best thing to do was to call his father—who had helped him out of many jams throughout his life—to see what he recommended.

It pained me to see Paul under the stress of our situation because it was his innocence and carefree zeal for life that first attracted me to him. However, when Paul picked me up for dinner that night, it looked as though a great weight had been lifted from his shoulders. He revealed that his father was glad we didn't elope and that he would do everything he could on his end to get us married back East so most of Paul's family could attend.

Paul and I hugged and enjoyed a dinner date and the movie, *Titanic* to celebrate the dream of beginning the rest of our lives together. The next day I purchased our plane tickets. To quote Antoine de Saint-Exupery: "Love does not consist in gazing at each other, but in looking outward together in the same direction." We found our unified purpose, and that decision would impact our world.

CHAPTER 15

A WEDDING CELEBRATION

 And now these three remain: faith, hope and love.
But the greatest of these is love.

—1 Corinthians 13:13

To Florida

We flew to Florida the second week of May, 1998 to attend a gathering at my parents' house to celebrate the upcoming wedding. I was torn by conflicting emotions as we approached Orlando International Airport where my parents would pick us up. On the one hand, I was excited to introduce my parents to my *"second chance"* at love, but on the other hand was nervous because, as devout Catholics, my parents abhorred divorce and were bitterly disappointed that my first marriage ended. As the plane approached the runway, I grasped Paul's hand and silently prayed that my family would accept Paul and embrace my new found hope in a life that was once so hopeless.

Any concerns I had about the reception Paul would receive melted away at dinner. Paul is extremely articulate and well versed in subjects ranging from fighting forest fires to classic literature. He's very engaging and likes to share his experiences with others. As Paul relayed a story about one of his bicycle accidents—he has had three ambulance rides, three surgeries and was in a coma for five days—I looked across the table to see my father sporting a humdinger of a smile. In spite of his stoic nature, My father seemed to take to Paul immediately.

My father had devoted his entire life to providing for his family and sacrificed his chance to experience a more adventurous life. It seemed as though he was experiencing Paul's adventurous lifestyle vicariously as he relayed one tale after another. After the meal I joked with my father that I could see his eyeteeth—Dad even smiles conservatively, rarely revealing teeth—and he responded, "Now, don't get carried away." I hugged him and thanked him for a great dinner.

My whole Florida family attended the wedding party, as did some of my parents' friends and some of my personal friends. Mom prepared a fabulous meal and Paul and I cut a two-tier wedding cake to make it official. As Paul gripped my hand and guided the knife through the cake, I was overcome with thankfulness. I had experienced much joy and sadness in this house, punctuated by the year I lived in it after my stay in the hospital before I moved to Colorado. I was extremely grateful to my parents for taking me back home then, as well as welcoming my new love to their home now.

Three days after the party, my parents dropped Paul and me off at Orlando International to catch a flight to Boston where Paul's parents would pick us up and facilitate the next stage of our wedding adventure. We parked at the curb and unloaded our luggage. I hugged my mother good-bye, then my father. I felt his shoulders tremble and as he let go of me. He said through watery eyes, "I'm sorry we can't make it to the wedding. We love you!" Wow, he said "it" and I hugged him again. "It's okay Daddy, I understand. You have stuff you have to take care of here. I love you too."

Paul's Parents

As our plane approached Boston, my heart and mind swirled with emotions and thoughts. On the one hand, I was calm and confident in the knowledge that my upcoming marriage was an integral part of the Lord's gracious opportunity for a second chance for me. On the other hand, I was nervous over how Paul's family would receive me. I wondered if they were apprehensive over the short engagement for, after all, I would become their daughter-in-law four days after first meeting them.

The walk through Logan International Airport to baggage claim seemed to take an eternity. The tapes in my head which proclaimed that I was not worthy and did not deserve a second chance at happiness began to play, but were ejected by my fervent prayer that the Lord prepare all of our hearts for our first meeting. It was all in His hands now.

After grabbing our baggage, Paul and I exited the airport to meet his parents on the curbside. I couldn't help but recognize the irony in meeting Paul's father for the first time in the same way that I last said good-bye to my own; I hoped the outcome would be the same. Just as we sat down on a bench, a car pulled up and two doors swung open. Paul's mother got out of the car and hugged Paul, while his father approached me. Paul's mother hugged me as Paul hugged his father then formal introductions were made. My fears vanished in this moment as I took one more step toward realizing my hopes and dreams.

Faith

Paul's father arranged for a picnic-style wedding at Paul's grandmother's house in Vermont. Although I had not met Grandma Dike in person, I felt connected to her through the Holy Spirit. She revealed in our first phone conversation that she had walked with the Lord her entire life and that He was her strength. This helped eliminate some of my anxiety over the faith issue. Although Paul went to church with me—sometimes reluctantly—he was still very skeptical about surrendering his life to the Lord. But I wasn't worried because I knew that God had his number and that it was only a matter of time.

Paul attended the Catholic Church growing up but had wandered away. I didn't know if his parents still attended mass, nor how they viewed evangelical Christians. I didn't want the faith issue to become a

Paul's side of the family-I'm next to Grandma Dike and Paul is next to me.

wedge like it had in my family. But I took comfort in the knowledge that Paul's grandmother would know my heart.

After arriving at his parent's home, Paul and I took a break from the wedding preparations to go rollerblading by the ocean. I inhaled the refreshing salty air and praised the Lord for this beautiful spring day. The ocean is one of my favorite places to spend time. I leaned back with my arms raised high in the sky and took a deep, breath of fresh sea air. Reaching out to Paul we skated hand in mitten as I wore many layers of clothing to insulate myself not particularly concerned about the comfortable temperature. However, when Paul and I returned to his parents' home, I began to experience that "crawling skin" feeling in my hands, legs, and feet. I took my roller-blades off to discover that my feet were blotchy red and swollen. As the skin got tighter by the moment, itchy hives ran up to my hips. When I removed my gloves I found the same chaos. I was particularly concerned about my ring finger that was twice its normal size as my wedding ring exerted pressure.

Cut Off The Ring?

Paul filled the bathtub with steaming hot water and gently lowered me in to it. Upon leaving the bathroom he turned and said with tears running down his cheeks, "Do you think we will have to cut the ring off?" I replied, "Definitely not! The warm water will do the trick." But inside I really wasn't sure. As he shut the door I knew he was scared. He had witnessed several bad outbreaks that I couldn't hide from him in our three-month courtship but they were usually in response to my trying to do too much or ski when I shouldn't have.

I sat in the bathtub wondering if my life would ever be uncomplicated. Here I was, on the verge of happiness and fulfillment, while an attack from my own body unexpectedly put me at risk and Satan's taunting threatened to pull the rug out from under me. I felt that dark cloud come over me and heard the words, "You don't deserve to be happy. Paul would be better off if you cut that ring off and just forgot about all this 'second chance' nonsense."

Unlike times past, I recognized what was happening and determined that I would stand my ground. I added more hot water to my bath and imagined Jesus' love enveloping me like the water whose warmth had finally penetrated to my bones and began to sing. After an hour in the tub, I heard a knock at the door and Paul's loving voice asking if I was okay. He came in and we talked through the shower curtain for a while. He handed me a towel and pulled me out of the tub. He helped me get to bed and covered me with many blankets so I could rest for a while. Finally, the swelling went down and I was able to rotate the ring around my finger. Everything was going to be all right.

Our Vermont Wedding

We all drove to Vermont in separate cars. Paul could tell I was as eager to meet his grandmother, as he was to show me off to her. When we pulled up this darling eighty-seven-year-old woman eased herself out the front door. I got out of the car and dashed over to hug my new grandmother. I could feel the warmth of her embrace and thanked her for opening up her home to host our wedding. She confided that while many in the family wondered if Paul would ever get married, she knew that God had selected a special woman for him and that she was glad to host the Lord's handiwork. Her words of wisdom meant so much.

Paul's father coordinated the activities associated with the wedding. The tent, tables, and chairs were put in place while one of the neighbors mowed the lawn and tended to the yard. Paul helped with these activities while I ironed out some of the details of the ceremony. Paul's brother and sister agreed to read scripture and we entrusted Paul's Uncle Ralph, his father's brother who is a music aficionado, with the music. For the past month I'd devoted much of my time to scripting the ceremony and even created a wedding program. The last detail to attend to was deciding who would conduct the ceremony. Paul's father said he had taken care of this and decided that the town's ninety-year-old justice of the peace would do it. At first I was not sure about this, but Paul's father revealed that "Hazel" had grown up with Grandma Dike and known her for over seventy years. This eased my mind for if she had been a friend of Grandma Dike's for that long, she must be all right!

The Big Day

May 16, 1998 dawned hot and steamy in North Ferrisburg, Vermont. After waking, Grandma and I enjoyed breakfast together and reflective conversation about our faith, family life on the farm over the years, and our joy for living and loving. I then began preparing for my "big day." As the morning passed, like most brides, the range of emotions I experienced amazed me. I was saddened that my family wasn't able to come, not even the ones from Massachusetts. Even though I told my parents that under the circumstances of what they were dealing with I didn't want them to add further stress to their life by making the trek from Florida to Vermont, my heart yearned for their presence. With no maid of honor or attendants, I was on my own. So I got on my knees

Our wedding photo on the bridge

and talked to God for a while and then asked Him to send His angels to attend to my heart. After a while, I got up and fixed my hair.

I hoped that if my parents were there that they would be proud. Proud of me for the person I had become, the person I wanted to be, and the union with this very special man. I thought of Paul and wondered what he was thinking and doing. Then I thought of the life I knew the Lord had in store for us, and I was so grateful because this second chance was only by God's saving grace.

By 11:00 a.m., Grandma Dike's deck was occupied with some fifty people whose faces I barely recalled seeing in photo albums Paul and I perused through on cold winter nights in Colorado. Paul's father was ready. Since my father couldn't be here, I asked him if he would walk me down the aisle—in this case, through the yard and over a tiny bridge—to the deck where Paul waited patiently for me.

The Bridge

As I walked over that bridge, I felt that it was not the only bridge I would cross today. I would cross bridges that would connect me to the joy and happiness of the future, as well as bridges that would reconcile me with the family and friends I often felt estranged from in the past. But most importantly, I hoped to cross a bridge that would forever lead me into the loving arms of my eternal Father where I would never feel separated from Him again.

I know that God detests divorce and the sins that led me so far away from Him during my dark days, but I now knew that He had forgiven me for my transgressions because I repented and laid them at the cross where all is forgiven! It was okay to be happy again. It was okay to love another and, to love myself. It was okay to hope and dream, for the Lord made this day and it was good.

Heading to the ship for our Alaskian cruise.

"Paul and Diane, I now pronounce you husband and wife. You may kiss the bride!" And the song, *How Sweet It Is,* by James Taylor, resounded our sentiments as we danced on the bridge of our future, together.

Honeymoon Cruise

For our first night as a married couple, we spent a romantic evening on Lake Champlain at Aunt Chick and Uncle Bob's home. Then Paul and I cruised to Alaska through the "Inland Passage" for our honeymoon. From the moment the ship left Vancouver, British Columbia, I had the irresistible desire to sleep. I am a water person and the rocking motions of the cruise ship relaxed me. After many years of struggling with sleep, it was great to lie on a bed and instantly drift into a serene dream world for as many hours as interruptions allowed. The only problem was that this was our honeymoon. Would Paul think I slept it away? When I told him of the situation, he told me not to worry; that he was happy that I was able to sleep and that he would spend his spare time working out in the ship's gym or participating in the activities offered on-board or at the ports-of-call. I slept on.

The cruise lasted seven days. We stopped in places with names like Skagway and Ketchikan. Although Paul said he enjoyed the vantage point the cruise ship offered of calving glaciers in Glacier Bay National Park, for the most part, he didn't like being confined to the ship. He said that when we passed beautiful scenery, he yearned to get close to it or, as he poetically put it, "I want to go climb that mountain or roll around in the dirt."

Marriage Gets Better Each Day

Erma Bombeck underscores that, "marriage is life's last chance for adults to grow up." The world needs men who have courage like my Paul. His dedication to our marriage has improved with each passing day. Men with courage take counsel and they take action; they may not do it perfectly, but they tackle issues and desert storms valiantly, taking responsibility for their actions head on. I am so thankful that through all the dark nights I held on because

This picture was taken as Paul was heading out the door to his first Christian retreat called, "Walk to Emmaus." He brought his camping gear and threatened to hike out. In the bag I'm holding is a special quilted blanket. It's theme is the great outdoors with fish, camping, tents, bears, etc. on it. The gift was to be opened when he arrived so he could be surrounded by my love. We snuggled under it on the way home. We now call it the born again blanket and remember that life changing moment when Paul made Jesus Lord of his life.

The day Paul gave his life to Jesus. Here he was professing what the Lord means to him in front of all the participants and family members that came to pick them up.

Paul was worth it. I couldn't imagine writing this book or embarking on this life's journey without him. Together, with courage, wisdom, commitment, love, and God, we have climbed to higher ground! While dating, I knew Paul was a keeper. He carried me when I couldn't walk. Since then he has gone through several health disappointments, surgeries, and close calls with me. He's rocked my world and inspired me to write two love songs—the one I sang to him on Valentine's Day and, *That's The Power Of Love,* which I sang to him for the first time during our wedding ceremony. One of the lines in the song is, "We are a better me as an us!" It is true.

It's been said that being born again takes but a moment; spiritual maturity takes a lifetime. I'm glad God is patient with each of us. After wrestling with the decision, Paul finally confessed Jesus as Lord. One cool Sunday evening on our way home from his "Walk to Emmaus" weekend in October of 1998, he dedicated and surrendered his life to Jesus. Right before we reached the Eisenhower Tunnel on interstate 70, I said to our friends driving, "Pull over I've got to do a praise dance!"

Right there on the side of the highway we all got out and danced around hugging and laughing and praising the good Lord. As a soft rain baptized us, I thought I might have heard the angels rejoicing, and felt the brush of their wings.

CHAPTER 16

Show Me How To Live!

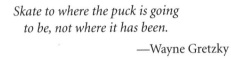

*Skate to where the puck is going
to be, not where it has been.*

—Wayne Gretzky

Gratefulness And Love

Right after moving to Colorado I prayed, "God, if I can't die and end this pain, if you're not ready to take me home, will you please show me how to live in spite of my challenges!" I believe Paul was part of the answer to that prayer. Paul really knows how to live. He has a passionate zest for life and an adoring sense of adventure. It's one of the things I admire about him. He worships the Creator by fully enjoying His creation through mountain and road biking, hiking, fishing, skiing, and running; enjoying the adventure that God has planned for him each and every day.

I've been allowed an inexplicable reprieve from death several times and blessed with several second chance's that I did nothing to deserve. I'm so thankful and while my body feels old from the ravages of the health challenges I've endured, love restores my youth. Like that Greek proverb, "The heart that loves is always young." I feel young at heart. I've been blessed with what many search their entire life for and healed by God's love. And I know, death cannot sink my battleship, only bring me into a harbor where I am forever home.

Paul and I work hard at experiencing a healthy, successful, and loving relationship. Vital to this process is applying the lessons that I've learned regarding how to take care of "my man," like many country songs sing about. Showing respect, appreciation, value, and cherishing my husband everyday regardless of how I feel doesn't mean that I avoid conflict about issues that are disturbing. I share my feelings honestly, in a kind way, to be sure we keep things from building up and causing greater trouble later on. When we have disagreements, we try to avoid bringing up past woes and focus on the current situation. Balance is so important, as well as not taking each other for granted.

I believe Paul is my gift from God and is an integral component of my opportunity to fulfill my God-given destiny. Together, we will fulfill our potential. As I say in the song I wrote for him, "We are a better me as an us." We are going to places we have never been, together with our arms wide open because God has a great plan for us. We believe each day, month, and year will be our best despite the challenges that come our way because we will face them together. Every morning, we start fresh and new, letting go of the mistakes or failures of yesterday, ready to embrace the possibilities of a new day. We say, "This is the day that the Lord has made and we will rejoice and be glad in it!"

The Language Of Love

Charles Swindoll wrote, "We live by encouragement and die without it. Slowly, sadly and angrily." If we believe that we are having one problem or friction after another, we know that it is probably because we have unresolved issues, that maybe we are not appreciating each other and/or we are not spending enough time in the Word. Arguments, disagreements, and misunderstandings are a natural part of any relationship. We choose to handle them carefully for ultimate resolution so resentment does not build up. We fight for our healthy love to stay, not to decide who is right or wrong! About every three months, Paul and I have to sit down and share our frustrations and feelings whether we want to or not. Sometimes it is painful to hear the truth, but we know that we must be willing to resolve negative emotions so our relationship can grow and thrive in security, peace, and love. We try to start with "I feel frustrated when... " instead of, "You are always so..." We both want to feel safe, appreciated, and loved. Picking the right time to discuss our thoughts is important and during these meetings we try to share our concerns and this approach seems to work for us. We've had our moments when impulsive, hurtful words have been spoken but it is our goal to avoid doing this at all costs. My prayer is that God would set a guard over our mouth and keep our lips from uttering ruin to each other. I desire that we would speak health, healing and promote life not destruction with the power of our words (Proverbs 13:3).

Sometimes Paul puts on a macho man façade. But I know he needs and wants to be appreciated. Sometimes he doesn't know how to ask for it so, to boost his manhood, I get behind him and say, "I'm proud of you. You're doing a great job. I really like the way you parked the car." Kenny Rogers sang about it in his love song, *She Believes In Me.* He said if he could get the girl, and she believed in him faithfully, he could change the world.

A Coach, A Teammate, and A Cheerleader

We are on the same team. Sometimes he needs a coach while other times he needs a cheerleader. I want him to feel good about himself because a happy husband equals a happy home. William James, the philosopher and psychologist said, "The deepest principle of human nature is the craving to be appreciated." On that same note, when I ask Paul how I can love him best, he usually replies, "Just leave me alone." This is a running joke between us, but alludes to a very important component to our marital success: the understanding and use of different love languages.

You Just May Be Right, Dear

I've learned Paul's love language and try to accept him just the way he is, while trying to bring out the best in him. I seek to get a perspective on his understanding of things when I can. I desire to meet his needs in whatever way serves him, not in a way I see fit. I focus on what I can do, not on what I cannot. We learned a valuable phrase to diffuse tense moments and disagreements from Merlin, the guy who runs the local balloon ride business. He said that when he and his wife disagree, regardless of who is right or wrong, he says to her, "You just may be right, dear." He probably doesn't know how much fun we have had with this lesson, but I know that it has sure come in handy for Paul and me when we disagree.

Paul, me, Jo & my nephew Billy in Merlin's balloon

Starting and ending each day with prayer helps too. Paul and I have respect for each other and take responsibility for our actions, words, and choices. Responding to my husband's needs and making him a priority can mean the difference between a happy, fulfilling marriage and a sad, lost, divorced one. I've been there and don't want to go there again! I strive to put God first, Paul second, and then myself. I look at our marriage as a triangle where we are at either end at the bottom and God is at the top. The closer we get to Him, the closer we get to each other. He created us and knows what is best for us. He helps us keep our heads and hearts in the right place so that we can stay in our most opportune place of blessing. We both have a responsibility to be where we are supposed to be, to do what we are supposed to be doing, to fulfill our purpose and plan in our generation. This is when we get the spiritual breakthrough that allows us to live lives that transcend mediocrity.

If we put each other first, we both win and glorify God in the process. I am focused on this goal and it causes me to live my best life now. This is why it is so important to be married to someone who believes as you do. The Bible says not to be unequally yoked for a reason: it is impossible for beasts of burden as well as people to move in the same direction if their focus and attention is on different things. If they agree upon a goal and the means to achieve it, they will surely get there and be all that they can be. Some say I changed Paul. No, I didn't, God did. He took Paul's wonderful heart and made it better.

Ecclesiastes 4:9-11 says, "Two are better than one, because they have a good return for their work: If one falls down, his friend can help him up. But pity the man who falls and has no one to help him up! Also if two lie down together, they will keep warm. But how can one keep warm alone?" Oh how thankful I am for the warmth of my husband!

Reckless Abandon

Approaching love with reckless abandon is what I've always done. I figure if you are going to love, love all the way, or not at all. I suppose it has always been part of my personality, from chasing the boys' home from the bus stop to give them a kiss, to loving my work, my husband, my dog, and the Lord. Love is a risk, but if it doesn't work out as I dreamed, it is a failure only if I fail to learn. Satan doesn't want us to have a successful marriage or a strong spiritual life. He will throw every sort of challenge into our path in an effort to distract us, to keep us busy, or to overwhelm us and weaken our love for each other and our stand for the Lord. We must not give him that power over us. Our marriage and our life depend on it. Unlike sports or television, there is no off-season in our stand and our need to study and know the Word of God. The times when I have faltered have almost always coincided with letting my guard down, and taking my focus off Jesus. We can maintain our strength, our position, and our hope on a daily basis if we stay in the Word. Allen E. Vartlett had it right when he wrote, "Seven days without prayer makes one weak."

If we are willing to give up the comforts of always having it our way for God's glory, we will gain so much more in Heaven. C. S. Lewis describes what I think is true living and the perseverance of reckless abandon:

> *Love anything, and your heart will certainly be wrung, possibly be broken. If you want to make sure of keeping it intact, you must give your heart to no one, not even to an animal. Wrap it carefully around with hobbies and little luxuries; avoid all entanglements; lock it up safe in the casket or coffin of your selfishness. But in that casket-safe, dark, motionless, airless-it will change. It will not be broken; it will become unbreakable, impenetrable, irredeemable. (Think, Exist, Lewis, 2008)*

Hiking in Glenwood Springs, Colorado

Intimacy Extracts A Price

To love will cost us something. Intimacy will extract a price. An unknown writer penned, "It will cost to follow Jesus Christ, but it costs even more not to." The same is true in our relationships with each other. Although I still suffer from my various ailments, the Lord restored my heart in so many ways thus allowing me the ability to receive the gift He has for me in Paul. I could have, like all of us I suppose, closed down, never to be hurt again. Paul is strong enough to be my man because he relies on the strength of the Lord. He massages my pain almost every night and guides me in my wheelchair with my backpack full of mittens, blankets, hats, scarves, and Bible. Without his commitment, love, and support, my life wouldn't be what it is today. Marrying Paul was one of the best decisions of my life. Our marriage is a joyful thing to behold. He lifts me up to more than I think I can be. I count on him and he can count on me. Our song, by Steven Curtis Chapman, is, *I Will Be There*. I know Paul will be there for me. He has already shown me this and I'm very thankful.

CHAPTER 17

GOD'S SENSE OF HUMOR

> *Friends are those rare people who ask how we are*
> *and then wait to hear the answer.*
>
> —Ed Cunningham

By Paul E. Dike

When I look back at meeting Diane and our whirlwind courtship, I can't help but think that God has a heck of a sense of humor. How else can I explain the juxtaposition of two completely different people in the tiny mountain town of Vail, Colorado? In the fall of 1998, I was the classic ski bum living the dream life: I skied 100 days a year, biked 100 days a year, hiked and fished a 100 days a year, and, quite frankly, was probably hung-over the remaining sixty-five days.

I had a good paying job that began at 4:00 in the morning, leaving the entire afternoon for adventure. I could live this adventure-based lifestyle because I was alone and, without beating around the bush, wanted to remain that way. I had experienced enough short-term and long-term relationships up to this point and had been hurt by the only women I really loved. I was not looking to meet anyone when I walked into a restaurant on Vail Mountain that fateful day. I stopped by to see how the new cookies were doing since, as the Purchasing Manager for the resort, I had just made the decision to change the cookie brand

on Vail Mountain. I walked up to the hostess station to see if the restaurant manager was there when a woman swirled around and flashed these big, white, perfect teeth. I no longer cared about cookies and my true life's adventure was about to begin.

A Smile That Changed My Life

A month later I met Diane at a Super Bowl party and we continued the conversation we started at the restaurant. I pulled my smoothest "Rico Suave" move thinking that this beautiful girl wanted the same thing as I. I pleaded for a ski date, which she first objected to then finally complied after I agreed to pick her up at the bottom of the hill she lived on—her rules of propriety prevented me from seeing where she lived on the first date. By this time I realized that this was no ordinary woman; that I would have to be on my best behavior if I was going to spend time with her. I picked her up for skiing then took her to the gym for a quick workout before we drove to Denver for a Colorado Avalanche hockey game. It was obvious that she wasn't lying about the old days when she spent much of her time playing various sports and working out in the gym. She promptly embarrassed me on the pull-up bar, than challenged me to push-ups. I took the fifth and declared that it was time to go to Denver.

During the two-hour drive to Denver I learned a lot about Diane: her higher education, her athletics, her strong faith, and her precarious health. To this day I do not know if I was more frightened by her faith or her illnesses. I grew up Roman Catholic but had not been to church on my own free will in fifteen years. All her illnesses seemed a little daunting, but I didn't really think much about them because she didn't look like she was sick. I figured I would take her to the doctor, fill her with prescriptions, and she would be as good as new. How wrong I was!

During the quiet times of the drive I couldn't stop looking at her. Her smile filled the car to overflowing, and it felt like we had known each other for a long time; that she actually cared about what I said and, perhaps more startling, what I felt. I don't know if my team won the game or not, but I do know that I won because I have been with Diane ever since; as her husband for all but four months of our whirlwind courtship.

My friends couldn't believe that I was getting married. At thirty-five, I was pretty set in my ways and thought I was as happy as anyone had the right to be. But there was just something about Diane that made me want to be with her. Call it charisma, call it panache, or call it what I know it to be today, the Holy Spirit, which emanates from her. I was a little leery of her "Christian Freak" faith. I was the college-educated skeptic who had wandered from transcendentalism to mysticism, while I worshipped the creation and not the Creator. I was very skeptical of so-called "Born Again Christians" but she seemed different, she seemed real. Her faith was disarming.

Suffering

Divisions and walls between people seem to crumble when Diane is involved in the conversation. This struck me the most on the RV trip we took in 2004-2005. Wherever we went, she met and became friends with people and couples of all ages and still keeps in touch with many of them today. I am not talking about superficial friendships, but the real deal where people share the secrets of their souls, where they look to each other for answers and support so they can make it through the challenges of another day. I believe Diane has the ability to reach this level of intimacy so quickly with the people God puts in her life because she has suffered in so many ways, at so many levels; even strangers feel comfortable sharing with Diane and can feel her genuine love.

Diane told me of her cryoglobulinemia, fibromyalgia, and all the other diseases before we got married and I saw their frightful attacks on her little body. Since I enjoy near perfect health, with the exception of various high-speed sports accidents, I hadn't heard of many of her maladies. Again, she looked fine, so I wasn't worried. I figured I could just read some books on the various diseases, take her to the doctor, and then help him figure out how to fix her. Well, I did read the books on fibromyalgia, chronic fatigue, and various autoimmune complexes and discovered the pickle we were in: there is no magic bullet, no direct cause and effect relationship between her symptoms and their underlying causes since autoimmune means that the body is attacking itself.

However, I was smart enough to know the role that stress plays in the diseased state and knew, after she told me about her life's pursuits, that she had burned the candle at both ends for far too long. I surmised that she just never had the chance to get better and I could provide her that chance. I had a good job so she could continue to massage on a part time basis. She wouldn't have to work a nine-to-five job, five days a week for us to make it financially; she would be able to pick and choose when she wanted to work, based upon how she was feeling rather than on the compulsion to honor a work commitment.

I will never forget when Diane revealed to me that she was diagnosed with bipolar. I had no idea what that meant so, again, I read books. I must admit that I was frightened. The highs of the cycle seemed pretty cool, but the lows, with talk about suicide, what was all that about? *Do I really know what I am getting into,* I wondered. Once again, Diane did not look sick in this way. She wasn't engaging in sexual adventures or taking spending sprees to Fifth Avenue. As far as being low, I had never seen someone smile so much and bring joy to so many lives. I concluded back then, and still believe today, that we are all mentally ill or bipolar in some way or another and those with the diagnosis just know that they are.

Looks Can Be Deceiving

Looks can be deceiving. When you look at Diane and see her smile, you cannot help but conclude that she is fine. She still hides behind that mask, but not to hide or run away from anything, but rather not to be a burden to anyone. She doesn't seem sick because she doesn't talk about it, but believe me, she is sick. Bad days follow sleepless nights and physical or emotional stress can lead to the flare-ups described and pictured in this book. Her legs look like someone splattered them with red paint, they bruise and swell, often times for no apparent reason, and she cannot walk. It's these times, when she does everything right and still suffers inexplicably, that the symptoms can take their toll and bring on depression. Who could blame her? In fact, just yesterday, I awoke in horrific pain and did not know why. I finally concluded that it was food poisoning from an undercooked burger I ate the night before. You're darn right I was depressed: I couldn't ride my bike or run because of the discomfort. Diane feels this aching pain all the time. So, she gets low at times, but she invariably lifts herself up to face another day and all who may encounter her are better for it.

Diane is a fiercely proud and driven individual, a chip off the old block, so to speak, because both her parents are proud and upstanding people. She was extremely athletic: strong in the weight room and phenomenal in the pool. It has been very difficult to watch her body fade away as she fights her assorted diseases. She no longer skis or rides mountain bikes like she did when we first married. In fact, much of the time she is confined to the home because she doesn't feel well, her feet are too swollen to walk without pain, or because possible cold and wet weather dampen any chance of her going outside safely.

Transitions and Painful Decisions

Six years ago she was prescribed a wheel chair and told to use it. For the most part, we kept that chair in the garage. Diane did not want to use it and, quite frankly, I did not want her to, either. It seemed to us that her choosing to use it was like admitting a personal defeat, like she was giving up. The years passed and the cries in the night returned after days spent just sitting or standing for too long. You see, it is imperative for Diane to keep her feet elevated when sitting and to avoid standing because when the blood pools in the feet it chills, and all hell breaks loose.

In 2006, we decided it was time she used the chair because simple outings—to the grocery store and even church—resulted in serious outbreaks of her various maladies. Paradoxically, the wheelchair has not confined her, but set her free. She can now participate in activities such as conferences and concerts that she had previously given up. It has been liberating to watch her grow past any stigma associated with a wheelchair as she tears off another layer of the mask. It has actually helped put "ability" back in her dis*ability*. She has been given some of her life back, opening up the opportunity for her to bless even more people as she travels the country sharing her testimony and message of hope from the safety of her chair.

Writing this book has been a labor of love for both of us. As I edited the manuscript, I was struck by the extraordinary life Diane has lived in spite of all her challenges. It has made me realize what a remarkable woman my wife is, and I want the whole world to know!

CHAPTER 18

A GOD THING!

Though our feelings come and go,
God's love for us does not.

—C.S. Lewis

Meeting Michael W. Smith

One day my pastor at Vail Bible Church was having some back problems, so I went to the church office to help him out; after the massage, he felt miraculously better. That Sunday, renowned singer and songwriter Michael W. Smith gave his testimony. I noticed that he had a neck problem. I just happened to have read and studied about that particular issue that week. I said, "Oh Lord, he has a terrible case of poke neck and I can imagine the discomfort he is experiencing. Please help him and if you want to do it through me, I am willing. Here I am Lord, send me."

Two days later, I came home from teaching water exercise classes to a message on my answering machine from Michael W. He said, "Diane, this is Michael W. Smith. We hear that you are an awesome massage therapist and we need some therapy up here." He left me his phone numbers and I called him back. Years later, I told him of my prayer and asked him how he got my name. Apparently, our pastor was playing golf with Frank Gifford and Michael. Michael mentioned that he really needed a massage, so my pastor gave him my number telling him, "God works miracles through this girl." How is that for a quick answer to a prayer? I really like it when God does that!

I later sang a song on Father's Day and was able to meet Kathy Lee and Frank Gifford. When I ran into them at an ice cream shop in Vail one afternoon, she told me the song I wrote and sang on Father's Day really touched her heart. Frank said he liked it too. I sat with them while they finished their ice cream and Kathy shared about her father in Florida. We hugged each other goodbye and I thanked them and the Lord for the encouragement.

Paul and I quickly became friends with the entire Smith Family and fell in love with their Tennessee associates. Among their friends are Jack and Joanne Kemp. Joanne visited a Bible study at our condo right after Paul and I were married but we met again through Michael. She quickly became a faithful client and friend. We often eat with the former vice presidential candidate and his wife when Michael invites us to join his group for dinner. Every time the Smiths come to town with

Amazing Friends-some of my "TN Family" right before dinner in Colorado!

their prayer group, family, or friends, they kindly include Paul and me in activities and dinners. I use to perform lots of massage work and ear candling in between.

Amazing People

My massage practice enabled me to work with many amazing people. One day while walking through Vail, a couple of gentlemen were standing at the locked door of a massage establishment. When they saw me coming, one said, "Hey, do you work here?" I said, "No, but I'm a therapist." He replied, "My name is Mike. Can you come by our place? We need some therapy." He gave me his name, phone number and location just down the street, and we enjoyed a friendly visit. I said, "Let me make sure my husband can bring me so I know everything is safe for me to work. We will call you and confirm the appointment."

With a little apprehension I followed up on this lead. Upon arriving home I informed Paul of the name and information of this man and work opportunity. Paul asked, "Did he look like a hockey player?"

"I don't know?" I giggled. "What does a hockey player look like?"

"Was he about this tall with red hair?"

"Yeah. How did you know?"

"That's Mike Keene. He used to play for the Colorado Avalanche and was traded to the Stars last season. Wow, that is so cool. How do these things just happen with you? I've heard that he is a real family man. Still I will help you get set up. I called Michael and told him we were on the way!

He was really nice and talked about his family throughout. Two and a half hours later he said, "We need to take you on the road with us. That is the best massage I've ever had." I praised the Lord and worked on him the next two years when his team was in town.

Road Trip

God was not done with his amazing grace. Paul and I took a road trip to Fort Collins, Colorado to camp and visit his alma mater and the most amazing thing happened. Throughout our trip, I popped many of my old cassette tapes into the stereo and enjoyed the stroll down memory lane. Most were made from taping the stereo in the days when I had no television. Suddenly tears welled up and a flood of emotion filled our car. Paul didn't know what to do as I was immediately transported to those dark and lonely nights when life seemed so hopeless; when death seemed the only escape from my constant physical, emotional, and mental turmoil. When the song *Take My Hand* finished. I pulled myself together

The whole gang! Joanne & Jack Kemp, Brad Quayle, the five Smith children and some of their friends, John and Susan from CA, the Webster's from CO, I'm at the top with Anna, Debbie and Michael (in front of me). Paul is on the far right.

and shared what my tears of gratefulness were about and how real and true the words of the song were to me: "You don't know what's comin' but you know the one who holds tomorrow—I will be your guide—take you through the night if you keep your eyes on Me." We probably listened to the song ten (or thirty) times really letting it soak in and talked of how God cared enough to work out every minute detail. Paul shared how thankful he was that I held on.

A short time after marrying Paul, some girls I became friends with told me I had to come to their church because their pastor, Tommy Schneider, and I were like brother and sister because we acted so much alike. So Paul and I visited Calvary Chapel Vail Valley on Mother's Day, 1999. My friends were right: I saw the resemblance right away. We loved our Vail Bible Church but we felt compelled to become members of this church family, too. Saturday nights we enjoyed Vail Bible and Sunday Mornings we celebrated worship at Calvary Chapel.

I sang a special or two and joined the worship team at Calvary with Bob Gross and Pete Nelson. Pete was in a band called "The Kry." One week, Jean-Luc Lajoie, one of the band's members came for a visit and to sing a song from their new album. They brought some new and old CD's to sell. After the service, Jean-Luc and I began talking about our French Canadian families, about places we had in common, and our Catholic upbringing. I really enjoyed our visit and felt a special connection, like somehow I knew him but I couldn't put my finger on it. In any case, we promised to pray for each other's dads as we hugged goodbye (his dad Louis, has been on my prayer list ever since). Dick Blaire joined in our conversation and out of the blue he asked, "Have you ever heard these guys?" I dropped my head with embarrassment and said, "I am not sure." He picked up a CD and said, "Here, this is for you, you're going to love it."

What Are The Chances?

When I got home I put the CD in the player, made lunch, and then it happened: the song *Take My Hand* started. I knew that song in three notes! I grabbed the insert information. Jean-Luc Lajoie and his brother Yves Lajoie wrote the words.

Wow! Amazing! What are the chances? Only God can do that! Are you kidding me? I wasn't sure if I wanted to laugh, cry, scream, or wave the American flag in front of my house like I did on September 11th! I called Dick and told him the abbreviated story of what this song meant to me. He said, "Wow! Here..." He passed the phone to Jean-Luc who listened carefully to my story. We had already made a wonderful association at church, but now this divine appointment would remind me forever of the promises of God and how I can stand on them, no matter what. We had a beautiful moment as I let him know that his song was instrumental in my not giving up. I thanked him for allowing God to work through him to write a song that helped a girl in the Central Florida swamps tie a knot at the end of her rope and hold on.

Weeks later I shared the testimony of how all those amazing details lined up and sang the song while Pete played the guitar. This is the testimony, in part, that I shared before I sang the song:

> *My hope and prayer is that what I share with you will encourage you in the truth that God loves you and cares about every detail of your life.*
>
> *There was a time not too long ago when I went through some of the darkest days of my life. I begged God to take me home. This living was too hard, too painful.*

I have no words to express the troubles that I brought on myself, that others inflicted on me or circumstances allowed but they were some of the most desolate days of my life and I almost gave up. I was so close to giving up that I could taste the relief that only death could bring. But God reached out to save me and He spoke to me through a song on a dark and lonely night.

The song, Take My Hand, *spoke to my very soul. I was scared and alone but He knew just what to do so I could carry on. Almost ten years later, God allowed me to meet and thank the man who wrote that saving song. It confirms in my heart and mind that God cares so much for all of his children that He will go to any length for them to know the depth and breadth of His unfailing love.*

I related what I have already written. I sang the song and praised God with every note and word. Just like a child holding Daddy's hand, I didn't let go of His because I know I can't stand on my own. I'm still holding on today!

How deep, how wide, how great is His love for you and me. Amazing.

CHAPTER 19

TO THE EDGE

It's not what you've got,
it's what you use that makes a difference.

—Zig Ziglar

Even though my life turned around after my encounter with the Lord and then meeting and marrying Paul, I still suffered from many conditions, particularly cryoglobulinemia. I had to face the fact that this disease wasn't going anywhere on its own. Paul wanted to help me beat it so we went on a quest to understand and figure out what to do about it and see if any new treatments had been developed.

Treatment

In the beginning I did everything that the doctors suggested to manage this disease. Their approach included standard procedures: surgeries, crutches, biopsies, blood tests, prescriptions, and hospital stays. I couldn't tolerate most of the medicines prescribed. They seemed to aggravate my condition or flare-up another disorder. The failure of the steroid treatment in particular made me doubt if traditional medicine had anything left to offer me. I had to learn to hold onto prescriptions and promises that were not of this world while giving everything that had potential here a chance. Fearful thoughts and a painful body kept me in need of a fresh injection of—confidence in Him—a steadfast confidence that He who began a good work in me would bring it to completion.

Paul knew that having children could be dangerous for me and was very understanding. He agreed that adoption was a viable option. So we attended classes to become certified foster parents and prepared to adopt some children. Not long after, I became extremely ill again and we made the painful decision on March 31, 1999 to go through with a doctor-recommended full hysterectomy. The irony of this procedure was that out of all the traditional treatments I received, this resulted in the most improvement to my conditions: it removed a variable from the lengthy list of things that aggravated my fragile homeostasis. After suffering for twenty years with this monthly challenge, I was freed from this recurring time of agony. I've been on natural hormone replacement ever since.

Alternative Treatments

We then ventured down the long and expensive road of alternative treatments including chiropractic, naturopathic, and homeopathic approaches. I've tried just about every "miracle" product known to man: vitamin IVs, peroxide IVs, straining my blood and blasting it with UV rays-UV blood irradiation, nutritional therapy, liquid vitamins, herbs, customized vitamins, aloe-vera, coral calcium, B-12 shots, enzymes, hydrotherapy, detoxification, biofeedback, bioelectrical therapies, DMSO and MSN, hydrazine sulfate, chelation, oxygen therapies, colon cleansings, juicing, and even coffee enemas. Recently, I started drinking fish oils. The elders of the church have prayed over me and anointed me as the Bible says to do. I'm on many prayer lists at churches throughout the world. Despite all these efforts, the various illnesses and conditions continue to plague me and even more join in as a consequence of my disabled immune system, even as I stretch my hand out to the hem of His garment.

Alternative Health Clinics

We searched for relief at alternative health clinics. Information about the success achieved at such "wonder clinics" floods the market. We still hoped to find a "magic bullet" to fix my health and I was willing to try expensive and often painful procedures. I couldn't help but think that I was missing something—a nutrient, a transfusion, a treatment, a mindset—and that if I could introduce that missing link to my regime, I would be cured.

I heard about a clinic called The Bright Spot in Wichita, Kansas. In 2001, my husband drove the 500 miles to Wichita where we spent three days as they conducted a barrage of tests. The doctor didn't seem over-whelmed by my laundry list of ailments and symptoms; this encouraged me. I liked the clinic's approach, which sought to combine the wisdom from many fields to create a regime that would send me on my way to better health.

The doctor found multiple problems including previous diagno-sis and: "H. pylori, toxic levels of copper, parasites, low vitamin C, low white blood count, Epstein-Barr virus, chronic fatigue, fibromyalgia..." and the list went on. I was still toxic even after months of treatment combining work with a local doctor and another holistic clinic. The biggest challenge with this clinic's regime was that the treatment plan they offered entailed many months of in-house therapy. This was prohibitive because of its cost. I lived far away and they had no rooms to accommodate guests who sought treatment. Thus, the Kansas doctor recommended a hyperbaric chamber treatment and another doctor in Aspen, Colorado, who subscribed to the same treatment philosophies.

Aspen, Colorado

My husband drove the 150 mile round trip from Vail to Aspen three days a week for an entire summer and fall in search of the elusive miracle cure. The treatment centered on the use of IVs for the administering of vitamins, nutrition, and chelation therapy. The Kansas clinic determined that I was deficient in the first two and toxic with heavy metals that the chelation therapy was designed to address. My blood was run through a machine that blasted it with ultra violet rays then returned it to my system. Lastly, the Aspen doctor put me on a strict diet void of many things that are common to the American diet including: sugar, wheat, red meat, and dairy products to name a few. I followed this strict regime and spent thousands of dollars on pills and potions. Yet, I noticed little change in how I felt on a day-to-day basis. In fact, in some ways, after four months of this treatment, I felt even worse.

From my first full year in Colorado to the present, Paul and I notice that my health takes a nosedive every spring. We think this is due in large part to the long winters which last from the first of November to the end of April. I can't push through and enjoy the winter wonderland of Vail outdoor sports anymore because it's too dangerous and I do not bounce back like I once did. I spend much of the season inside the safety of our home, working from my bed. I work on my computer and try to stay involved with projects but the ensuing depression adds to my physical distress and pushes me to the edge. A simple cold turns into a respiratory infection, cough, walking pneumonia, with ear pain, sore throats, swollen glands, cough, laryngitis, difficulty swallowing. The weakness continues because of irregular heart-beats, myocarditis, pericarditis, palpitations with another interesting symptom: an increased susceptibility to electrostatic shock. It is likely a change in the electro-potential in my cells/nervous system. Some of toxins are likely sodium channel agonists and can change the electrical potential of my body. Thus, increasing the likelihood of electro-static shock which could explain my constant problems with computers malfunctioning. I can't even wear a watch. Then of course the body ache and perpetual flu continues to make working, socializing, shopping, and performing daily chores difficult. Slowly I've had to abandon my various jobs and the house work, cooking and cleaning has fallen on Paul's shoulders. In January 2003, I became desperate. I had to do something to relieve my suffering. I was frantic for a cure!

My Aspen doctor was as frustrated as I was with the lack of improvement in my condition and suggested that I try one of the "health clinics" in Mexico that have reportedly cured many who were desperate for help. We were distressed because food and medication was going through me without a hint of digestion and I was getting weaker. Something had to be done. The doctor gave me a glossy brochure of one of the clinics depicting vibrant looking patients congregating around a pool, and a table topped with fresh, healthy looking food. There were also pictures of sophisticated looking equipment and claims that the treatment offered there was "cutting edge;" so advanced that it was not yet approved by U.S.F.D.A.

I researched all the clinics I could find information on. Based on this research and my Aspen doctor's recommendation, I decided to go to Tijuana, Mexico, hoping that this drastic measure would finally bring the miracle cure that had eluded me all these years

South Of The Border

The decision to go to Mexico was a difficult one to make. I spoke to the American doctor who seemed to run the facility, or, at least whose research on curing the incurable the clinic's protocol was based upon. He assured me his regimen, if followed, would not only improve my health but probably cure my many diseases. He said there was nothing like his clinic anywhere in the world. I must admit that I began to get excited, even hopeful about the prospects of being cured, and the possibility of returning to the vibrant lifestyle I knew fifteen years before. Covered intensely in prayer, I headed to Mexico ready and fully expecting my complete healing.

The Mexico clinic was not what the doctor said it would be, but one positive thing I took home were the many divine appointments I had in the midst of many sick and suffering people. Since phlebitis, inflammation of my blood vessels, plagued my arms and legs from the intensive IV treatment I received in Aspen the Mexican clinic scheduled the surgery for an IV port to be inserted into my chest so I could receive my treatment regime. I could feel the doctor's hands tremble while he cut into my chest just below my right clavicle bone. He assured me that he was a doctor, but I started to have my doubts as he fumbled around to find the right blood vessel to hook into. Finally he found it and connected the port to a major vein and stuck a hose into the vein; this port would be used to transport my daily nutrients and to administer the chelation therapy that nearly killed me.

Chelation

Chelation therapy is used in conventional as well as alternative medicine to remove heavy metals from the body. Through blood work done in Aspen, Kansas, and Mexico, the doctors could see that I was toxic with several heavy metals. The problem with chelation therapy is that it takes out the good metals as well as the bad. This is why it is imperative to follow it with a mega-nutrient cocktail to replenish any vital metals and nutrients lost. The side effects I previously experienced from the pill form of chelation therapy included severe headaches, upset stomach, overall intensified body pain, and the inability to move from nausea.

I was supposed to get three chelation treatments a week. I remember that on the third treatment of the first week, the nurse increased the speed of my IV drip. As a result of the nurse's mistake, I became extremely ill later that night. I went into convulsions, lost control of my bodily functions, and almost died. They placed ten blankets and several hot packs on me, but could not get my temperature to rise as my blood pressure dropped. They held down my arms and legs while I jerked forcibly. They didn't call the doctor at home, but when she came in the next morning to find me looking half dead, I was told that she ran to the office in tears, filed a complaint with the administration, and quit working at the facility that very moment. I never saw her again.

Just as I was beginning to recover they continued the treatment regime that included: over 50 pills a day, potions, ointments, acupuncture, suppositories, enemas, IVs, electrical current zapping, cleansings, tea baths, B-12 shots, and blood work. It was a like a medial carnival but it wasn't fun. However, I insisted, "Bring it on-I want to be well!"

My nurse and what appeared to be a nurse-in-training took me to a room with a big machine and table to give me a colon cleansing. Once I was set up, it seemed like they were having some difficulties but from my compromised position, I couldn't tell what they were doing. They inserted what felt like a cold sharp knife, and then I felt the cold water shoot into me. Cold is the worst thing for me and now I was getting injected with icy water. I shouted in horror for them to stop but they just said, "Esta bueno," meaning everything is all right. Through my antics, they finally realized that everything was not all right. However, it was too late and the damage was done. This treatment caused my insides to revolt and three days of hemorrhaging and ulcerative cryoglobulinemia colitis ensued. I was as withered and worn-out as my child-hood rag doll and thought I was might die for a second time. I knew this wasn't going to be a picnic but I really started to worry about the efficacy, or lack thereof, of this treatment. Nevertheless, I reasoned, *God doesn't make mistakes. He knows exactly what He is doing.* This stabilizing truth was the superglue that held me together. However, I still wondered: *Did I make a mistake coming here? Why am I here? This isn't how I dreamed it would be. What could possibly be the purpose for this torture?*

I received a call of encouragement from my dear friends, George and Carol MacKenzie, nearly every day. They prayed and let me know that they had not forgotten me. They relished in the joy that several of the patients had rededicated or dedicated their lives to the Lord for the first time when I was able to witness to them. One evening after dinner I gave a spontaneous concert in the treatment hall. I stood up and announced, "Pilar has just given her life to the Lord. I know the angels in Heaven are rejoicing. Amazing Grace, how sweet the sound..." Each patient that could joined in the singing and when we were done we let out a cheer like that hospital has never heard before (as I was told by the staff). They began giving me requests... I cry as I think of the stolen moment of peace we all shared as I sang until the sun went down and my voice gave out. The Lord was answering the prayers of friends and family back home and this helped me to carry on, gave me strength to hold on to hope, and trust that my trip here was about more than just a physical healing for myself. It was about the eternal destination of my critically ill new friends.

Paul's Visit

During my third and supposedly last week at the clinic, Paul came down to Mexico to see me. He was distraught and suggested that I return to Colorado with him. I didn't want to leave early, even with all the mistakes and setbacks because I didn't want to wonder one day, *"What if I had only stayed? Maybe I would have been healed."* We had the best few days we could under the circumstances. He cradled me while I received the treatments we both expected would bring my healing. We had church in my room most of the day and when I could he helped me take a walk around the hospital to check in on my new friends. I'd touch and stroke the suffering person's arm, hold their hand and let them know they were not alone, and tried to impart hope and encouragement by singing their favorite song. I welcomed new patients when they came, missed those that headed for home to the States, and mourned when others went home to Heaven.

I Didn't Want Him To Leave

Now, it was time for Paul to go home. Holding him close, I didn't want him to leave and he didn't want to leave either. With tears pouring down his face, he walked out the security gate. I stood in my pink slippers, blue hospital gown, and white robe while I grasped my rolling IV pole. He pressed his hand to the taxicab window signaling the "I love you" sign in sign language as I stretched the same until we could not see each other anymore. The air was heavy with sadness. Pilar, struggling with the last stages of cancer, came out to walk me back to my room; she understood my mourning. At about 11:00 a.m., I took a shower, attempting to wash my tears away. I reached for a towel on the rack and felt a snap and heard a pop emanating from my right shoulder. A sharp intense pain followed immediately which brought me to my knees. The pain radiated from near the port in my chest. I struggled to reach the HELP button mounted by the shower. A male nurse responded and covered me up as he helped me to my bed. My new doctor could see I was in obvious pain and checked the hose that was sticking out of my chest.

She wouldn't look me in the eye when she told me, "Everything looks okay?" I could see she did not seem so sure as she headed out of my room. I couldn't go to lunch because it was too painful to move so

Paul in Church while I was in the hospital in Mexico. My friend Nedra and I came up with the idea of blowing up a silly picture of me sitting in my usual spot, where Paul would find me when he came into church. Pastor Tommy said, "It kept freaking me out, like you where really there and waving at me during the message."

they brought my lunch to my room, but I couldn't eat. With each painful breath, I prayed to God to help me. I had to remain calm and take shallow breaths. I tried to focus on the scripture cards on my walls and reviewed the many pictures made for me at a benefit concert, featuring my dear friend, John David Webster, presented by, Calvary Chapel Vail Valley. It was the end of the day and I asked for the doctor one last time. She told me I would be fine, and that she would see me in the morning.

I couldn't help weeping in pain all night long. I prayed for God's will to be done, but like David in the Psalms and Job, I cried in anguish: *"God, my soul is troubled; I am in deep distress; how long will my enemies seem to triumph over me and my body fail me? Where are you God? I need you; the night drags on and I feel so alone; how long will I be tormented and crushed? Help me Jesus; have mercy on me. Have you forgotten me? Help me, please help me!"*

Angels From Vail

The next morning, like angels sent from God, Jo Ellen and Greg Nash, friends from Vail, came walking into my room. They weren't sure it was me. I was drenched in sweat with a swollen face from the wrestling that had occurred all night long. I could see the fear on their faces. My breathing was still shallow and they noticed the tears streaming down my face. I gave them the best smile I could and thanked God for sending them. After she demanded that the staff do something, an x-ray was taken revealing that my clavicle bone had snapped like a dried up

John David Webster...

Benefit Concert

Hear the awesome, inspired music of
John David Webster

Sunday · April 14th · 6:30 pm
Berry Creek Middle School

Concert is free!

An offering will be taken to benefit
Diane Dike and Michelle Gross
to offset extreme medical expenses
incurred recently for Diane's medical
treatments and Michelle's
surgery to remove a brain tumor.

For additional details call 748-1103

Calvary Chapel Vail Valley

calvary

Poster of John David Webster's benefit concert.

chick bone. Jesus did answer my prayer and cries for help by sending the Nashes. They bathed me, fed me, and combed my tangled hair. With my heart hanging low it was hard to say yet another good-bye.

Going Home

In the end, the "hospital" sent me home with a broken bone, inflamed colitis, osteoporosis, severe weakness, and a suitcase full of expensive healing potions. All the symptoms from my other maladies were magnified as well. The future looked grim. Both conventional and alternative medicine had failed as my three-inch medical file grew thicker. Science knew of no cause or cure for my maladies. All treatments proved to be unsuccessful and I came home in a wheelchair, in worse shape than when I arrived at the clinic: I was devastated.

At the airport Paul picked me up in his arms like the Good Shepherd carries a broken little lamb. It took us some time to lick our wounds. Paul needed to contact the Aspen doctor so that he could treat me for my bone problems and continue the nutrient IVs. I ended up giving myself the IV treatments in our home because the car ride to Aspen three times a week was just too much. With each passing day, I rehabilitated myself with isometric exercises, walked, climbed our stairs, and did the best that I could when I could do it. Building up my strength so I could give massages again was my goal. I was determined to be a productive member of society and wanted to contribute to recuperating our finances of which we spent well over thirty-five thousand dollars of so far this year. Helping others forget their pain helped me to forget my own. When I am focused on the person on my table, I can better forget my own issues, even when it comes at a physical cost.

What I wanted to do more than anything was give a huge praise report of the healing I received from the treatment, the prayers of the faithful saints, and most of all from God. Instead, I was able to share something much more important with my church family about my "mission" trip to Mexico: the healing of hearts and salvation stories.

My survival is a testament to the power of faith and how God helps those who love Him enough to rise above and fight on against all odds. The day I left Mexico, one of the nurses told me in broken English, "We will never forget your outrageous joy, the hope you shared with the hopeless, you're singing like an angel... You are a light beckoning us to do better. Christo is alive in you. Muchas Gracias!"

CHAPTER 20

Massage Therapy on Tour

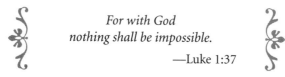

*For with God
nothing shall be impossible.*
—Luke 1:37

Over four months after I returned from Mexico, the Smiths came to town. Paul and I joined Michael's family at the Cordillera Club for dinner. Anna, Michael's daughter, and I made big plans for the next day and couldn't wait to get back together. I often spent the night at their Beaver Creek home and slept in the bunk room with Anna and Emily, giggling the night away. But I decided to go home this time and come back in the morning.

We Should Pray

I awoke early the next morning in severe pain. Paul had left for work at 4 a.m., I was alone. Feeling sweaty, I went to the bathroom to wash my face when suddenly a sharp pain struck and my innards felt like they were going to fall out. Close to fainting, I sat on the toilet and tried to get hold of what was happening; blood began to gush out of me while I fought the nausea. I crawled back to bed with a towel, holding my stomach in pain. I waited a while to see if it would get better, but it gave no indication that it would. I thought, *No, not today! Let me go back to sleep and start over.* I reviewed yesterday's activities: I hadn't sat on the ground or eaten anything cold; I wore warm clothes... I just couldn't think of anything that could have brought this on except for sitting in the restaurant or standing for too long.

Finally, barely able to speak, I called Paul at work around 9 a.m. He came right home, picked me up, put me in the truck, and rushed me to the emergency room. I was in so much pain. Anna called to get going on our day's activities just before I left. I had to tell her what was happening

Anne, Murray, Debbie, Me, (on the couch) Anna & Tyler standing in the back.

and how sorry I was that we couldn't get together. She told me that her grandfather, Murray, was on the way to the hospital as well with a heart problem. I said, "Please forgive me Anna. I'm so sorry about our plans. I will pray for Murray and look for him there. I love you."

Tommy, our pastor from Calvary Chapel, met Paul and me at the emergency room; Michele Gross, our prayer team leader and friend, came as well. Murray and I were admitted and we ended up on the same floor, just down the hall from each other.

Soon my doctor stopped in. I was behind the curtain wailing in pain as blood passed through me into the bedpan. It felt like I'd been stabbed. When the episode passed, the doctor suggested that, "We should pray." If you've ever had your doctor say this, you know that it's both comforting and unsettling. But out of all my team members, I want my doctor to pray anytime he sees the need. Paul, my doctor, and I lifted our hearts up in prayer. We had done all we could do and I was now in God's hands. The Smith family came by later that evening to visit Murray and kindly visited me, too.

Michael came in with his parents, Barbara and Paul, his doctor and our good friend, Dr. Ron Leoppke, and Ron's wife, Robin, and Anna. They couldn't hide their alarm; I looked terrible. Michael came over and knelt down on the hard floor next to my bed, right at eye level, and said, "D!" There wasn't much to be said so we wept and we prayed. It was a deep and tender moment.

As they turned to leave, Michael said, "Feel better soon; we will be praying for you! Love you BIG time." He saw I had a CD player and the next morning delivered a plethora of musical encouragement. Later, Debbie (Michael's wife) and her mom, Anne, came for a visit. I recalled the cozy moments I'd shared with each of them while ministering massages to their weary bodies. Now, they were taking the time to minister back to me.

What A Difference

The next day as I laid in bed looking at Vail Mountain out the hospital window, I thought of all the wonderful times I had in this valley with the Smith family. As Michael W.'s CD, *Freedom* played, I wondered if my body would ever stop revolting. I wondered if my body would ever experience true freedom! Then, the telephone rang; "Hey D! How are you doing today?" "Michael, hey Bro. I'm doing better. Thank you for the CD's. I'm listening to you right now. Just like so many other times when I've been in the hospital, your music is encouraging me to carry on. Thank you, I sure love you." "I love you too D. You keep getting better okay. We hate to leave you but you call me if you need anything." They were on the jet getting ready to fly home to Tennessee. He called me every day while I was in the hospital and after I got home.

Just like his toe-tapping song, *Lead Me Home*, I thought it might not be long before my sun went down and maybe the Lord was leading me home. I could hear Him calling and I knew if I left the earth I wouldn't be leaving home, I would be going home. In the desert of silent suffering, God used Michael's voice and anointed music as a tool to help me follow Him even when I couldn't see the path. However, the vultures of darkness were not going to get a crumb of self-pity to chew on from me.

Murray finally made it out of the hospital, but his sun did go down and he recently went home to be with the Lord. I fondly remember walking into his hospital room one evening. Tears streamed down Anne's cheeks as she watched him sleep. We didn't have to say a word. We held each other for a long time. The next morning she brought me an angel and said, "This is to remind you that I think you really are one." Anne always says, "I love you to the moon!" I reply, "I love you to the moon and back!" We have had some incredible moments over the years sharing our deep heartfelt dreams and disappointments. She is a true friend and a treasure, beautiful inside and out. I was sad the day they left me there in the hospital, but was happy they were able to go back home to Tennessee.

Barbara and Paul Smith in their home after I shared my testimony with her Bible study group.

I know prayers matter and are heard by our Heavenly Father. Because of the prayers and support from my entire Tennessee family and local church family, I recuperated.

Afraid Of Losing You

The Smiths came out three months later and invited Paul and me to have dinner with the whole group at the same restaurant. With fifteen of us gathered around the table conducting several conversations, my dear friend, Jan Harris, asked about my last hospital incident. When I got to the part about Michael kneeling on the hard floor next to my bed, I looked across the table and saw tears in his eyes. He buried his face in the white napkin. I thought, *Oh no, I've said something wrong.* I got up and hugged him saying, "I'm so sorry Michael." All he could get out was, "We were afraid we were going to lose you." Dr. Ron said, "We all thought we were going to lose you."

Hiking in Beaver Creek, CO-In the back, Bill, Don, Michael, Debbie, then, Laura Lyn (LL wrote the Afterword in this book), me and Paul.

After a day of hiking, dinner in Beaver Creek, with my friends!

Wow! Epiphany! They love me? Why is it so hard for me to accept that? They love me as I love them! Undisguised tears of joy streamed down my face. It was during this trip that Michael came up with the idea of me joining him on tour as a massage therapist and prayer warrior. Just over six months after my disappointing visit to Mexico, I was given the chance to reach the summit and enjoy its view!

On Tour!

My first tour began in October of 2002. Even though I faced many health challenges that could incapacitate me without notice, Michael W. took me anyway. He had a plan in place: if I had any emergencies during my time on the road, he would have me flown to Dr. Ron or have Dr. Ron flown out to me on his private jet. Fortunately, this was never necessary. Touring seemed to give me a new lease on life. I thrived and felt alive. I praised the Lord with 15,000 people each night. WOW! Only God can do that! This filled me up with a supernatural strength and with God's help—no matter how tired, tender, or dreadful I felt—I was able to perform my duties while having the time of my life.

I was told that God himself was working through my hands. I counted more than ninety-nine times in the Bible where God directs us to lay healing hands on one another while we pray. God said in Isaiah 49:16 that He engraved us on the palms of His hands. I always started and finished my massages with prayer and played worship music

In the crowd with Max Lucado during the concert.

Meeting President Bush, #41 at one of Michael's concerts in Texas. He said, "You are very good! You know what you are doing." When I gave him a chair massage while we listened to Michael during the show,

Basketball player-David Robinson-I can't remember if we were laughing about how short I am or how tall he is but it was fun to meet him.

Point of Grace and Kari back-stage while on the "Christmastime" tour in 2002

throughout. Sometimes I started at 8:00 a.m. and gave massages off and on all day, finally finishing on the bus at midnight as we traveled to the next show. It was supernatural.

Through reviving others, I was revived as well; and my passion for life was renewed. Meeting all the people and feeling useful, a part of the team was good for me. I treasured the time that I toured. I started on the "Come Together Tour" with Third Day and Max Lucado. On our days off, we flew to Michael's house in his private jet to enjoy activities with his family. I was on tour for about two weeks and Michael saw how good it was for me. He called Paul to see if he could keep me for another week. Paul assured Michael that it was okay to keep me as long as he wanted. Paul and I talked about five times a day and he shared in my joy and triumph. Upon returning to Colorado a week later, I hoped and prayed that Michael would bring me on tour again.

Remarkable

Soon I was out on the "Christmastime Tour" with Kari, Point of Grace, and of course, Michael's wonderful band. This tour was fabulous! It was a dream. I was able to spend Christmas with the Smiths, met their neighbors and friends including the Donahue's, Chris Rice, and so many other wonderful people. Earlier in the year, I'd prayed for the New River Church Michael recently started in his farmhouse. Now I was able to attend it in its new building and meet its passionate members.

When I was on the road, I slept great as the rocking motion of the tour bus agreed with me. I couldn't get enough of the lifestyle, people, fans, and music. At times I felt amazed that I was associated with the music and artists I listened to many years ago while aimlessly wondering with my doubter's heart and troubled mind. I thanked God for this remarkable opportunity and soaked in every moment.

I met endless interesting people including, David Foster, Bart Millard—Mercy Me's Lead singer and writer of *I Can Only Imagine*— The Katina's, basketball star David Robinson, and President George H. W. Bush-#41! I was even able to give the former president a short neck and shoulder massage during Michael's show in Texas.

Then Michael took me to George Lucas's ranch in California where he recorded the album, *Healing Rain*. I felt that song in my soul. Michael is a genius with the rare ability to catch a moment and put it into extraordinary words and a divine melody. While on tour, every move I made, I made for God. I caught myself thinking at times, *Lord,*

Right in front of Billy Graham speaking with a packed stadium behind me. Michael W. spots me and says "Hey D!".

if you take me now, I would go with a big smile on my face. Thank you for helping me to hang on during the really bad times; this was worth

The wonderful highlights, divine appointments, restful sleep, and answered prayers made the time I spent out on tour among the very best of my life and fulfilled the prophetic words, that my best days were ahead. On days we were not on the road, Michael's parents and I spent time together. We adopted each other. I'd spend the night at their house, enjoy countless meals, go for walks, and I called them every week until I started writing my books; now, I try to talk to them at least once a month and more often through emails. We stay with them when we are in town and to honor Barbara when she became a great grandmother,

At George Lucas Ranch in California. I was invited to come while they worked on The Healing Rain *Album. Mr. Lucas's office was in the building behind us; as well as, a library, restaurant, and museum with artifacts from his films.*

Always cheering the team on from the sidelines looking out to 15,000 fans! A heavenly moment I cherished each night!

I asked her to write the foreword for my first children's book, *Gracie Comes Home*. She accepted and did a beautiful job.

After spending up to three weeks straight on tour, I can truly say Michael, my heart brother, is one of the most thoughtful, generous, and caring people I've ever known. I consider him among my closest friends. He is faithfully in love with his family and our Lord. I'm extremely fond of his five talented children, wife, family and awesome parents. Michael opened up a whole world of friends and family in Tennessee that have changed my life forever... It's like a dream come true! I toured off and on for three years but my health finally intervened. I couldn't imagine anything more wonderful than the adventure of touring until I met Gracie. Her cute little nose burrowed through the layers in my life and settled in my heart. It was our destiny to be together.

Michael W. meeting my Dad back stage after his concert in Lakeland, FL at the very church I gave my life to the Lord in so many years before.

CHAPTER 21

GRACIE, MY LIFESAVER!

*My goal in life is to be as good of a person as my
dog already thinks I am.*

— Author Unknown

Gracie, my gift from God knows about suffering, too. When I'm over-whelmed I look into her calm brown eyes, and slowly, carefully, she raises her little paw up to my chin, we hug and snuggle and I feel much better.

In 2003, while sick in bed, I said this simple prayer, "Lord, is there a little puppy dog out there that needs me as much as I need her? If there is, please show me where she is, if it is Your will." I pulled the covers over my head and wondered *where did that come from? I can barely take care of myself, never mind a dog.*

Even though I told no one about my prayer, a friend called me from the local animal hospital two days later and said, "Diane, there's a broken little dog down here who needs a home. I want her, but the Lord

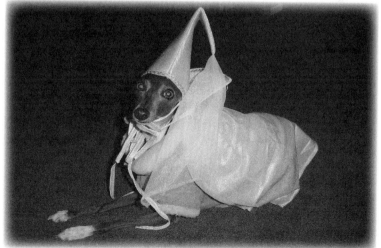

keeps telling me she is for you." Have you ever had a call like that before? I went to the hospital immediately. The doctor told me that the fragile, little Italian Greyhound had gotten caught in the clutches of a child's gate while trying to escape the solitude of the bathroom she was kept in and broke several of her tiny bones.

We stood looking at each other. She looked like a tiny fawn with hot pink casts on her front legs. In the midst of all her trouble, she still seemed happy and had a wonderful disposition. I wanted to take her home right there on the spot but the doctor told me, "No, it's too soon." I went to the hospital every day to hold her, to take her out for fresh air, and to nurture her broken little life. It was the beginning of a warm and intimate friendship. I told Paul about this little ball of hurt, but he was adamant about not getting a dog. Whenever I broached the subject he replied, "I never had a dog and don't want a dog. What are we going to do with a broken dog?" Grasping his arm, I said, "Paul you must meet her!" He finally agreed.

Divine Providence

Gracie was born in Kansas and shipped to a Denver pet shop when she was about seven weeks old. Two months later, a man going through a divorce purchased her for his son, and they named her Roxy. He came home from work on her third afternoon in his home to eat lunch and to check on her. He found her in a heap of trouble. Somehow, she had climbed over the gate and apparently got her legs hung up as she fell to the other side. She wailed in pain from broken ribs, a ripped-off tail, and broken front legs. He scooped her up and rushed her to the hospital. She died on the operating table but they were able to bring her back (I say, "Because God had a plan for her life"). After she made it through surgery, he informed the doctor that it would not work out to keep her and would he please find her a good home? Several people entertained the idea of adopting Roxy but, for one reason or another, everyone backed out.

The doctors couldn't guarantee that she wouldn't have complications or even be able to walk. Between her stay in the Denver pet shop and the hospital, Gracie spent the first four months of her life in a cold, isolated cage and the veterinarian feared that such a beginning for a dog of her breed could lead to behavioral issues. I was familiar with rough beginnings, but also knew that with God's grace and a second chance, anything was possible. I was not dissuaded by the doctor's concerns.

I didn't think she looked like a Roxy. I almost named her "Happy" because of her wonderful temperament, but finally settled on Gracie because God gave me what I needed instead of what I deserved; that is grace, His unmerited favor. Gracie reminds me of God's unconditional love and grace every day. Yes, I named Gracie before I had Paul's approval to get her. I couldn't help it. We were bonding and I was sure he would change his mind about the matter once he met her.

Life-Changing Decision

Her new name marked the beginning of a new chapter in her life and mine! The day that Paul was to come to the hospital, I took Gracie outside to the park. All of a sudden, people started coming out of the stores adjacent to the park to see what the story was behind this adorable little dog with two big casts on her legs. I told each person her story and that we were waiting for Paul to see if I could adopt Gracie. Finally, I saw Paul coming and said, "Here he comes." The crowd started clapping. Paul's eyes gazed to Heaven. I know he must have thought that he was walking into a "setup" since he didn't recognize anyone. He sat down on a bench as everyone stared. I put Gracie down and with all her might, as if we had

Paul, Gracie & me the day Paul said, "Yes," in the park-Picture taken by Kay Barr

rehearsed it, she limped over to Paul, picked up her two broken legs, and put them on his knees. She looked into his eyes, and he melted. "Okay, you can have the dog." The crowd applauded and some shed a few tears.

The next day the doctor said, "You can take her home if you promise not to let her walk too much" out of fear that she could re-injure herself. He also told me not to kennel her or leave her home alone because she could chew on her casts and bandages. So, I trained Gracie to let me carry her in a baby harness that my friend Karen Peck gave to us.

It was difficult at first because Gracie didn't like being confined. Before long though, she came to find comfort in the closeness and constant companionship we shared. During the weeks of her rehabilitation she counted on me for everything: we became inseparable.

A Dog In Church?

Tommy, our pastor, is a dog lover. I told him the story and asked him if I could bring Gracie to church and he replied, "Absolutely, it's a wonderful thing you're doing!" Because of my blood disease, my extremities are always cold, even in the middle of summer. At church, Paul reached out to hold my hands to warm them as he usually does and, much to his surprise, they were warm. He almost fell out of his chair then looked at me. I pointed to Gracie. Her temperature is 101-102.5 degrees and she kicks out some heat. Since she is practically hairless, I can get to her warm body therefore, she feels much warmer than other dogs.

In Mexico today, and for as long as 3,500 years, some people believe that the "xolos," (pronounced show-low) or Mexican hairless dogs, can provide temporary relief from aches, pains, stomach cramps, and other problems so they use the dogs as heating pads (Gordon, *Paws for Comfort*). Having Gracie on my person mitigates my disability in a similar way. My body lives in a state of "fight or flight" in an attempt to maintain my already fragile homeostasis. The result of this is a double whammy: my already cold extremities get colder and when my blood falls below body temperature, I experience the acute flare-ups of my chronic conditions, which can lead to death. By holding her in the upgraded Snugli© (a patented harness for babies given to us by Kirsten Webster) against my chest, Gracie's lifesaving heat helps to regulate my homeostasis and increase the circulation of warm blood to my extremities. Furthermore, I can put my hands in the Snugli© against her body to warm them anytime I need to. This dynamic explained my suddenly warm hands. Initially, I trained Gracie to stay in the Snugli© on command for her safety and healing, but it ended up being a lifesaving act for me, too.

A Medical Device

Gracie as a perfect medical device, she does not need to be charged to perform her duty. She is consistent and reliable. Throughout the years of battling my illness, I tried many heating devices but couldn't get it right. They were often too hot—a real danger for me because I also have peripheral neuropathy—or were not hot enough, long enough to allow me to complete the task at hand. Unless you have cryoglobulinemia, vasculitis, fibromyalgia, Raynaud's phenomenon, or other circulatory challenges, you may not understand how valuable a lifesaving service Gracie performs by staying on my person thus, regulating my body

temperature. As Charles Schulz said, "Happiness is a warm puppy," and nothing compares to the blessing Gracie's warmth is to me. She does for me what I cannot do for myself.

Could She Be A "Service Dog"?

You've probably seen golden retrievers or German shepherds guiding the blind but there are different kinds of dogs that help people with many kinds of disabilities. Before I adopted Gracie, I received a magazine from the National Fibromyalgia Association (NFA). Inside was an article about a woman who utilized a small Service Dog to help her deal with fibromyalgia pain (Gordon, *The Healing Power of Puppy Love*). It was a good story, but I didn't really think too much about it at the time. I found the article and read it again with a sense of urgency.

Paul and I realized that we might have an even bigger blessing in our hands than just a great pet, and started researching about service dog programs on the Internet. We started making some calls. When I explained my desire to transform Gracie into a Service Dog, some people said, "No way, it will never work with an Italian greyhound. The breed is not a good breed for service." Others gave me the following negative reports: "You'll never be able to house break her—vital if she is to become a service dog—since she was kenneled for her first four months." "Italian greyhounds are too anxious." "Gracie is too small and frail; she was broken, physically and perhaps emotionally and will be too difficult to train." Many were eager to tell me about the difficulties rather than the possibilities of utilizing Gracie as a Service dog. Although I was discouraged by such feedback, I trusted my instincts and faith in a sovereign God who directs our paths by allowing events and people to enter our lives; it was no accident that Gracie and I were brought together at this time and place.

Undeterred, I found web sites for several groups including Owner Trained Service Dogs and Top Dogs that encouraged me to pursue my goal. I talked to them about the disabilities associated with my rare disease and the tasks Gracie could be trained to perform to help mitigate my condition. I educated myself on the legal aspects, rights, and procedures and started doing what needed to be done to train and qualify Gracie as a "Service Dog."

Americans With Disabilities Act

The Americans with Disabilities Act (ADA) is the federal legislation that defines and protects the rights of disabled people to utilize service dogs. It defines a "service animal as any guide dog, signal dog, or other animal individually trained to provide assistance to an individual with a disability." Service dogs can assist people with a wide range of disabilities, both visible and invisible. Through research, I discovered that people often have to wait several years to obtain a purebred, professionally-trained service dog, and that they can cost thousands of dollars to breed, train, foster, and purchase. I knew that I couldn't afford that expense, and that I couldn't wait that long. Tomorrow is not promised so I went for it; how could I deny this gift that literally fell into my lap?

A dog is not a service dog until it is individually trained to perform tasks that assist a person with their disability. I individually trained Gracie by deliberately rewarding her for the correct response to my commands and requests. A task is considered learned when she performs it reliably whenever needed. A trained task mitigates or lessens the effects of my disabling condition. This is the legal basis for granting access rights to disabled handlers under the Americans With Disabilities Act. The adequacy of training is largely a matter of trust because federal laws do not require proof of training. But if a dog is under control and is actually performing tasks for someone, then, under the law, these types of working teams are eligible for public access and protection.

The law allows a service dog to accompany its owner in public places. Businesses are NOT allowed to decline a person admittance or segregate him or her because of a service dog. However, places of business are allowed to ask two questions:

——-Is that a service dog?

——-Are you disabled?

How does that dog assist you? This question is presently being debated in the courts. When I am asked this third question, I reply, "She is a medical alert and retrieval service dog." I am not required to share personal information about my medical problems.

Wherever state, local, or federal laws conflict, whichever one provides the most protection to the disabled service dog team applies. Just because a team may not look disabled, it doesn't mean that they are not or deserve to be mistreated. If you see someone with a service dog of any size, please, DON'T TOUCH, speak to, whistle at, offer food, or try to distract the dog with animal sounds. The animal is on duty performing a serious job and deserves respect. A service dog with this special training should be viewed as assistive technology or medical equipment, not as a pet.

Training!

Initially, I focused on potty training. Because of her rough beginning and her breed's reputation for difficulty in mastering this behavior, I knew it could be a challenge. However, from the beginning, Gracie displayed an eagerness to learn and within two weeks, she was box trained. This is

beneficial because I don't have to go outside in bad weather for her to "take care of business." I also trained her to go on command. She can bulls-eye a newspaper or whatever I tell her to go on. She has not had a single accident in public while on duty.

At the same time, we focused on socialization skills by allowing Gracie to interact with other people and dogs. She has never acted aggressively, noisily, or inappropriately

One of our first family photos taken together. You can see her big casts. Taken by Karen Peck

while on duty or in training. She just looks to me as if to say, "Is this okay?" I give her the nod and say, "It's okay, good girl." The socialization skills are important because people, especially children, often try to pet Gracie when she is working. An aggressive response (nuisance behavior) would not only be legal grounds for asking us to leave the premise, but would also reflect poorly on the service dog community. When we are in public, she is all business and focused on me.

The potty and socialization training were essential if Gracie were to become a service dog because in order to perform her primary task of enhancing my circulation and regulating my body temperature, she has to stay on my person for extended periods of time. If she has to go while we are flying on an airplane, she communicates this (we have such a close relationship we understand each other quite well). I simply take her to the restroom, put an absorbent cloth on the floor that she eliminates on, and then dispose of it. Under normal circumstances she has considerable control and does not need to go very often while on duty.

Workin' Like A Dawg

Since my disabilities sometimes confine me to my bed or my wheelchair, training Gracie to retrieve items like keys, water bottles, tape, pens and pencils, cell phones, and remotes—just about anything she can get her mouth on—was essential. She will drag bags and pillows or bring me a box of Kleenex when instructed; she will even dig my cell phone out of my purse. She is raring to go and ready to learn new tasks. We are asked all the time about details of her training as others seek secrets to help them with training their dog for service or just to be a good pet. We are working on a book with more detailed information on how I trained Gracie. For now, you can read Appendix A, our published magazine articles, or visit our web site at http://www.DianeDike.org

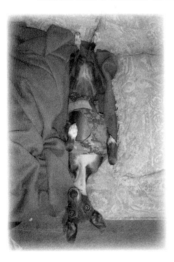

Gracie can work for as long as I need her to. I try to give her playtime every day, she has lots of toys and knows them by name. She does all the things doggies do when she is off duty. One of her best friends is Sabrina, the cat. She also has a great time with a couple of teddy bear hamsters. She plays chase with some of the birds that hang out around the house, and tumbles about with her two dachshund boyfriends. She finds it irresistible to run like the wind with her Italian greyhound friends.

Roger Caras was so right when he said, "Dogs have given us their absolute all. We are the center of their universe. We are the focus of their love and faith and trust. They serve us in return for scraps. It's without a doubt the best deal man has ever made."

CHAPTER 22

MY GIFT FROM GOD

 *The greatest healing therapy is
friendship and love.*
—Hubert H. Humphrey

There is a scripture in Hebrews 13:2. "Do not forget to entertain strangers, for by so doing some people have entertained angels without knowing it." Do you think some angels have fur on their wings? Maybe our former pets and service animals will be waiting for us at the Pearly

Gates, as afterlife ambassadors. After all, they live forever in our hearts. Here on earth they perform many important tasks at hospitals, in nursing homes, as prisoner rehabilitation specialists, matchmakers, medical help, rescuers... there is a deep connection between people and their dogs.

The Italian look

Alert
Perhaps Gracie's most amazing service is alerting me to dangerous and imminent flare-ups. She demonstrated this ability at the most unexpected of places, a warm Florida beach. When I got up to take a walk, Gracie began to tug relentlessly at my towel. At first, I thought she was just excited because I said, "walk" and she is always ready to go. But, after taking a few steps, she didn't stop. She tugged so hard on the towel, trying to get me to lie back down, that she tore it. Needless to say, I got the message, "Don't go!" Twenty minutes later, the flare-up exposed its ugly self. My sister Joanne and parents

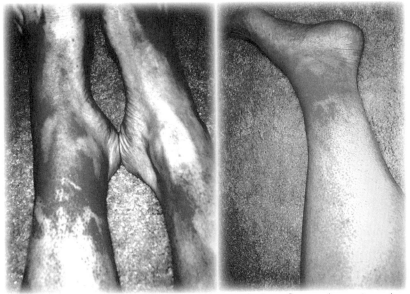

Gracie's most amazing service The above pictures depict a flare-up I experienced in Florida. Gracie warned me of this episode twenty minutes before it began. This was the first time she alerted me and she has been 100% ever since! Her alerts are right on and life saving! We watched as my legs painfully filled up with blood, bruised and swelled. It felt like I was being burned from the inside out. I couldn't walk for days. See more pictures and in color on the web: www.DianeDike.org

watched in horror as the blood hemorrhaged into the superficial layers of skin on my legs. If not for Gracie's act, I could have wandered too far and been stranded on a deserted part of the beach, unable to walk back to safety. Gracie demonstrated what is known as "intelligent disobedience." She will not follow my command if she intuitively knows it will be bad for me. If she says, "No," I now know that it is for a good reason. That reason could be to literally save my life!

Chemistry

Gracie senses changes in my internal chemistry and warns me up to forty minutes before I even know that I am in danger. I've encouraged this alerting behavior by rewarding her with praise, and sometimes by giving treats. Her alert response includes: excessive licking of my face and hands; sudden restlessness while in her harness; tugging at my clothing; and even whining until I take appropriate action such as lying down, getting to a warmer place, or sitting down and elevating my legs. Such timely response to flare-ups is essential if I am to keep the damage to my body to a minimum. She even alerts me to impending pass-out attacks from hypoglycemia (low blood sugar) up to twenty minutes before I black out. If I am out in public, this alert is very valuable because if I fall, I could hit my head or otherwise injure myself. Sometimes she wakes me in the middle of the night to let me know my blood sugar is about to get too low. Since I have had Gracie, I have had fewer severe attacks, and NO injuries from falling or passing out. More importantly, I have not been hospitalized since we have been together. During presentations everyone cheers and rejoices with us when I share this remarkable news.

Working Overtime

Gracie displayed her aptitude one day when I helped a friend who had a bad reaction to medication. Megan began to have trouble breathing and a panic attack ensued. I let Gracie out of the Snugli© and she began to lick her sweat, then laid on her chest area, which calmed her breathing. A few minutes of petting and hugging Gracie allowed the crisis to pass for my troubled friend. When the paramedics arrived outside the apartment complex, Gracie went to the only open window and began to bark with determination until they came to the right place. After the paramedics took over, Gracie came back to me and snuggled on my chest as though it was "just another day at the office." This event amazed everyone present and only confirmed my faith in her innate and trained abilities.

I try not to over analyze all that Gracie does for me but simply thank God. Before I became seriously ill, I witnessed the benefits a dog could have on my special education students, the elderly in nursing homes, and patients in hospitals through my work with Millie. Bern Williams said, "There is no psychiatrist in the world like a puppy licking your face." Back then, I didn't truly understand the role a dog can play in a disabled person's life. Now I know the benefits and improved quality of life a service dog can bring to my life, and appreciate the importance of my role in helping to educate as many people as possible about service dogs and how to better treat those who utilize them. Paul, Gracie and I travel the country training establishments on disability awareness and etiquette. It can save them thousands in litigations for mistreatment.

As for the depression, I have had fewer serious bouts since rescuing Gracie. As a result, I say that Gracie rescued me right back. How can I feel down for long with her beautiful brown eyes looking up at me? When she puts a paw on each shoulder and gives me a hug my troubles melt away, the benefits she offers are never-ending; she is the best medication ever. Her non-judgmental and unconditional acceptance of my

challenges is just another way that I enjoy a taste of how much God loves me.

One-Of-A-Kind Constant Companion

The commitment to own and train a service dog is not to be taken lightly! It has worked out wonderfully for me but has not been without it's challenges. However, much good has come from the bad in our pasts. My heart and blood disease open the opportunity for Gracie to help me. Her brokenness made it so no one wanted her until I came along. Our research shows that Gracie is the world's first rescued Italian greyhound Service Dog helping a woman with a rare and incurable blood disease called cryoglobulinemia.

My friend Kirsten recently wrote this letter of encouragement to me and I asked her permission to share it here with you.

February 14, 2007
Hey girl!
I am so proud of you!
I can never begin to imagine what a daily struggle it is for you to get out of bed and continue on with the day. As I looked through the symptoms of your disease I thought back to our week together and how I saw those symptoms play out at different times. It's so crazy that when something cannot be readily seen it can be hard for people to comprehend the depth and seriousness of it. I remember walking around with you and Gracie and seeing the looks on people's faces. It takes a strong and confident woman to not care about what others think. I am sure that was a process for you, but I love how you handle it.
I loved how when the time was right you told your whole story, but if the time wasn't right you didn't say a thing. I know you constantly struggle. I wish I could take it all away, but I love how

you have allowed the Lord to use it to make you who you are. Because of the Lord in you, you have allowed this disease to become a strength.

I love that you are going for it and writing these books and getting your story out wherever the Lord will allow it to go. You are an incredible woman, Diane. Most of all, I love your transparency and that you don't pretend. Keep on going girl!!! If I can help in any way let me know. Know that we will want copies when your books are ready. Follow the Lord's footsteps. They are taking you to amazing places!!!

I love you! We love you!
Give our love to Paul and Gracie as well,

Kirsten and John David (Webster)
www.johndavidwebster.com

I deeply appreciate and treasure my friends and family who have stood by me during the challenging transition of acquiring a service dog, training, studying the law, and learning how to accept her help. The support has made all the difference. Annie Johnson Flint expresses it this way, "God has promised strength for the day, rest for the labor, light for the way, grace for the trials, help from above, unfailing sympathy, undying love." That is what He has done through Gracie, through friends, and through my family. Instead of receiving a healing, I get to be one of the few women in the world walking around with a dog strapped to my chest for medical reasons. It's not easy; yet, God has not given me the spirit of fear, but of power, love, and a sound mind!

My Special Little Pal And Faithful Friend!

Her name is "Gracie." She is graceful and a faithful, companion;

which was what I needed instead of what I deserved. Gracie and I will be true pals until one of our hearts gives up its labor of love. Through Gracie, God soothes my fears, lifts my spirits, and licks away all my tears. Suddenly, as I wrote this story it occurred to me, God answered my prayers after all! Could Gracie be the little pal I prayed for each night as a child. My friend Max Lucado said: "Hope is not a granted wish or a favor performed; no, it is far greater than that. It's a zany, unpredictable dependence on a God who loves to surprise us out of our socks."

According to Carolyn Alexander, "Dog ownership is like a rainbow. Puppies are the joy at one end. Old dogs are the treasure at the other." I pray Gracie will have a very long and healthy life; she is my rainbow, my joy, and my treasure. Two things strike me about the word "dog": One is that dog spelled backwards is God. Second, D-O-G can stand for Depending On God. Gracie is definitely my gift from God and she reminds me to always depend on Him. God sent me this little angel and bundle of love as a reminder that he has not abandoned me, and I am so grateful. I tell Him everyday, *"Lord, thank you for the gift of Gracie! Bless her with the long life, health, and happiness she so deserves! Please keep her safe and protect her all the days of her life. She has taught me many lessons and gives so much, unconditionally! Thank you for the spiritual hug you give me daily through Gracie! In Jesus name. Amen!"*

I think the following note from Paul describes my relationship with Gracie better than I can myself:

> *Gracie has given Diane much of her life back. The heat she provides and the circulation she enhances allows Diane to do things many of us take for granted. She can walk outside on a windy day, and even go into an air-conditioned store more safely and not worry about passing out in the frozen food aisle. The two go everywhere together and it's a marvel to watch. Gracie is Diane's faithful friend, whom you can tell does what she does out of love, not compulsion.*
>
> *It seems Diane had the same impact on Gracie that she has on people. God made only one Diane and only one Gracie. But it's the two of them together that testifies to the fact that miracles still happen if we are willing to look closely enough. Take advantage of any chance you have to meet and know this can-do woman and incredible dog. I know you will fall in love with them just like I did.*

CHAPTER 23

LIFE CAN BE UNFAIR . . . BUT

*A faithful friend is the
medicine of life.*

—Old Proverb

Trusting Him

Throughout this journey good and bad things have happened in my life. When bad things happen to good people, life doesn't make sense. However, God promises that all things will work together for good for those who love Him and are called according to His purposes. How can we find any good in the suffering, financial expense, and stress of devastating news or illness? The only way is by trusting Him.

God has a different perspective and when bad things happen to those who love Him, they can serve a purpose greater than we could ever imagine. One conclusion I've come to that helps me deal with the waves of trouble that roll into shore, is that even when life seems unfair, I can grow, and learn and stay on my knees in humility. Illness is the vehicle God allowed in my life to help me discover what I am really made of, what I really care about, and what is really important to me. I have been sifted like sand.

Can illness lead to the discovery of unexpected strengths or courage beyond what you thought possible? Can it lead to compassion or a deeper love enabling you to live life in new and enlightened ways? My heart of compassion for others bubbles over and I don't want anyone to sink into the pit of suffering where they feel all alone and without hope. I know what it is to make terrible choices and to lose everything that ever meant anything to me. Even while writing this book, I'm learning to

My friend Max Lucado

be honest with others and myself, and to embrace my challenges rather than run from them. In turn, others feel safe to share their challenges with me, and we grow through them together. They feel safe to tell me the secrets of their souls because I am sharing my own with them first. There is freedom in speaking the truth and feeling safe enough to do so. It opens a connection that only knowledge of suffering can. Psalm 41:2-3 proclaims in victory that, "He also brought me up out of the horrible pit, out of the miry clay, and set my feet upon a rock, and established my steps. He has put a new song in my mouth-praise to our God."

Freedom

Colin Powell understood that, "The freedom to do your best means nothing unless you are willing to do your best." I feel a freedom that I've never known. A freedom to be who God created me to be—comfortable in my own skin— rather than ashamed or filled with guilt and condemnation when I fail to meet my own impossible expectations. When I first became ill, I felt profoundly diminished, different, and even ashamed that somehow I deserved it because God was mad at me. I didn't know then that what challenges the body can strengthen the soul if I don't give up! I focused on the curing of my disease, spending endless hours, money, and time, and despaired when a cure or healing didn't come. I asked, "Why, God? I am doing everything I know to do." It was not the focus on my healing that God desired, but rather focusing on the healer, which would move me toward wholeness, no matter the circumstances. *The biggest challenge is, when you want to hear "yes" and all you get is a "no," can you still believe? Can you still trust?* The apostle Paul begged the Lord that the "thorn in his flesh," the messenger from Satan, that harassed daily, might depart from him but the Lord denied his urgent requests. Sometimes the answer is, "No."

Grieving

Every great loss has demanded that I choose life. I needed to grieve in order to do this. The Bible says blessed are they that mourn: I'm blessed... I bet you are too. Understanding how to appreciate and experience the heights of joy and the depths of sadness is a part of living. Truly living involves immense sadness and great joy; there is no way around it. If we don't mourn, the pain not grieved over will stand between life and us. Grieving helps us to let go. One by one, you let go of the things that are gone and mourn for them and build again.

I used to say, "It's all good" but that really isn't the case. However, my faith in God and His Word assures me that He can turn everything around for good. By faith, I cling to my hope that God will turn it all around for good somehow, someway. When I can't make sense of the overwhelming circumstances most of us will encounter at some point in our lives, I think of Joseph in the Bible. It's amazes me that even when all seemed lost, Joseph kept the faith and God turned it all around for good. This encourages me and gives me hope on the rough days.

Be A Good Student Of Life

A good teacher is also a good student who never stops learning. As I encountered one disease, surgery, and sickness after another, I felt like the bumper cars of life were smashing me. Picking myself up after each blow seemed futile since I often just got knocked down again. One thing a devastating experience like being diagnosed with an incurable illness teaches is never to trust immediate reactions, emotions, or feelings. It's dangerous to make life-changing decisions based upon them because those feeling are not trustworthy. Leaving my husband Scott the way I did was a terrible mistake. It affected more people than I was able to understand at the time. I became a victim because of my terrible decisions and so did those who loved me.

Once you've made mistakes, forgiveness is the first step to humbling and restoring integrity in your life. I've learned just how important forgiveness is. If we don't forgive, unforgiveness becomes a bitter root that will keep us from ever being whole. We can't go over and over the hurts, mistakes, and injustices because they will eat us alive. That is condemnation and there is no condemnation in Christ Jesus. Conviction can guide our hearts to make right what we can and then let it go. God never said it would be easy, but He did promise He would always be with us. Because of fear of rejection or failure, I have not always lived up to my full potential and

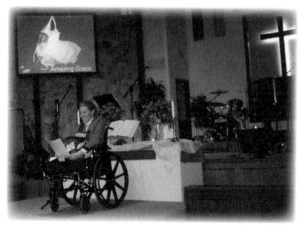

Gracie and I sharing our story with College students in, Lake Wales, FL

thus felt guilty and condemned because I was not being all God created me to be. But now I know that in my distress, if I pray to the Lord, He will rescue me and my goal of honoring Him above all else can still be achieved.

When Facing Challenges

When facing challenges, I can't overemphasize the importance of surrounding yourself with advocates and separating yourself from detractors, as well as not feeling guilty about performing this vital task. Whether you are trying to overcome addictions, disappointments, devastating news or diagnosis, "Pleasant words are a honeycomb, sweet to the soul and healing to the bones" (Proverbs 16:24). You may have to cut out of your life programs, people, and things that are not helping but only hurting you. It's a tough and painful thing to do, but it must be done if you are going to fight the good fight and live.

Since I don't always look ill, use a wheelchair, and have an unusual Service Dog, I often get looks of judgment. I have had people I thought were my friends find it difficult to accept the chronic nature of my ill-

One of my best friend's Jan Lack. She has Huntington's disease.

Celebrating Jan's birthday with my Mom and Dad right before Mom was diagnosised with cancer

ness, like I should just get over it. They stopped inviting me to do things because of the "perceived" trouble a wheelchair or an unusual Service Dog can create. It's hard not to take this personally. Mark Twain said, "Having spent considerable time with 'good' people, I can understand why Jesus liked to be with tax collectors and sinners." Those who have been in the trenches themselves sometimes offer less judgment and

Celebrating Jan's birthday one year later. She lost 50 pounds. Huntington's is taking its toll.

more grace. The difficult lesson I've learned is that I can't make people love me. However, I have also learned that I am not responsible for their reaction to my person or situation. I do the best that I can. I try to educate and help them understand my life condition and try not to be a burden. But ultimately, it is up to them how they perceive me. All I can do is what Jesus did when He was not welcomed; shake the dust off my feet and move on!

The most important thing is that I am not living with the disapproval of the lord. What will the Lords appraisal of our lives be? His thoughts are all that really matter. I desire to be steadfast, immovable, always abounding in the work of the Lord" (1 Corinthians 15:8). May the fire of my devotion light the way for this scripture to be true: "I have fought the good fight, I have finished the race, I have kept the faith" (1 Timothy 4:7).

Be Careful

Cruel things have been said to me, "You've not evolved, you're really not sick, you just think you are, so you manifest the symptoms." "You must not have enough faith." "God is punishing you." "Are you tithing?" "It must be your fault or your sin, otherwise God would heal you." "You must like being sick or you could visualize your healing and be well." As I look out on this snowy morning, at the clouds hugging the mountains from my bed, I can assure them I am not manifesting the bloody diarrhea, bloody legs, and chronic nauseating pain. And I hear Jesus say, "Forgive them for they know not what they do." And, "My grace is sufficient for you, for my power is made perfect in weakness." Therefore I will not be ashamed of my weaknesses, so that Christ's power may rest on me (2 Corinthians 12:9).

When facing your challenge or diagnosis, be honest enough to let others know. Don't be too proud to accept help; you will need it! When you graciously accept it, you enable those who help you to experience the joy and satisfaction that comes with serving others. If you are the caregiver, like my husband, the task can wear you down physically, spiritually, and emotionally. You need support and to be honest with others in order to take care of yourself so that you can continue to care for your loved one. If you don't have the support you need, the burden will become too heavy and you may inadvertently cause your loved one to feel even worse and add to their feelings of hopelessness.

Try to lighten up when you can. A good sense of humor is essential. I smiled when I read this sign recently:

Welcome to the Psychiatric Hotline

If you are obsessive-compulsive, please press 1 repeatedly. If you are codependent, please ask someone to press 2.

If you have multiple personalities, please press 3, 4, 5 and 6.

If you are paranoid-delusional, we know who you are and what you want. Just stay on the line so we can trace the call.

If you are schizophrenic, listen carefully and a little voice will tell you which number to press.

If you are manic-depressive, it doesn't matter which number you press. No one will answer.

Don't be too serious or heavenly minded to be of any earthly good. When you're ill, irritability, anger, and disappointment can dominate your emotional spectrum. It's easy to lash out at the closest target. When this occurs, often times it doesn't have anything to do with the moment at hand or the insignificant trigger. It usually is the result of exhaustion, suppressed frustration, fear, or anger at the disease, the feeling of helplessness, or pain. Men want to fix things while women often want to control them, and when either can't do one or the other, it becomes a recipe for trouble.

Stop!!! Face your feelings and deal with them head on; go to a support group, do what you need to do to let it go, move forward with life, living and breathe. Don't play the victim role. Go punch something (preferably not a person) or play an inspirational song. Praise and worship music almost always pulls me out of a low time. Pray for someone else and don't fixate on yourself and your problems. Illness can make us too self-absorbed. Do whatever you can to get a better perspective. Don't follow Melissa Manchester's suggestion of holding it all in and learning how to hide your feelings. Be real. Cry, let it out! Have a melt-down. God can handle your spiritual fits. Whatever you do, never give up! Keep learning the lessons that God is teaching you through the life that is all around you and then be still and know He loves you and He is God... you are not.

A Deep And Scary Crevasse

Counting sheep for sleeplessness is okay for some, but not for me... Remember, I'm no good at math! What works for me is prayer. I chatter on with the Lord until, before I know it, I'm asleep. Psalm 23 is one of my favorites to recite in the middle of the night. I was struggling with sleep the night of January 27, 2008, but prayer only seemed to generate questions. During the evening church service, my friend, Eric Alexander, gave a presentation. Eric is a world-class skier, climber, and mountain-eer, and he recently defied the odds and scaled Mt. Everest leading his blind friend, Erik Weihenmayer to the summit. This incredible duo's story made "Time Magazine," with Erik gracing its cover. During his presentation, Eric mentioned that Gracie and I were an inspiration to him, an example of courage and teamwork that few in life achieve. This touched my heart, but as Eric showed a video clip of Erik working his way across a deep and deadly crevasse on a wobbly ladder, I saw cour-age as I'd never seen before. Blind and held from certain death by what looked like a flimsy rope Erik had to rely on his guide's voice and direc-tion to make it safely across to solid ground.

I don't know why this bothered me so much, but I couldn't get it out of my head. Dozing in and out of sleep that night with this video clip relentlessly replaying it disturbing images in my mind, I suddenly sat up in a cold sweat around 2:45 a.m. I pleaded with the Lord, "Why is this bothering me so much?" After a few more hours of restless prayer, I crawled out of bed at 7:30 a.m. It was then the Lord revealed the answer. *This is something you deal with everyday!* Gasping, I realized this was true!

Every moment of my life, I hang over a deep and scary crevasse, yet I am held safe and secure by a simple rope of hope and am guided by the still small voice of the Lord. With these two supports in place, I've avoided slamming into the icy walls of certain death and, despite my knee-knocking fears, have victoriously reached the far side of God's empowering faith. Not that it isn't a struggle. There are days when that rope looks awfully threadbare and Jesus' voice is hard to hear. During these times, I have to remind myself that what looks wobbly is really stronger than anything my earthly eyes have ever seen. Trusting Him, I walk by faith. The Lord never fails. And the neat thing about it is I get to live. Live to tell about how I've wobbled across and fallen into His safe arms of love, forgiveness, hope, restoration, and sanctuary.

Life is a Grand Canyon-size adventure. None of us has control over the day we are born. What makes us think we can control the day we die? Let us hold tightly to the One who is and walk where He leads us, carefully counting on His Word. He never promised it would be easy and life can be unfair, but we serve a great God who is Master of every single thing in the universe... and He knows what is best for you and me!

Anne Severance, Gracie, me and Barbara Smith- Enjoying time together in Beaver Creek, Colorado

Hiking in Colorado with my TN family--Robin, Chris, Jan, Debbie, Michael, me - Gracie was enjoying running around with everyone

CHAPTER 24

BE STRONG
AND COURAGEOUS!

I press on that I may lay hold of that for which Christ Jesus has also laid hold of me. Brethren, I don't count myself to have apprehended; but one thing I do, forgetting those things, which are behind, and reaching forward to those things, which are ahead. I press toward the goal for the prize of the upward call of God in Christ Jesus.

—Philippians 3:14

Heroes

When I was a child I regarded Wonder Woman, Superman, the Bionic Woman, and the Six Million Dollar Man as heroes. Now I know that a hero is an ordinary person who chooses to rise above his or her circumstances with a warrior mentality and fights to work with God to make something good out of their lives in spite of overwhelming obstacles, challenges, and heartbreaks.

Gracie

Gracie is my hero because she has done just that to join me. She defied the odds and naysayers to become not only a good dog, but also a working dog with a mission to help improve the quality of my life; helping me do things I can't do without her. I believe this life of service has given more meaning to her life and, of course, to mine. We all have that kind of potential to make a difference and be a hero! I mean, where did you go today? Better yet, where did God send you to be His hands, heart, grace, and mercy and how did you represent Him? Take nothing for granted. Everyday is an opportunity to be a hero.

Saint Paul

My husband, Paul, is a hero. He married me knowing I was broken. He had faith in me and faith in himself to overcome the fears of partnering with a chronically ill mate. He helped me to be more than I thought possible, and I believe he has grown into more of a man than he thought

possible. Paul was afraid, but he did it anyway. Look at all the blessings we would have missed. I call him "Saint Paul."

My heroes have inspired me to carry on. An old Indian Proverb says, "When you were born you cried and the world rejoiced; live your life in such a way that when you die the world cries and you rejoice." One of my most fervent prayers is that when I die, my life will have counted for something and to someone; that it will be a celebration because I didn't live in vain but fulfilled my purpose in such a way that God was glorified in my generation. I feel He is counting on me. Like my pastor in Florida, Mark James, taught me, I'm an ordinary person but I can make an extraordinary impact.

You Can Be A Hero

I pray that my story encourages someone facing obstacles, disabilities, diseases, depression, or divorce to press on and not give up. I trust you realize that you can reach out and take His hand and really live regardless of the circumstances, prison walls, or challenges you face. You can rise above them all in truth and be free. Live every moment, find outrageous joy, and leave nothing to chance. God is working out His plan even now in the midst of your trial. He did it for me, I know He can do it for you! *God made only one of me but He made only one of you*, too! And you can be someone's hero.

The great heroes of the Bible impress us with their strength, confidence, and depth of faith. God's Word tells us that we can do great things like they did because we have the same God in us, and for us! King David made huge mis-

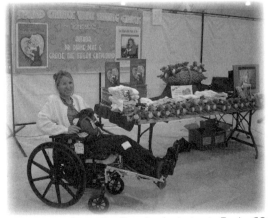

Preparing for a book signing in Eagle, CO

Sharing our story with an after school program in TX Gracie and I are in the center

takes but was also supremely confident in God; firm in the knowledge that God would give him the strength to overcome his obstacles. You can accomplish anything through the power of Christ. I hope this will encourage you to take a stand for God even if you are afraid. Just do it! He took one for you through Christ's death on the cross. Don't ever think that God only does great things for other people or those stalwarts of the Bible. That same powerful God will help you!

The Challenge

Samuel Ulman said, "Years may wrinkle the skin, but to give up enthusiasm wrinkles the soul." Suffering has played an integral part in my life. God could heal me in a second. I certainly have the faith of a mustard seed and have stretched to touch the hem of His garment. Through it all, I have become both a warrior and a worshiper. I have determined that none of my testing and suffering will be wasted. The "no pain, no gain" mentality underlying my years as a weight lifter and sports enthusiast applies to my life except that it's faith that is flexed rather than muscles: the more I study the Word and flex my faith, the stronger I get!

Sharing our story with an after school program in Colorado

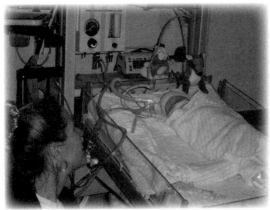

Delivering a "Love Kits" and praying for this baby in critical condition at Dell's Children's Hospital, TX.
This baby lived!

As Elisabeth Elliot said, "I am very aware of the fact that pain is necessary to all of us. In my own life, I think I can honestly say that out of the deepest pain has come the strongest conviction of the presence of God and the love of God." (*Gateway To Joy*, Elliot, 2005). Pain and suffering get our attention like nothing else. C.S. Lewis wrote, "God whispers to us in our pleasures, speaks to us in our conscience, but shouts in our pains: It is His megaphone to rouse a deaf world." Despite our pain or circumstances, God wants us to be strong and courageous!

Yet, sometimes the "no pain, no gain" approach can come in conflict with the Word of God. The Bible says in Philippians 4:13: "I can do everything through him who gives me strength" and 1 Corinthians 10:13: "No temptation has seized you except what is common to man. And God is faithful; he will not let you be tempted beyond what you can bear. But when you are tempted, he will also provide a way out so that you can stand up under it." When we choose to carry more than God would have us, we are in conflict with His Word and get out of balance. That is what I did and still do sometimes, but the God of the Bible lightens our loads and offers restoration.

Be Bold!

So be bold! Live the life Joshua directs in Joshua 1:9: "Be strong and of good courage; be not afraid, neither be thou dismayed: for the Lord thy God is with thee whithersoever thou goest." Again! "Be strong and of good courage... for the Lord thy God... will not fail thee, nor forsake thee." Deuteronomy 31:6. NKJ.

My hope is that you are encouraged to stand, fight the good fight, and carry on with all the Lord blessed you with. You have the power to make a difference and change the course of another person's day, week, or life. Let's go make a difference in the world for good. Just look around you. I bet there is someone who could really use your encouragement, your help, and your love. You are needed. You are never too young, too old, or too broken to be all He created you to be if you do it with His strength, guidance, and direction. This is what the *Gracie Challenge* is all about. Please join us www.DianeDike.org. He wants you to come before the throne of grace and make your requests know to Him and a peace that surpasses all understanding will guard your heart and mind.

The Power Of One

I'm Satan's worst nightmare because I will not give up. I'm armed and dangerous with the truth and the truth has set me free! The Word of God is energizing. I truly believe that is why I have been able to make it. I sleep with my Bible; I play scripture all night and praise and worship music all day. I do what it takes to keep my eyes on Him, not my circumstances or how I feel. This is how I survive, how I overcome, and become more than a conqueror.

Along with this book, I have written Gracie's children's book series, *The Adventures of Gracie and Diane* and started a ministry called, *Second Chance with Saving Grace.* It's a non-profit organization whose mission is to travel the world sharing the Good News of God's grace and love to broken people. I hope that my life experience will encourage others to carry on despite, and because, of their suffering and challenges. (See Appendix C)

Blessed And Grateful

I celebrate and know that I'm truly blessed and am grateful for all that I can still do, what I still have, and the opportunities that I have been allowed. So the real question is, "Why is God so good and gracious to me?" He loves me... He loves you. He loves us too much to leave us alone.

I've always prided myself on being independent but have had to acknowledge that I can't make it alone and sometimes have to "cry out loud." There are many lessons to learn through the good, the bad and the ugly. I am learning to live while dying... we all are. I may get knocked down but with God, I won't get knocked out (2 Corinthians 4:8-9). Paul said, "Our present troubles are quite small and won't last very long. Yet they produce for us an immeasurable great glory that will last forever!" (NLT 2 Corinthians 4:17). Job's situation didn't change until he changed his attitude. Am I holding on to things and allowing my past to poison my future? If I am going to go forward I must stop looking behind. My best days are just ahead. Yours are, too! You're just a fraction of an inch away from your dreams coming true!

God is first place in my life and He has taken me places I couldn't have dreamed possible. Not long ago, in an intimate conversation with Grandma Dike, she exhorted while shrugging her now frail shoulders,

"God made only one of me." The most important thing to her is that her family would come to know Christ as their friend and Savior too. As I listened, I felt God's love and pleasure for her. Then it occurred to me: He feels the same way for me. I'm just as loved, treasured, and precious to God as Grandma Dike. How am I going to apply this truth to my life? What am

Grandma Dike, Gracie and Paul in Vermont

I going to do about it? My answer is this book, Gracie's adventure series, my non-profit organiza-tion, *Second Chance with Saving Grace,* and *Gracie's Challenge* (to the world to-*Be a light in the dark-ness!* This is just the start and the result of applying what God revealed to me that day.

In His great name I pray you will "be strong and of good courage, do not fear nor be afraid... for the Lord your God, He is the One who goes with you. He will not leave you nor forsake you." Deuteronomy 31:6

CHAPTER 25

To The Future...
With Love

*There is nothing like a dream
to create the future.*

—Victor Hugo

A Final Note From Me To You.

Wow, what a journey, huh? I've been authentic with you in an effort to show you how bad things had gotten for me and how lost I'd become. The editors had me take out several parts and told me it was just too heartbreaking to have all those details in one book, "It's more than the reader can take." Maybe I will share those details at another time. But isn't it wonderful no matter how lost I was God, had not lost me. He never gave up on me. He pulled me from the rubble of my life and set me high upon a rocked. When I arrived at the top of that mountain I held my arms high to praise the Lord... thanking Him for all He'd done.

There is still so much that I do not understand but I can face tomorrow because I know the One who holds it in the palm of His hand.

Taking Mom and Dad out to eat when we took care of them in Feb. 2007. Mom was going through chemotherapy-Dad is still dealing with Parkinson's and a hernia operation. We are thankful for our time together!

Because of that, it is well with my soul. If I understood it all, what would I need to have faith for? I choose to celebrate life because I've learned walking with Jesus doesn't depend on my legs, it depends on my heart. I know in my day of trouble I can call upon Him and He will answer me.

Continually On The Move

Paul, Gracie, and I live in the Vail Valley of Colorado. We just sold our third home and bought a "Green" home. One that has been rated with high efficiency. The builder said, "The best way to live green is to start with your home." We want to be responsible stewards with all our resources as we prepare for our *Second Chance with Saving Grace* USA book tour. Being back on the speaking circuit and sharing God's goodness wherever I am allowed, teaching disability awareness and etiquette to businesses, and continuing *The Adventures of Gracie and Diane* book series are more than fulfilling; they are a dream come true. Book One, *Gracie Comes Home* is published and doing really well. We are waiting on the illustrations for Book Two which is called, *Gracie Discovers Her Purpose. Even as Book One is printed in Spanish and English-soft cover.*

Paul and I recently spent three months caring for my parents in Florida. Mom is fighting multiple myeloma cancer while my dad battles Parkinson's. Both of them experience episodes of forgetfulness and I fear they will soon

Jan, Gracie & me

need greater assistance than the family can provide.

Jan, one of my best friends inspires me as she fights Huntington's disease. It pains me deeply to watch her suffer from this cruel affliction. I wish I could take away her thrashing and frustration; she has lost almost ninety pounds from the uncontrollable movements of her body. My darling Paul had shoulder surgery, precipitated by his shoulder dislocating several times. I recently flew to Massachusetts to sit at the bedside of my beloved Aunt Pat as she prepared to go to Heaven. Much of the time she was in great distress because she had unfinished business. But I was thankful to be able to read the Bible, sing, hold her hand, change her, turn her, fix her hair and lay next to her when she was

Our last photo with Tyler in Vermont-Paul, Aunt Chick, Tyler, me, and Uncle Bob

anxious and scared all through the day and night. Then, Tyler Palmer, our thirty-seven year old, dearly loved cousin died unexpectedly on January 27, 2008, while skiing. He is so missed by his family, friends, fiancé, and especially his wonderful Mom, our Aunt Chick.

Yes, we packed up our treasures and moved this month in the middle of all of this. Our lives are a high-traffic area. Do you know what I mean? I'm not going to lie to you, there is nothing easy about this thing called "living," not for most of us, but it could be worse and aren't you thankful for this life in any case? Although my faith has matured because of much suffering, each day still offers its challenging typhoons... Daily I focus on God, He leads me beside the still blue waters and renews my weary soul. Still, in the midst of finding His rest the disease rages on. I've had several severe flare-ups of cryoglobulinemia and was close to going in to the hospital for the first time since I've had Gracie. Instead, Gracie's divine service provided the help I needed and we made it through another excruciating night. Sometimes friends and family get mad at me for not going to the hospital. I try to explain, you see, they have to keep the IV bag warm, the room warm and a warm blanket on me, and not wake me up all during the night if I should get to sleep. That just doesn't usually happen. I'd rather pray, and wait it out in the comfort of my own home. It takes a move of God to get me to go to the hospital and that works for me.

We get emails daily from and about those who are suffering. We help by sending "Love Kits" with letters of encouragement and the tools we think will help them overcome. (A "Love Kit" includes a t-shirt to give them something to wear, a Gracie baby to give them something to love, a book with the audio, and a handy bag to carry it all in). Life's circumstances are certainly overwhelming right now but, unlike the past, I do not focus on what I can see but on the One who is my anchor through the category five storms. I don't get blown away very easily anymore. I stand on the promises of the Word of God which is sturdy ground

Dancing with Paul Smith at the Christmas party at Michael's house

and am refreshed enough to carry on—remembering that— Greater is He that is in me than He that is in the world, and if He is for me, who can be against me: He fights the battles for me even as I write this book. My passion for life, Paul, my family, friends, and Gracie continues to grow as I become all He created me to be. I am more than a conqueror. Amen!

Along with the challenges, I have also experienced miracles. In fact, so many miracles surround me right now that I couldn't even list them all. What has been meant for evil is turning out for good right before my eyes. Wow! Only God can do that!

I Know I'm Not "Normal," It's Okay!

I know I'm not normal: I hug strangers and smile at children in cars passing by, I'm an oddball. Yet, most nights I can lay down in peace knowing I lived today the best way that I know how. If I meet my Maker, I am ready. I am thankful. Yet, there is so much I still want to do so I ask Him for time now instead of begging Him to take me home. It's unusual to push a chair and then sit in it yet, I am even thankful for the wheelchair because it enables me to keep living and participating in life. If Paul has to push me in on a gurney, I'm still going to participate in living this life to the fullest and share our message of hope anywhere I'm invited. I may not have always made the best choices, but I am finishing strong. I'm learning to think new thoughts and renew my mind daily. Worry steals the joy of today so I try to remember all that He has done and all that He can do, no matter what! I rely on His promise of hope and purpose for my life.

Where Are You Today?

Whether you are on the mountaintop or in the valley, I hope you have enjoyed my triumphant adventure with its divine appointments and challenges. I've cracked open the door to my life to show how I've overcome with a smile, a Service Dog, and a second chance. But most of all, I have overcome because of a Savior who is my friend and walks with me daily. He's a revolutionary man who has given me a revolutionary hope! May you experience renewal, restoration, and a new found energy through eyes of faith. "Let us hold unswervingly to the hope we profess, for He who promised is faithful." (Hebrews 10:23) May you be amazed and give praise to God. Being filled with awe and saying, "We have seen remarkable things today" (Luke 5:26).

Learning to celebrate the lessons of life may give us a deeper appreciation for the difficult times, especially when love gets tough. I've shared a portion of my life's journey with truth and hope. so we can learn from my past, find hope for tomorrow, and enjoy the present.

I do not have to live in denial of my circumstances any more, but stand with hope in spite of them. I defy my circumstances with a trust in a God who never forsakes me, and I know He will take me through. Exercising my hope in Him lifts me up and strengthens my soul. Now I am soaring by faith, setting my sights on heights that are far and above anything I could have imagined. A scientist that I'm working with to tackle my complicated medical problems asked me recently, "Diane, are you spiritual?"

"Yes, I am."

"Do you know that God has a divine plan for your life and you are right on schedule?"

"Yes!" I exclaimed.

"Then trust that, trust Him."

The fact that I sometimes walk in unbelief became clear to me, again. If I'm worrying, I'm not trusting. That speaks volumes about what I really believe. To be truly be free, I must believe. I do not have to beat myself up for not being good enough. Believing He can do what He says He can do, what He says I can do, that He is who he says He is, and I am who He says I am, is key. And when the world overwhelms me I pray,

"*Help me Jesus believe and overcome my unbelief! And give me the strength to face this difficulty, learn what you would have me learn and overcome.*" He can do it! I dare you to have belief in Him. Give Him the opportunity and you'll see how awesome and powerful He is. God wants to bless you, and He can lift your head above any trial!

Remember that you are not beyond the reach of Jesus, the one who was willing to sacrifice everything for you. Meet with Him at the foot of the cross and join your heart to His at any cost. **God made only one of you.** He can clear a way when there seems to be no way because all things are possible with Him. Be the wonderful you He created you to be. Embrace who you are and where you are. God has a divine plan for you and you are right on schedule. Trust Him! He is counting on you to do what only you can do! He loves you no matter what! Give Him your best and trust Him with the rest.

Shine your light in the darkness. Just do it! Enjoy it! You matter! I look forward to hearing your story! May God bless you exceedingly and abundantly above anything you can ask or think. May God himself, the God of peace sanctify you through and through. May your whole spirit, soul ad body be kept blameless by the sacrifice of Christ until He returns. Please keep us in your prayers and when you get the chance, tell us your triumphant story!

Your Friend,

♥ *Diane xoxo*

Lord, help us to find hope to believe even when dreams fade and hope to endure as we put the truths we have learned into practice. May we always remember that those who wait on the Lord shall renew their strength; they shall mount up with wings like eagles, they shall run and not be weary, they shall walk and not faint, in the lovely, gracious name of Jesus Christ. Amen!

From Pain to Pearl

All the days ordained for me were written in God's book before one of them came to be.

—Psalm 139:16

Learning To Stand, Even in a Wheelchair

As you have read, even with my best effort, I couldn't fix everything and everyone, or be good enough. I couldn't make others be happy or even myself. The secret to happiness is a heart full of gratitude and to hunger and thirst for the holiness of Christ; hunger for Him and His Word as you would an oasis in the scorching desert. My friend and pastor Craig Smith says we are "failing forward." We are going to fail because we are human, but with Jesus we can still move forward. In His strength I'm moving forward.

I want to know Christ and the power of His resurrection but that entails the fellowship of sharing in His sufferings, becoming like Him in His death (Philippians 3: 11). We can't say, "Um, ya God, I want all the good you have for me but, I do not want to experience any bad!" (Job 2:10) Now each time a crisis hits—as long as I'm alive they will—I do not curse God and run away from Him and my troubles; I've learned to respond by asking the sovereign God, "What would you have me learn, speak Lord, I'm listening. Please show me the way."

I was resurrected out of my old life. Life still is not perfect and never will be here on earth, but I'm heading in the right direction. I've got my eye on the prize—eternal life. In Heaven, He will wipe every tear from our eyes. There will be no more death or mourning or crying or pain, for the old order of things will have passed away (Revelation 21:4.) I can't always handle the load that I would like, be as physically active as I desire, or just live without thinking so much, but I'm going to live while I'm alive the best that I know how. I'm going to love and forgive and laugh and live victoriously!

Do you think events that seemed meaningless, or even wasteful, could take you to amazing destinations as surely as the dusty twisting and turning path you have followed? No matter what difficulties life brings, no matter how hard, painful, or unfair life can be, it's worthy of celebrating. Today, I choose life and celebrate living! God's touch on my body has not caused a physical healing but He has brought wholeness in my heart that only He could craft. I realize I am helpless without Him. My faith must rest in Him and Him alone.

Life offers its wisdom generously, and everything in it can teach us something. If we choose to learn, life's lessons can deepen our capacity for compassion, intimacy, and forgiveness. An acorn has everything in it that it needs, placed there by the Creator, to become a big oak tree. But it must break open to become what it was created to be; maybe it's the same for you and me?

I've learned that accepting Christ requires a daily laying down of my life, and that what I want—healing and deliverance from my mental and physical suffering—is not the most important thing. What is most important is fulfilling the purpose and plan He created me for. That is where I will rest in peace, no matter what.

The following lists a few things I have come to know:

✿ Life is to be enjoyed not endured-Look, watch, and listen carefully.

✿ Through God, all things are possible. Seek His best!

✿ Listen and say sorry when someone is hurting

✿ Share a message of hope with the hopeless.

✿ Always do your best.

✿ Share your story

✿ Be fair

✿ You're not an accident.

✿ Dunking my warm chocolate chip cookie in milk is yummy-enjoy!

✿ Balance is important so take a nap, snuggle, and hold hands whenever you can.

✿ I never want to be separated from God again.

✿ Life is difficult, but God is faithful.

✿ Encourage others.

✿ Forgive more, complain less and love.

✿ Always keep your promise and be careful with your words.

✿ I must evaluate my spiritual health on a regular basis, stay account-able, and most of all, stay in the Word!

✿ It is not about me, it is all about Him; yet He is counting on me to make a difference and do what He created me to do. Each of us is impor-tant. We matter. He loves us. In fact, He is passionate about every detail of our lives.

✿ Love is not given because it is deserved...

✿ It's okay to be an oddball.

✿ Never Give Up!

✿ Love is a verb.

✿ Believe.

✿ Faith is my foundation. I am reconciled and redeemed; a grateful prodigal. Yet, if I were to be on trial for being a Christian, would there be enough evidence to convict me?

✿ *God made only one of me and He made only one of you, too.* He is counting on us to be who He created us to be and do what He created us to do in this generation. No one loves the way you do or looks at things the way you do. You are special. You are one of a kind. You are loved. You are important! (Yes, I have my cheerleader hat on and I hope you are getting fired-up to live and be all you can be!)

The Miracle Of Light

Hanukkah is about the miracle of light. God's menorah is made of people; like candles we are to shine His light into the darkness. This is what *Gracie's Challenge* is all about. There is a place for God's light in every one of us; it's either shining or waiting to shine, even if in a simple smile. *We may never know the good that a smile can accomplish.* God sent Jesus to bridge the gap between Him and us. Sometimes it takes being in the dark foxhole to discover the place in us that carries the light. Live out loud; look for places to shine and it will make a difference in this world.

Suffering is a part of being alive, and we don't truly live by avoiding it. Hiding ourselves means that we will suffer alone and miss the chance to bless others and to receive their blessings. In the presence of suffering, everyone needs to find refuge and the Lord puts people in our lives for that reason. Matthew 5:14-16, as quoted from *The Message Bible*, says it well:

> *Here's another way to put it: You're here to be light, bringing out the God-colors in the world. God is not a secret to be kept. We're going public with this, as public as a city on a hill. If I make you light-bearers, you don't think I'm going to hide you under a bucket, do you? I'm putting you on a light stand. Now that I've put you there on a hilltop, on a light stand—shine! Keep open house; be generous with your lives. By opening up to others, you'll prompt people to open up with God, this generous Father in Heaven.*

The Medical Chart

My medical chart documents what appear to be the worst times of my life and is held together by all the jarring questions that were never answered. I was intensely angry about how I was shuffled around from doctor to doctor and charged a fortune to be a guinea pig, or a prime example of what modern medicine could not do; this added to my end-less frustration. Maybe the painful stuff of life was the sandpaper that God used to help get rid of my rough edges. I certainly feel purged and refined. Through the weeping, whining, losing, shining, praying, grow-ing... I've learned to depend upon His Word and know that there is HOPE beyond trials; I have become a tested and true believer who is very thankful to be out of dysfunction junction!

I get asked during interviews if I believe God allows us more than we can handle? I'd have to say, "Yes." If He didn't allow it, at times, we might get too self-righteous or self-reliant and forget our need of Him. Daily, we all have the opportunity to be God's instrument and demon-strate His awesome love and power by helping those He has put around us. My desire is to spread His Good News through my life. He has turned my mess into a message and my test into a testimony.

As I wrote this book I felt like quitting many times. I thought, *who cares?* And every time I read through it, I realized that I'd left some-thing out. There was another layer of onion whose peeling away led to more unwanted tears. The deeper I go, the more I remember what I once wished to forget. However, God prodded me to continue and trea-sures burst through the surface to become moments of clarion truth along this journey. I realized that I didn't want to go too deep because

I was afraid truth about my sin would bring me rejection and judgment, it's easier to play it safe. Yet, God said the truth would set me free. If I'm to stand, to be truly whole, I must acknowledge and sometimes share the secrets of my soul so He can use them for good, so you will know you are not alone. Growing up meant not worrying about how others respond but caring if I am doing what He instructed me to do.

Oysters' Response To Pain

Harry Emerson Fosdick thinks the most extraordinary thing about the oyster is the irritations that get into the shell... and when the oyster can't get rid of them, it uses the irritations to do the loveliest thing an oyster ever has the chance to do, make a pearl. If there are irritations in our life today, there is only one prescription; make a pearl... and it takes faith to do it. (*Secrets of Success*, Fosdick, 2007)

If you were an oyster, what would be your response to pain? A pearl, or complaint and bitterness? Numbers 11:1 says, "When the people complained, it displeased the Lord." Complaining is like worrying it doesn't do anyone any good. Would you demand that God fix it or else! I guess in the beginning that is what I did. I threw a tantrum because He was not doing it my way, according to my plan. Whooee, I had a lot to learn.

I can relate to an oyster. An oyster is soft and sensitive to the circumstances surrounding it, it creates something of great value in the place where it's most vulnerable. That is my desire. Not to be a dumpster full of garbage and stink, dragging my troubles behind me, but to recycle it all into something of use for the Kingdom of God. I choose to get better, not bitter and I will accept whatever God decides is best for me and try to glorify Him in it no matter what. Char-ching! A pearl is in the making.

A piece of sand can enter our lives and alter us so profoundly that we can't go back to the way we were. Yet, we can make a pearl out of our experiences, trials, tribulations, and irritations when we truly live by experiencing everything that life has to offer. We can kick against our circumstances all our lives or accept who, where, and what we are by grasping the magnificent lessons to be learned. Then we can let go of the anger, blame, sense of injustice, and finally, the pain itself until all we have left is a deeper sense of the value of life, and a greater capacity to live it.

Live life on purpose! Live it boldly! Live it profoundly! Live it out loud! Embrace who and where you are! Sometimes the very things that threaten our lives may strengthen it. Loss, pain, and crisis can activate the will to truly live and can be our wake-up call. I want to live and I'm not going to hold back anymore. Char-Ching!

Chronic Trouble

People with chronic troubles or illness may be getting a wake-up call. Yet, too often they become trapped in a state of invalidation, not by the force of their disease, but by the power of their beliefs about it. Disease can be brutal, lonely, constricting, and terrifying. But, with the right tools and the Bible in hand, you can overcome the challenges it presents and live a fulfilling life of hope, promise, and joy.

The Message Bible reminds us in James 1:2-4 to,

"Count it all joy! Consider it a sheer gift, friends, when tests and challenges come at you from all sides. You know that under pressure, your faith-life is forced into the open and shows its true colors. So don't try to get out of anything prematurely. Let it do its work so you become mature and well developed, not deficient in any way."

Daily we are tested and sifted like sand. Are you ready? Can you count it all joy? He loves you too much to not help you grow.

It's Easy!

It's easy to follow Jesus when everything is going your way. The only way to truly know what is inside is to get squeezed: that is when we really find out what we believe! To stay spiritually fit your faith will get a work-out and you can remain strong with the solid food of God's word. There are no shortcuts to a fulfilling life. Fulfillment can come when we experience and transcend the diseased state. Pain marks the

Me, Gracie, Anne, Barbara, Grandma Kate, Debbie- The Girls out to lunch in TN

place where self-knowledge and growth can happen in much the same way that the tangled web of fear does. Untouched by the hand of God, we will suffer anyway; we just will not be transformed by it.

Most of us wear masks to hide our pain, distress, and true selves. For many years, I wore a mask. I wanted to hide my shame and fear about never being able to lead a "normal" life again; about not being good enough; about my failures and shortcomings... Removing many layers of my mask has been a painful task, but writing this book has not only helped me to come out from behind them, but also afforded me the strength to throw them as far as the east is from the west, never to be picked up and worn again. If I can do it, I know you can, too. I hope to strengthen your courage; if I do, then my life has not been in vain. We can transcend time by finally fulfilling our life's purpose. The Word says we have not because we ask not; God can do anything and all glory goes to Him.

Purposeful Life And Suffering

Martha Washington wrote, "I have learned from experience that the greater part of our happiness or misery depends on our dispositions and not on our circumstances." My husband taught me during our days of mountain biking together that I (and my bike) will go exactly where I am looking; I broke several ribs to remind me of this truth. The same is true in life. If I am looking at the troubles in my life, that is all I will see and my heart will follow these troubles right into the pit.

If I focus on the promises and the many good things God is doing in my life, that is what I will see, and that is where my heart will go. It's up to me. If I really believe Romans 8:28, "that in all things God works for the good," what am I worrying about? When I worry—and I know it's hard not to in our humanness—I show a direct lack of faith in my Savior, my friend, my confident, my provider, the one who has brought me through everything.

He Rescues Those Crushed In Spirit

I would like to give Rick Warren a big hug! Years ago our friends gave us his book, *The Purpose Driven Life*. I have studied and found much wisdom in it. He confirms that there is a purpose in our trials:

> *God uses problems to draw you closer to Himself. The Bible says, "The Lord is close to the brokenhearted; he rescues those who are crushed in spirit." Your most profound and intimate experiences of worship will likely be in your darkest days—when your heart is broken, when you feel abandoned, when you're out of options, when the pain is great—and you turn to God alone. It's during suffering that we learn to pray our most authentic,*

heartfelt, honest-to-God prayers. When we're in pain, we don't have the energy for superficial prayer. (Purpose Driven Life, Warren, 194).

I don't know if I've ever worshiped the Lord with a greater depth of gratefulness than when, with a shattered heart and abandoned. But it was in this darkness that I realized that God was all I had to hold on to. Jesus' payment for my sins was, and is, my only hope. Prayer is a deep longing in my soul to connect and communicate with my friend and savior in an authentic manner. Mahatma Gandhi said, "It is better in prayer to have a heart without words than words without a heart" (*The God Light*, Gandhi, 2006). I think God enjoys it and I am blessed when I find the appropriate words to match my contrite heart, but sometimes all I can do is fall on my face before Him. Yet, I'm mindful that whether I am singing, meditating, dancing, praising, or performing the mundane chores of daily living, I need to do it prayerfully and thankfully unto Him. Max says, "Worship is the 'thank you' that refuses to be silenced."

Beauty from Ashes

Often I attempted to accomplish much in my own strength, draining my very soul with impossible expectations. I don't have the energy to live a superficial life and must make the best use of the time I have left. I can only do this in His strength and by grasping the fact that He is my Savior and He is with me everywhere I go. He came to save me, not condemn me. He loved me so much that He died for me. So beauty can come from the ashes of my life and God can be glorified. Isaiah 61:1-3 says:

The Lord has anointed me...
To comfort all who mourn... To give beauty for ashes,
The oil of joy for mourning,
The garment of praise for the spirit of heaviness;
That they may be called trees of righteousness,
The planting of the Lord, that He may be glorified.

God knows what is best and how to get us where we need to be. We are not accidents. Everything in our world has a purpose. Do you know your purpose in life? It's to glorify God in all you say and do, no matter what!

All of us can be like so many characters in the Bible including Abraham, Noah, Moses, David, and Peter. They didn't live perfect lives but they had perfect testimonies because they walked with God. Each o

Some of my TN "Family." We rode two tour buses to Memphis to watch Michael in Concert, in 2005.

us has the opportunity to please God, even with our imperfections, to have a perfect testimony by walking with Him!

"Joni Eareckson Tada comments, 'When life is rosy, we may slide by with knowing about Jesus, with imitating Him and quoting Him and speaking of Him. But only in suffering will we know Jesus.' We learn things about God in suffering that we can't learn any other way." (*Purpose Driven Life*, Warren, p.194).

Inspirational singer and author, Sheila Walsh, expands upon this notion and gives examples of its truth found in the Bible:

> *Suffering is seldom an item on our list of requests to the Lord. But when it crosses our path and we are able by His grace to keep on walking, our lives become messages of hope to the world and to the church. Besides Job, there are plenty of examples in Scripture of people who suffered physical pain or loss and spiritual perse-cution. David suffered politically and spiritually. He was chased by Saul's men, captured by the Philistines, and threatened by the followers of Baal. The apostle Peter, who lived in the New Testament era during a period of intense religious persecution, was eventually martyred upside down on a cross. In each case, we read of these men's commitment to God and their under-standing that God's glory would be seen through their sufferings* (Life Is Tough But God Is Faithful, *Walsh, 57, 1999).*

Trust

If we believe in God for only the blessings He can give us, our belief in Him is not based on trust but on our own selfish desires, and our own concept of what we think God owes us. Jesus is not a Jeannie in a bottle that we snap our fingers and He magically does as we tell Him. Suffering was not His dream for our life but trials and tribulation are now inescapable in this fallen world until He returns. We may never understand the, "why." That is where faith comes in. Do you think it takes more faith to trust Him in a storm or when you are enjoying calm waters. Have you ever been broken, lost, or sick and still you looked up to Heaven and said, "Blessed be the name of the Lord. Oh, God, I love you." I my weakness, I pray, He is shown strong.

Living Out Romans 8:28

I cling to Him because that is all that really matters and what will last forever. I don't care about personal fame or financial gain. I believe it's my purpose to offer encouragement to hurting people, and I am going to do everything that I can to help others in spite of myself. That is why I have created, *Second Chance with Saving Grace, Inc* and it's many outreaches. Actions speak louder than words.

Jesus is always there to help and He often desires to do it through our hands and feet. I desire to live out 2 Corinthians 1:4 and comfort all who are troubled, as I was comforted, so they can pay it forward too. Jesus will walk with us through the most difficult times. I know this to be true because He did it for me. I'm called to reach out to others with His love. I challenge you, I dare you, to try to do the same. Look for people and ways to help someone *everyday*. And if your motive is to

The guys in the mountains during one of our hikes-Chris, Don, Dr. Ron, Bill, Michael W. and Paul

bring Him glory, it will transform you. It will transform us all (join the *Gracie Challenge* today). Now that is real living and it fires me up! Come on everyone, just like a wave at the football game, let's stand and raise our hands, join in the fun, work together as a team, and love each other. What a difference we can make if we work together! I'm so thankful to live! My only fear now is I will run out of time to accomplish all the hopes and dreams I have to reach out and help others.

The Support Of The Church

There is nothing pretty about sin; it's ugly and someone always has to pay. My tragedies have changed my priorities. Spiritual warfare is important. If we could see the spiritual world happening all around us, we would not take it so lightly. The greatest lie of Satan is to convince us that he is not real, and that just knowing about God is as good as knowing Him on a deep and personal level. Even Satan knows that God exists, but he is still condemned to prowl the earth in search of others to share the misery he brought on himself by refusing to submit to God's will and authority. We must put on the armor of the Lord and stand firm in the Word by meditating on it day and night. Just like Ephesians Chapter six teaches us.

Although I pray persistently, I still need the loving critique of others to hold me accountable. That is why I feel belonging to and attending a church and small groups is vital to my spiritual walk. Together, we are powerful, especially when we realize God loves us. He promised to be wherever two or more are gathered in His name. His mercies will renew us daily if we will let them. I like what Billy Graham said about church: "If you ever find the perfect church, please don't join it. You'll mess it up!" Indeed, there are no perfect people or perfect churches out there but let us be the church, anyway! The church may be a majestic mess, but it's majestic, indeed! I do honestly believe that the Body of Christ is the "hope of the world." Please be an active participant. Let us walk hand in hand to the promised land. It's about teamwork not perfection. It's about people coming together to form a family, not a building.

The Church Is Alive And Well

I really enjoy going to church and I'm so thankful for my church family here and all over the world. In fact, I rarely meet a stranger because, I consider us all family. Over the years the church has made all the difference. I don't think of the church as a building with a name brand; no, it's the people who, however imperfect, come together to stand with each other so if one falls down, the other can help pick him up. When we don't join in, we miss the blessing of each other. When members of the Body of Christ unite, they are stronger, more likely to achieve goals, and are more successful and effective as individuals. The last part of community and opportunity is unity. When the world sees us standing together, we symbolize the truth of an old song that I often hum in my heart when I see the good in us as a team. Peter Scholtes wrote, "They will know we are Christians by our love." True disciples of Jesus are not known by speeches, or politics, or theology, but by their love. "By this all will know that you are My disciples, if you have love for one another" (John 13:35).

To borrow from John Donne, "No man is an island all to himself." We are connected. We need each other. We all share the destination of death, and it's not as scary if we walk the road together. Troubles force us so deeply into our own vulnerability that we reach a place of knowing that such vulnerability exists. With great loss can come the ability to be more compassionate as we utilize the unexpected strength gained from breaking through obstacles and living as overcomers. The bell tolls for each of us. Frances Ridley Havergal declared, "Satan scatters but Jesus gathers." Let's pray for one another, eternity is hanging in the balance. I pray for the worldwide church of Jesus Christ to truly put Christ first and live together in peace and let it begin with me.

The Bible

John MacArthur wrote these words and I have them written in the cover of my Bible:

> *The Bible contains the mind of God, the state of man, the way of salvation, the doom of sinners, and the happiness of believers. Its doctrines are holy, its precepts binding. Its histories are true and its decisions are immutable. Read it to be wise, believe it to be safe and practice it to be holy. It contains light to direct, food to support, and comfort to cheer me. It's the traveler's map, the pilgrim's staff, the pilot's compass, the soldier's sword, and the Christians' charter. Here paradise is restored, Heaven opened and the gates of hell disclosed. Christ is its great subject, our good its design and the glory of God its end. It should fill the memory, test the heart and guide the feet. Read it slowly, frequently, prayerfully. It's a mine of wealth, a paradise of glory, and a river of pleasure. It's given in life; it will be opened at the judgment and be remembered forever. It involves the highest*

responsibility, rewards the greatest labor, and condemns all who will trifle with its sacred contents. Christ must be received by faith. Once the heart is changed the rest will fall in line to give God glory (How We Got The Bible. MacArthur, 1997).

Wow! This tripartite Godhead is like the four-leaf clover when it infuses the believer. Each leaf is separate yet connected to make one leaf. It's the union of the Father, Son, Holy Spirit, and the contrite heart that gives the believer the hope and courage to triumph in this fallen world. Sometimes this life seems to be filled with too much pain, suffering, trials, and tribulations. However, we have the choice to focus on our circumstances or to focus on God and find joy in our salvation. It' difficult to focus on this truth when I am in the midst of the daily pain of my disease or an acute flare-up, or when bad things happen to good people or innocent children yet, I choose to believe. We live in a fallen world where bad things do happen but we know from the Bible who has the last word, and who will make all things right again. The Bible says this, God promises this, and I believe it.

Inspiration

Throughout my travels and years of teaching, I have met some wonderful people who have overcome tragedies in their lives: hurricanes; loss of loved ones; financial disasters; and physical, mental, and spiritual sickness. The courage and tenacity of the special needs children I taught helped keep me afloat in the rough sea that almost drowned me. The perseverance of the terminally ill patients I visit in the hospital remind me that life is precious and worth fighting for. I can't hear too many stories about people who choose to triumph over their circumstances, and glorify God in the process and I look forward to hearing yours.

Inspiration From The Bible

I am especially encouraged by the way the Bible tells the stories of many people by including their terrible sins, guilt, shame, failures, and mistakes, as well as their triumphs; this gives me hope. Jesus came from the lineage of David and Bathsheba, the very woman David coveted, committed adultery with, and then had her husband killed for. Even still, our forgiving God called David a man after His own heart. David "displeased" and let God down just as I have through the years. Upon his confession and repentance, David writes this grateful Psalm:

Have mercy on me, O God, according to Your unfailing love; according to Your great compassion blot out my transgressions. Wash away all my iniquity and cleanse me from my sin... Cleanse me and I will be clean; wash me, and I will be whiter than snow... Hide Your face from my sins and blot out all my iniquity. Create in me a pure heart, O God, and renew a steadfast spirit within me. Psalm 51:1-3,7-11.

I say, Amen!! And thank God for being good and gracious; not turning His loving head away from a sincere cry like that? As He has forgiven me, so I forgive.

Living Life To The Fullest

The guidelines and/or rules of the Bible are not to hinder our happiness, but to teach us how to live our lives in such a way that true happiness and contentment are possible. Stephen V. Rexroat said, "Read His instructions with great care and you will see behind the initial 'no' an eternal 'yes.'" An old English proverb states it so well:

Above all else love God alone;
Bow down to neither wood nor stone.
God's name refuse to take in vain;
The Sabbath rest with care maintain.
Respect your parents all your days;
Hold sacred human life always.
Be loyal to your chosen mate;
Steal nothing, neither small nor great.
Report, with truth, your neighbor's deed;
And rid your mind of selfish greed.

—McGuffey Reader

There have been times when I've talked to God, and thought and acted in ways that weren't godly. Now, if my thoughts do not line up with the Word of God, I rebuke them and get my mind back on the truth of who I am in Christ. I am His warrior and will continue to fight. Each day is filled with appreciation for the sunsets God paints, a gentle hug from my husband or a friend, a smile, a snowflake, a warm blanket, and snuggling with my Service Dog, Gracie, as my passion for Jesus Christ sustains me. In the end, that is really the best any of us can do: glorify God in all we say and do and appreciate all that He has done and is doing for us even if our circumstances are not what we hoped and dreamed they would be.

You Matter!

Are you in the midst of challenging circumstances? Have you wondered, "Is life worth living? Do I matter?" I am a fellow sojourner with you. I've made many mistakes, learned difficult lessons, and shared some of them here with you. No matter what calamity strikes, don't be afraid because you are not alone. Take His hand, go where He leads and bless His holy name. The key to life is walking with Jesus. Accepting His second chance by being born again with His love, forgiveness, and His saving grace. That doesn't mean there won't be trouble, but the difference will be in the way that you see things and deal with circumstances. I'm living proof that God can save and set someone free, even if He chooses not to completely deliver me from all my challenges.

My friend Ilene sent this email:

> "Psalm 34:19 'Many are the afflictions of the righteous, but the Lord delivers him out of them all.' Then I opened my daily devotional (currently reading Charles Spurgeon). Here's today's message: 'Now for a little while you may have had to suffer grief in all kinds of trials. These have come so that your faith-of greater worth than gold, which perishes even though refined by fire-may be proved genuine and may result in praise, glory and honor when Jesus Christ is revealed.' 1 Peter 1:6-7 'A tried saint brings more glory to God than an untried one. I think in my own soul that a believer in a prison reflects more glory in His Master than a believer in paradise, that a child of God in the burning, fiery furnace, whose hair is yet unscorched and upon whom the smell of the fire has not passed, displays more the glory of the Godhead than even he who stands with a crown upon his head, perpetually singing praises before the Father's throne. Nothing reflects so much honor on a workman as a trial of his work and its endurance of it. So it is with God. It honors Him when His saints preserve their integrity. Peter honored Christ more when he walked on the ragging water than when he stood upon the land. There was no glory given to God by his walking on the solid shore, but there was glory reflected when he walked on the unsettled water. If we could but add more jewels to the crown of Christ by remaining here, why should we wish to be taken out of the world? We should say, 'It is blessed to be anywhere where we can glorify Him.'"

Wow! Good words to keep things in perspective. I'm passionate because I know what it is to live in the darkness trying to fill the void. Come into the light. May you continue to fulfill the amazing call God has on your life, no matter what!

It all comes down to this one thing; that God may be glorified in me, through me, and by me all the days of my life no matter what!

There are two kinds of people according to C.S. Lewis, "Those who say to God, 'Thy will be done,' or those to whom God says, 'All right, then, have it your way.'" I challenge you to invite Christ into your heart and discover for yourself His transforming power. (See Appendix D and I will walk with you) Do you feel like you are walking through the valley of the shadow of death? No matter what you are facing, you are not alone. Jesus accepts you just as you are. It doesn't matter what things are against you or if you are poor, disabled, divorced, or in prison. Jesus is extending His hand of love and help to you. I don't take this lightly and believe it could be the very reason he kept me alive. He wants you to know, He is walking you through. Focus on Him and what He can do, not on yourself and what you cannot do. Your faith will give God glory and open the door for God to do mighty things in and through your life. He promises that all things work together for good for those who love Him (Romans 8:28), and that we are more than conquerors through Him who loved us (Romans 8:37). Everyday is a unique and irreplaceable gift but when we stumble and fall, we can take the hand of the One who can lead us to solid ground. Never give up hope no matter what! He has a plan for you. You matter. When troubles are all around keep your eyes on Him and trust that everything is going to be okay. In the light of His promises and Word obstacles shrink. If God can help me make it and live a more powerful life, He can help you make it, too. It's not too late—you still have time. Nothing is impossible for Him. You are special, *God Made Only One of You!* Char-Ching!

A Prayer for us:
Dear Lord,
Thank you for your faithfulness to equip us with everything we need to be successful in this life. You are the God of infinite possibilities walking with us even in the hard times. Help us understand that neither death nor life, neither angels nor demons, neither the past nor the present, neither height nor depth, nor

anything else in all creation, will be able to separate us from Your love. Help us to know Your love never runs out and in You ALL is forgiven! Give us grace to triumph over our trials and a sense of purpose and hope in our pain. Assurance that we are not alone and Your good plans for us are not aborted even in our most awful mistakes. And when we come through our challenges may we maintain compassion and encouragement for those who are in the midst of tribulations. On this rugged journey from earth to Heaven I give You praise, glory and honor today and always. Lord, have Your way in me. I'm standing on Your promises trusting You. Please cause my life to impact others so they will meet You for themselves and believe. I will hope continually, and will praise You yet more and more. I ask all this in Jesus most pow- erful, pre- cious and awesome name. Amen!

Does God not see my ways and count my every step?
—Job 31:4

AFTERWORD

*You must be the change
you wish to see in the world.*
—Mahatma Gandhi

By Laura Lyn Donahue

Your website is fantastic. I've enjoyed navigating around and looking at the photos, reading the emails and being blessed by the blessing that you are to so many. I really see you as a golden angel. You shine with the glory of God. His glory exudes from your very being. You are a rare gem, and I am always blessed when I am in your presence.

I remember the day that I met Gracie. In September of 2003 Don and I had come to Colorado to celebrate our 10-year anniversary. Our trip was coming to an end and several of us girls decided to have lunch in Edwards at a sushi restaurant. You had mentioned Gracie to me and told me her story and how she had come to the animal hospital with broken legs and a sad life.

When we met in Edwards, you were so excited because the hospital was there as well. You picked up tiny Gracie and brought her to meet us. The smile on your face—wow—instant bond—instant connection... I knew you were going to take this broken puppy home. Your mothering instincts poured out over this puppy, and Gracie knew what you knew—Diane and Gracie were meant for each other. God's plan had ordained the two of you to be together.

We all know stories of animals that have come into the lives of individuals and have provided healing—emotional, physical, etc. I am even aware that the actual act of petting an animal can bring a person's stress level down. It's no doubt that God gave us animals as a blessing. I don't doubt that God gave you Gracie. He is the Great Physician. Why is it extraordinary that He would use one of His very own creations to minister to the life of another? Doesn't He do this every day? Are we paying attention?

Your story is extraordinary because you prayed; you waited; you listened. You brought little Gracie home not too many days after I met her. Your life has never been the same. Perhaps some may balk at the idea of a tiny dog and a tiny woman ministering health, heat and healing to one another, let them. I stand witness to a precious story of faith and the ability to endure against the odds. I have held your little heater on a very cold day and felt for myself some of the wonderful warmth that she gives to you.

God uses all things for His glory—a beautiful woman with a rare disease and a tiny, orphaned dog waiting for her ordained owner—the two of you, an unlikely pair, an unlikely story—a Divine appointment. Since the day that I met you, I knew that you were an angel put on earth by the very hand of God. I know that I am right. The evidence is over-whelming.

I am so glad to be a small part of your tapestry—woven by the very hand of God—perfect in His eyes—ordained by Him and given to you for a specific purpose. I will praise Him for your willingness to walk by faith even on days when you cannot walk at all.

May God continue to use you for His glory. I pray for you daily.
I love you.

Laura Lyn,
Nashville, Tennessee
Mother of four and wife of Don Donahue
Rocketown Records Label President

. . . there is joy in the presence of God's angels . . . Luke 15:10

APPENDIX A

TRAINING GRACIE

There is no man living who isn't
capable of doing more than he
thinks he can do.

—Henry Ford

As defined by the Americans with Disabilities Act—I have a condition that substantially limits a major life activity and my dog is trained to do specific tasks, which mitigate my impairment—Gracie is considered a Service Dog. The ADA (American with Disabilities Act) requires such training for an animal to exempt them from restrictions that apply to pets. There is no national certification program or ID cards required for these animals to be allowed access to all places the handler goes.

My philosophy for training Gracie is based

Gracie retrieving my water bottle.

on more than three decades of teaching special needs and regular education students, from pre-kindergarten to the collegiate level. As a teacher, I always tried to discover what motivates my students and, in this case, Gracie. I taught Gracie in small increments and with positive reinforcement. Dog training is not

Gracie retrieving my shoe.

something you do just one time but is a daily adventure of learning, teaching, and growing. Upon getting Gracie, I realized that training her to be a well-behaved pet, let alone a Service Dog, would be a challenge because of her breed and the difficult start she had. I took her right where she was and helped her to grow into the special working dog I knew she could be. Like all of us, she had her own unique style of learning and potential. I simply tapped into that style and potential to achieve the desired result: a well-behaved, balanced dog of service for my specific needs. I am by no means a professional dog trainer. All I can do is tell you what worked for us. I get emails and questions weekly from

interested people who need help training their Italian Greyhound or any dog in general. In a future book I will share how God taught me to live like the overcomer I am with Gracie, and how I specifically trained her. She has brought me back from the brink of death several times. I'm so thankful for a friend who will come when I call and help me when I fall.

Gracie retrieved my computer bag. On the "sit" command waiting for the next request

It should be noted that I did consult with my veterinarian before embarking on the adventure of training Gracie to be a Service Dog. I also did much research and called many organizations connected to training service dogs including: The U.S. Department of Justice, Delta Society, IAADP, Paw-a-bility, Top Dogs, and several trainers. Essential to helping Gracie become a working dog was creating a plan, following the law, growing in our bond and trust, and making the best use of our time together. Also, please remember that a service animal is an animal trained specifically to help a person perform a task that they're not able to perform otherwise. Please do not take your pets into establishments that say "No Pets" and call it a service dog. It is illegal and considered fraud. For a more detailed list of tasks Gracie has been trained to perform for my particular disability, or for more information about service dogs and programs, please go to www.DianeDike.org Also, you may contact: www.deltasociety.org , www.iaadp.org , and the U.S. Dept. of Justice http://www.usdoj.gov/crt/ada/animal.htm, http://adionline.org/

Gracie waiting for my in the locker at the Vail Aria Club and Spa while I take a shower

MEDICAL INFORMATION

 The word "hope" I take for faith; and indeed hope is nothing else but the constancy of faith.

—John Calvin

Disease: What is It?

According to the Wikipedia, encyclopedia, "a disease is an abnormal condition of an organism that impairs bodily functions. In human beings, 'disease' is often used more broadly to refer to any condition that causes dysfunction, distress, social problems, and/or death to the person afflicted, or similar problems for those in contact with the person. In this broader sense, it sometimes includes infections. (Wikimedia, 2007).

What is Depression? Bipolar/Manic Depression

Everyone has times when they get down. Death, stress, and illness can all bring on depression. Most of us have moments of mild, temporary depression. But if it lasts more than two weeks and interferes with daily functioning, then a serious mental or mood disorder can result. In such cases the price tag of depression can be life itself.

When depression becomes the dark cloud that will not lift, when the color and meaning of life are darkened, clinical depression is often the result. The two most common forms of depression are unipolar and bipolar. The former is characterized by an unabated depressed state where patients lose all zest for life and often contemplate or even attempt suicide. Bipolar or, manic depression, is just as serious but is character-ized by drastic mood swings from extreme euphoria and hyperactivity to a loss of interest in life and suicidal ideation. Those who suffer with bipolar disorder can go as high as they can go low. It's a roller coaster of great pain, great happiness, great joy, great sadness, and too often leads to self-destructive behavior.

The Department of Health and Human Services lists some of the symptoms of depression as:

- A persistent sad or "empty" mood
- Feeling of hopelessness and pessimism
- Feelings of guilt, worthlessness, and helplessness
- Loss of interest or pleasure in ordinary activities
- Fatigue, decreased energy
- Sleep disturbances
- Loss or gain of appetite and weight
- Thoughts of death or suicide; suicide attempts
- Restlessness or irritability
- Difficulty concentrating, remembering, or making decisions
- Physical symptoms, including headaches, digestive disorders, and chronic pain, that don't respond to treatment

As you can see, depression is a serious illness with emotional, physical, and behavioral symptoms. Depression can make it difficult or impossible to work and disrupts social and family life. A combination of alcohol abuse and depression can lead to deadly results. Add mania to all that and you have chaos. Bipolar/manic depression can be characterized with excessive talking, racing thoughts, grandiose ideas, terrible decision-making, hypersexual behavior, and extravagant spending. It's irritating to me when professionals who have never experienced depression only prescribe pharmaceuticals, as though prescription drugs are the answer to the problem. Sometimes the drugs can mask the real problems that need to be dealt with and, even worse, have the opposite result of the desired effect. Depression, whether unipolar or bipolar, is an emotional, spiritual, physical, and behavioral problem that needs investigation.

Depressive tendencies with no apparent cause can be hereditary. Other causes can be influenced by hormone balance, premenstrual syndrome, and thyroid problems. Traumas such as illness, death, divorce, drug or alcohol abuse, and childbirth can lead to depression. I had to realize that I was not to blame. My depression started when I was a child. A child certainly does not deserve to be depressed.

Depression was a dark hole that I came to know intimately, and after a while, I was too tired to climb out. I needed someone willing to stick a hand down into the pit and pull me out. Jesus did that. I went to hell and came back realizing I can't always trust my feelings. If I feel unworthy and worthless, that does not mean that I am.

I have been on many antidepressants including: Prozac, Zoloft, Paxil, Wellbutrin, Effexor, Nardil, Elavil, Eskalith, and a powerful cocktail of anti-psychotic drugs. I called them my happy pills, but no matter how many I took, I didn't feel happy. The experts don't understand the long-term side effects of these drugs. Short-term effects for me were devastating. When I was on antidepressants I was more suicidal than when I was off them. Prescription drugs messed me up and I crossed over ungodly thresholds.

I held myself to impossible standards and was not satisfied with success or myself. I took everything personally and nothing ever seemed good enough. I thought that I had no friends; that no one cared, and was so afraid of the bad, that I shut out all the good too. I repeatedly self-sabotaged my life in a vicious cycle of dysfunction and punished myself on every turn. (Do you hear those tapes in my head?) I often thought I was a weirdo and that no one really liked me. I now know that I am diferent, who isn't? It's okay to be the one of a kind me, God made me to be.

For more information please go to Depression and Bipolar Support Alliance web site: http://www.ndmda.org/ and the Mental Health of America web site: http://www.nmha.org/go/about-us.

What is an Autoimmune Disease?

Autoimmune means the body is attacking itself. Autoimmunity is the result of a hypersensitive, overactive immune system. The immune system is supposed to protect the body by responding to invading microorganisms, such as germs, cancer, parasites, chemicals, bacteria, and viruses, by producing antibodies from white blood cells that will recognize and destroy foreign invaders. The American Autoimmune Related Diseases Association is a good resource for understanding the various types of this disease. Their web link is: http://www.aarda.org/. Also, NORD, National Organization of Rare Diseases is a good resource for learning about difficult to diagnose and treat diseases. The web link is: http://www.rare-diseases.org/. It's important for families who experience autoimmune problems to inform their doctors of the family history. There is a genetic component to many autoimmune diseases although such a predisposition alone does not seem to cause the autoimmune disease. Stress, viruses, bacteria, sun exposure, trauma, hormone fluctuation, chemical exposure, and allergies to food or pollutants can trigger this diseased state.

What is Fibromyalgia and TMJ?

Fibromyalgia is a syndrome characterized by the following symptoms and conditions: multiple tender points, fatigue, stiffness, non-restorative sleep, irritability, depression, impaired memory, headaches, dizziness, blurred vision, sensitivity to temperature change, irritable bowel syndrome (IBS), Temporomandibular Joint Stress (TMJ), teeth grinding, restless legs, cramps, itching, rash or dermatitis, and chronic aching. (Myo = muscle; algia = pain.) Today fibromyalgia is accepted as a distinct illness that affects about five percent of the population, with women outnumbering men, eight to one. At one time it was thought to be a type of rheumatism that afflicted people with hardened painful places. The symptoms can come and go, leaving the patient frustrated and confused and doctors thinking they are hypochondriacs. To be diagnosed with fibromyalgia, the patient must exhibit pain in at least eleven of eighteen trigger points. The onset of the condition is not always clear. Sometimes it results from an accident, the flu, other autoimmune diseases, repetitive strain, and inflammatory or degenerative problems. There is no known cure though it sometimes can be managed with medications, massage, appropriate exercise, maintaining body temperature, and reducing stress levels. To learn more about Fibromyalgia go to the National Fibromyalgia Association web site: http://www.fmaware.org/

Although it's generally not life threatening, except for the depression and suicidal ideation that can accompany it, fibromyalgia can significantly decrease quality of life and increase other health problems, lower immune system function, and impair social relationships. There are varying intensities of this syndrome from mild to severe. I have a severe case. The first signs of this problem and the teeth grinding occurred when I was fifteen and I used to beg my Mom to massage my back. I couldn't sleep at night and then all of the above began.

I don't know if the jaw grinding led to this problem, or if it just came along with fibromyalgia, but TMJ (Temporomandibular Joint Stress) has given me much discomfort over the years. My jaw often aches and can be particularly painful while eating or talking. The intense pain can radiate to under my ears and up the back of my skull, connecting back to my temples. It can make thinking clearly almost impossible and brings on headaches that can develop into migraines. My friend Robin enjoys a chuckle when I tell her I'm too tired to chew anymore. To learn more go to: the American Association of Oral and Maxillofacial

Surgeons http://www.aaoms.org/tmj.php and the American Dental Association web site: http://www.ada.org/public/topics/tmd_tmj.asp

What is Chronic Fatigue Syndrome (CFS)?

Chronic Fatigue Syndrome (CFS) and/or Epstein-Barr Virus (EBV) can lie dormant inside body cells for years, and then, under certain conditions of immune dysfunction, emerge and cause a variety of troublesome symptoms. Some of the symptoms can include debilitating fatigue, headaches, depression, low-grade fevers, poor concentration, sleep disturbance, body aches and pains, and other flu like symptoms. Factors that contribute to CFS are trace mineral imbalances; poisoning with metals; hypoglycemia (low blood sugar); food and chemical sensitivities; exposure to toxins; heart disease; cancer; surgery; autoimmunity and so on. I've had a difficult encounter with all of the above. According to the Center for Disease Control and Prevention "More than 1 million Americans suffer from Chronic Fatigue Syndrome." To learn more go to: http://www.cdc.gov/cfs/

What is Endometriosis?

Endometriosis is a painful condition that affects a woman's uterus. Internal blisters can build until they erupt and cause much pain and scarring. In my case I became feverish, clammy, and then passed out; vomiting and irritable bowels usually accompanied such episodes. Because of this affliction, my menses could be very debilitating. My flow would suddenly stop and a stabbing pain would ensue until I was overcome. I would then have to take strong pain medicine and go to bed with a heating pad for a few hours. The blister like pouches of blood would then burst and flow would follow; although very fatigued, I could function again. The blisters can cause significant scarring and lead to infertility. I finally had to have a complete hysterectomy on March 31, 1999. This decision was a painful one. However, my doctors had recommended that I not have children because of the cryoglobulinemia that could cause complications to both the child and me. Now, I'm on natural hormone replacement therapy.

Also see: http://www.medicinenet.com/endometriosis/article.htm

What is Costrochondritis?

Costrochondritis is a stabbing or constant chest pain that runs along the sternum and into the rib cage. It feels like you are having a heart attack and it's hard to breathe. My holistic doctor can usually find the main hot spot, and apply pressure to the inflamed connective tissue, bringing relief. I have found that episodes of costrochondritis can be brought on by stressing the area through lifting weights or children, a virus, coughing, breathing cold air, poor posture, and gas. The anti-inflammatory and prednisone medications I have been prescribed are hard on my stomach, exacerbate my cryoglobulinemia, and give me hives. Thus, they are not a good option.

What is Polyarticular Arthritis?

PA is an arthritis that affects more than five joints. There are two kinds: one with rheumatoid factor and one without. Thankfully, doctors believe I have the one without. Arthritis pain in my joints and its severity depend on stress levels, and the amount of time I spend standing or am immobilized from my other conditions

What is Raynaud's Phenomenon and Purpura?

Raynaud's phenomenon (RP) (ra-NODES) is an autoimmune vascular disorder caused by spasm of blood vessels in response to a person being exposed to either hot or cold temperatures, or emotional stress. The symptoms I've experienced include aching pain, tingling, itching, prickly feeling, feeling cold, numbness, loss of color, and turning blue. Purpura refers to the red and purple spots that appear on the skin because of the rupture of blood vessels nearest to the surface of the skin. It results in blood and plasma appearing under the surface of the skin, mucous membranes, and lungs, sometimes breaking through into sores that heal with difficulty. Purpura is a common symptom of vascular bleeding disorders, which is characterized by increased bruising and fragile vessels throughout the body. My fingers, hands, toes, feet, and legs turn all colors of blue and purple with white spotting. It hurts, and it's not very pretty.

To learn more go to:

http://www.medicinenet.com/raynauds_phenomenon/article.htm
http://www.arthritis.org/conditions/DiseaseCenter/raynauds.asp

What is Neuropathy?

Neuropathy is a condition that results in inexplicable pain and numbness to various parts of the body due to a dysfunctional nervous system. Neuropathy affects my cardiovascular system by interfering with nerve impulses that regulate my blood pressure and heart rate. When my blood pressure drops after sitting or standing, it often causes me to feel dizzy or faint. Experiencing autonomic neuropathy and angina or chest pains that could be a warning sign of heart disease has come along with it. When an episode occurs, I take a nitroglycerin pill. According to the Mayo clinic some complications can include:

- Injuries from falls caused by lowered blood pressure when you stand
- Mental and physical fatigue due to low blood pressure
- Malnutrition and weight loss from digestive system difficulties
- Fluid or electrolyte imbalance from excessive vomiting or diarrhea, a condition in which your body loses minerals you need
- Relationship problems due to sexual dysfunction
- Urinary problems, including urinary tract infection
- Cardiovascular complications, such as irregular heartbeat (arrhythmia)
- Kidney failure from bladder problems that aren't treated properly

(Mayo, 2007)

Neuropathy complicates all of my medical conditions in the cruelest way. When nerve damage affects the activity of the sweat glands, it makes it difficult for the body to regulate temperature. This would be bad enough in itself but when accompanied by a blood disease that makes me hypersensitive to temperature changes, I truly don't know whether I am coming or going most of the time. If I stand too long or get up too quickly after sitting, I get drenched with sweat and feel faint. Then, nausea sets in and the stomach pain increases. My body is in a constant state of fight or flight and it's amazing to me how it carries on. Other times, I wake in the night to profuse sweating. Eating, sleeping, walking, talking, thinking... I can't think of anything that is not affected by these sensations that overwhelm my body.

We've thought since nerve damage can affect digestion. My stomach sometimes empties too slowly which often causes my blood sugar levels to fluctuate. I experience persistent nausea, gas and bloating and irritable bowel disease is an ongoing challenge.

I experience peripheral neuropathy that has damaged the nerves of my limbs. The sensations can be overwhelming at times including: numbness, tingling, burning, cramping, extreme sensitivity to touch, and the list goes on. The most insidious effect is that I often can't even feel my extremities getting cold which is dangerous because of cryoglobulinemia. Extremely vulnerable to changes in temperature is where Gracie has been instrumental in helping me mitigate this situation by keeping my internal temperature constant and alerting me to drops in environmental temperatures.

What is Vasculitis

Vasculitis is known as the "hurting disease." It results from inflammation of the blood vessel walls. Arteries and veins in all parts of the body may be affected. Patients can feel sick, fatigued, have a fever, rapid pulse, diffused aches and pains, nerve infarctions, pain from insufficient blood to the extremities, generalized weakness, and skin ulcers. It may result in damage to the skin, joints, lungs, kidneys, blood, eyes, brain, nerves, sinuses, nose and ears, and the gastrointestinal tract. Complications from vasculitis can include stroke, blindness (uveitis), and aneurysms. I have had sores in my nose for the past ten years. My nose aches, bleeds, and feels raw daily, like it's rotting away. Before I moved to Colorado, I had ulcerated sores on my legs for over two years. My friend used to squeeze vitamin E capsules into them to try and get them to heal. They would start to look better after resting during the night but, by the end of the day, they would open, oozing puss and gunk again. The little red spots that mysteriously appear on my legs often break through the skin and become sores. Healing even from a paper cut can take weeks. For more information go to http://vasculitis.med.jhu.edu/whatis/symptoms.html Also: http://www.answers.com/topic/vasculitis

What is Cryoglobulinemia?

Cryoglobulinemia has many painful, scary symptoms. I have a high tolerance for pain, but this exhaustive list of sensations can get the best of me. I find it difficult to concentrate, follow directions, and I tire eas-

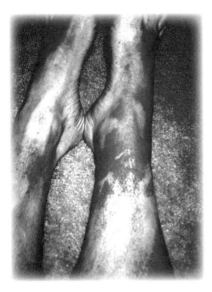

ily. On an average day I experience some or all the following symptoms:

• Swelling of hands, ankles, legs and feet
• Feet hurt to walk on-like walking on shells or rocks most all the time and worse when an episode is flaring the condition.
• Scaly head and face (dermatitis, psoriasis, candida)
• Depression (mild to severe)
• Leg and arm heaviness
• Runny nose (blowing and coughing episodes)

- Allergies (stuffed up ears and nose)
- Swollen glands in throat, armpits, and groin
- Weight loss, muscle loss, poor appetite
- Low blood pressure, high heart rate, cardiac spasms
- Swelling in joints, connective tissue and especially hands, legs, ankles, feet with extreme neck stiffness and pain
- Numbness, tingling, or weakness in the hands, arms, legs, and feet
- Pitted ulcers in my nose (with bleeding), mouth, skin, and slow-healing sores, blood in urine
- Gastrointestinal pain, irritable bowel with periodic bloody stool
- Intense muscle and bone pain
- Floaters (black spots in eyes), halo vision, dry eyes
- Episodes of cryoglobulinemia colitis with intestinal bleeding.

Go to www.DianeDike.com to find our web site for more information, further pictures, and related links.

Since I created my educational web site, others who suffer with cryoglobulinemia have confirmed this long list of symptoms. Many have lost parts of their bodies due to this insidious disease, as well, the quality of there life is greatly diminished Still some only have this as a secondary disease managing it well enough. I try to stay away from processed foods, sugar and MSG. Eating fresh fruits, veggies, fish and lean meat and organic as much as possible. I take many health products, fish oil and get massages regularly. These along with other methods mentioned help me to manage this disease pretty well so far.

As I understand it, the test for cryoglobulinemia is very sensitive. If they don't do it exactly it right, it will come up negative. They have to draw the blood into a tube that is at body temperature or they will lose the globulins. Then they must keep it at body temp for an hour and check it several times. A hematologist recently told me I must have a Complete Blood Count done at body temp too. Otherwise, it can cause false readings on platelet count, white blood count, and several other items.

To see further effects of this disease, and to understand the importance of taking care of and limiting the outbreaks go to: http://www.endoskopischer-atlas.de/k39ae.htm. It is important to limit fare-ups as much as possible and why I use the wheelchair to elevate my legs and feet, and take extreme measures to limit temperature changes.

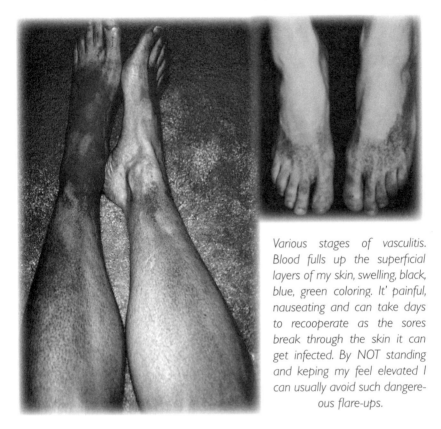

Various stages of vasculitis. Blood fulls up the superficial layers of my skin, swelling, black, blue, green coloring. It' painful, nauseating and can take days to recooperate as the sores break through the skin it can get infected. By NOT standing and keping my feel elevated I can usually avoid such dangere-ous flare-ups.

What is Cryoglobulinemia Colitis?

This is much like ulcerated colitis. It hits me most often when I am exposed to internal and external temperature changes. If I sit on something cold, stand too long, sit too long, eat food not completely cooked, etc. I can experience profuse bleeding, cramps, inflammation, and pain, sometimes requiring hospitalization.

Again, since having Gracie, I experience this condition less frequently and have not been hospitalized once. It's effects are similar to Chrohn's Disease. To see what it looks like, visit this web site: http://www.endoskopischer-atlas.de/k39e.htm

What are the lymphocytes that indicate a lymphoproliferative disorder?

Not all lymphocytes are the same. An increase of lymphocytes in the blood can occur because of a viral infection such as Epstein-Barr virus infection or caused by Lymphoproliferative disorders (LPD). LPD and increased levels of lymphocytes is more serious when combined with a dysfunctional immune system. Some examples of an LPD according to Wikipedia encyclopedia include: leukemia, acute lymphoblastic leukemia, multiple myeloma, hairy cell leukemia and autoimmune lymphoproliferative syndrome (ALPS). The outcome can be deadly and at the very least challenging.

Summary-Life

The above list of diseases and syndromes can be overwhelming. I include them since I was diagnosed with each of them at one time or another and deal with their symptoms. I also included them because I know that many readers may be experiencing one or several of them right now or know someone who is. The one thing they all have in common is the impact they have on their victim's physical, emotional, and spiritual well being. It's vital for those of us who suffer from chronic illness to reach for meaning in the events that have disrupted our lives. Such meaning helps us to see in the darkness closes in and strengthens our will to live by helping us come to know more intimately who we are and what is really important to us. Over time, meaning, hope, and love can heal many things that are beyond a cure. People who have viewed themselves as victims may be surprised to realize they are heroes. I spent years dreaming of a safe place even envying the turtle's ability to pull it's extremities under the safety of a hard shell, never to go out again until it is safe. However, I am determined never to live that way again. Each day I will climb my mountain thankful for whatever picture God paints for me to see. *This section in no way is meant to take the place of seeking professional medical help

Mom is fighting multiple myeloma cancer

SECOND CHANCE WITH SAVING GRACE

*If you judge people,
you have no time to love them.*

—Mother Teresa

Second Chance with Saving Grace, our non-profit organization is receiving tax-deductible donations. We are a team working together to make a positive difference in the world by visiting schools, children in hospitals, prisoners, churches, and other organizations with our message of HOPE and ENCOURAGEMENT; as well as, educating businesses on disability

awareness and etiquette as it relates to the treatment of people who utilize service animals. If you would like to schedule a visit or presentation to your establishment, please contact us on our web site, www. DianeDike.org.

Our Mission: Educate, Enrich and Encourage! We help people and animals grow from brokenness to wholeness, with Love!

The Importance Of Reading!

Research has proven that reading difficulties and illiteracy contribute to school failure and drop-outs, increasing absenteeism, juvenile delinquency, crime, teen pregnancy, drug use and other problems that impact our community. Studies have shown one of the easiest ways to increase literacy among pre-school and school age children is to read to them. So Gracie and Diane created the audio version of *Gracie Comes Home* so they can read to children every day!

Reading Gracie's story to children and teaching them about Service Dogs

Colleen and Rick Gardner of the Gardner Foundation at the Dell Children's Hospital where they donated Gracie books and Gracie Babies to sick children

Helping Hand Home for Children, in TX where the Gardner Foundation donated sixty books to the children during our special story time

Project Cuddle

Through project Cuddle, an outreach program that connects with at-risk children suffering from abuse, abandonment, illness or who are hurting in any way. Gracie, Paul and Diane mail and/or hand-deliver "Love Kits." A love kit includes: a personal note; a copy of *Gracie Comes Home*, Book One of the children's series, *The Adventures of Gracie and Diane*; a t-shirt depicting the cover of Gracie's book or her "Aviator" picture; an audio CD of *Gracie Comes Home* including fun sound effects; a Gracie beanie baby and a handy bag to carry all the gifts in or hook on to the back of their wheelchairs. We do the same for adults. Instead of the Gracie Book we send, *God Made Only One of Me*.

We Will Advertise You!

Donations to help us with this important work of $1,000 or more can be recognized on the t-shirts, in the books, and on the web site. (Please include a business card or logo information if you would like to be recognized). If your troop, civic group, school or organization would like to know how to become an **Ambassador of Love** and join our team helping us deliver these gifts in your home town, please contact us.

SCwSG c/o Diane Dike
P.O. Box 673
Eagle, CO 81631

or online www.DianeDike.org

We are thankful for our supporters and we will gladly send a thank you band to all who would like one and the best part is-it glows in the dark! Wearing this band is a symbol of your commitment to be a light in the darkness!

If you need help with a fund-raiser we have programs to support you. Be watching for cuddle blankets and other projects coming soon!

Thank you for your prayers and support!

Gracie &
Brownie

A New Life in Christ!

*For a small reward, a man will hurry away
on a long journey; while for eternal life,
many will hardly take a single step.*

—Thomas à Kempis

"Who am I? Why am I here? Where will I go when I die? What must I do to be saved?" Are questions that need to be answered by each of us. Have you felt adrift with the pressures, the winds, and waves of life stressing your rope of hope? When troubles rage, God is an anchor you can count on. I know there is a place of peace and hope, no matter what is going on around you. When life doesn't make sense you can have hope in the midst of your storm, in the midnight hour, and when you have muddled up your life. Jesus' invitation has stood for 2,000 years to whomever will come to Him but you only have your lifetime to step out in faith and accept His offer of grace. What are you waiting for?

The author of confusion, Satan, tries to corrupt the simplicity of the gospel message by making it seem as though faith is not enough. He plays into our desire to be in control and our need to earn our salvation, something none of us is capable of doing. Salvation is achieved by faith—the other things will fall into place as you grow in your relationship with Jesus Christ. It's all about Him, there is nothing for us to boast about. Do not let fear and guilt become a disability that keep you away from the promises of God and the good plans He has to bring meaning to your life. No matter who you are, what age you are, or what strengths and weaknesses you have, He is waiting for you. You have a Savior who loves you, died for you, and is awaiting your arrival in Heaven. God's Word, the Bible, provides clear answers to many of your questions; for the rest, you have to have faith that He will do what is best for you.

Let's look at what the Word says. If you once gave your life to the Lord and have fallen away from a personal relationship with Him, I pray your will rededicate your life to Him today and get reconnected. Email me or write to me and let me know your decision! *—Diane*

Acknowledge Your Sin

"But the tax collector stood at a distance. He would not even look up to heaven, but beat his breast and said, 'God, have mercy on me, a sinner.'"- Luke 18:13

"for all have sinned and fall short of the glory of God," -Romans 3:23

Repent

"Repent, then, and turn to God, so that your sins may be wiped out, that times of refreshing may come from the Lord" -Acts 3:19

"...except ye repent, ye shall all likewise perish." -Luke 13:3 KJV

Confess Your Sin

"That if you confess with your mouth, "Jesus is Lord," and believe in your heart that God raised him from the dead, you will be saved." -Romans 10:9

"If we confess our sins, he is faithful and just to forgive us our sins, and to cleanse us from all unrighteousness." -1 John 1:9 KJV

Forsake The Past

"Let the wicked forsake his way, and the unrighteous man his thoughts: and let him return unto the LORD, and He will have mercy upon him; and to our God, for He will abundantly pardon." -Isaiah 55:7 KJV

Believe On The Lord For Your Salvation

"For God so loved the world, that He gave His only begotten Son, that whosoever believeth in Him should not perish, but have everlasting life." -John 3:16 KJV

"Jesus answered, "I am the way and the truth and the life. No one comes to the Father except through me." -John 14:6

Receive The Gift Of Eternal Life

"He came unto His own, and His own received Him not. But as many as received Him, to them gave He power to become the sons of God, even to them that believe on His name." -John 1:11-12 KJV

If you declare with your mouth, "Jesus is Lord, and believe in your heart that God raised Him from the dead, you will be saved. -Romans 10:9 KJV

If you have not made your eternal decision, you can make it right now! It is so profound, so eternal, yet in many cases, so simple. Give your life to the Prince of Peace, and His peace will open doors for you that No one can shut! He'll take you places that you've only dreamed of. Please pray this prayer right now:

> **"Lord Jesus, I believe You died for my sins and I'm sorry for all the things I've done wrong. I ask You to forgive me. I receive You now as my personal friend and Savior. Teach me to think and live your way. Amen."**

Immediately, you are equipped with everything you need to fulfill your passion and purpose in this life. All you have to do is walk in it and continually seek Him! The angels are rejoicing for you, right now! Yahoo! As your relationship grows you will realize God has given you the gift of a new life of peace and victory. You are now connected with the peace that surpasses all human understanding. By faith, receive what God has already done for YOU! God promises that joy is found in His presence, and if you've accepted Jesus as your Lord and Savior, then His presence lives inside of you! Focus your mind and heart on the Father and begin to praise Him for what He's done, doing, and going to do in your life. He inhabits the praises of His people. His presence will manifest wherever we are and the enemy cannot loom over us in the presence of our Mighty God! Don't let the cares and worries and stresses of this life overwhelm you! Learn about and obey the Word of God. Walk with Him, and His purposes will become clearer. As a result you will live a fruitful, abundant life. Your helmet of salvation will protect you from the enemy's lies and you will live the life of strength and victory God has in store for you!

What do you need that you do not have? Do you need restoration, healing, deliverance, faith... ? Worship Him. When you do, things will change and your perspective will improve. Not only will you become more effective and wiser, but you will also become more emotionally steady. You will make powerful decisions based on truth. Who doesn't need that? You say, Diane, how do you know this? Because I lived it and what He did for me, He wants to do for you! This is exciting stuff!

Let's thank Him and praise Him together. *"Lord, we worship You right now! Be glorified today in our act of obedience and love. You are a good and faithful God. We thank You for working in our lives today. We need You. We are nothing without You. Thank You for dying for each one of us. We want to bless You today with all that we are, all that we think and all that we do. Thank You for hearing our every prayer. We want to be like You. In the gracious and honorable name of Jesus we pray.* (Can I hear a resounding) *Amen!*

Just know that every tsunami will eventually retreat, every cloudy sky will clear, and every tornado's wind will calm. He will guide you into safe harbors once again. You have a special journey to make. Like Gracie and me you are one of a kind. When God created you He went to great lengths to make you exactly the way He wanted you to be. I encourage you to make your life a living tribute to Him by realizing your value, and not only who you are, but also Whose you are, then your very existence will give God praise. Gracie does that by just being the wonderful dog that God created her to be. You, too, can honor God by accepting who you are and making the decision to be the best you can be. Faith is a gift from God, but trusting is a choice only you can make.

There could be warning signs that a tsunami is heading your way. It's time to leave the self-destructive disastrous ways of sin and disobedience behind. Go to higher ground where God's forgiving grace can keep you safe. Get up every morning and say: "I'm the apple of God's eye. I'm His masterpiece and He is counting on me! Nothing is too hard for Him and He loves me." Regardless of your swirling circumstances, if you learn to have the correct viewpoint about who you are, then you will live a life of victory and that is what God wants for you. Sometimes the worst that happens to us can open the door for the best that God has in store for us.

The enemy's lies may try to crash on the shores of your mind but he will have NO power to torment you anymore! God wants you to experience His endless supply of supernatural joy, peace, and strength no matter what! Don't waste another minute feeling overburdened and discouraged. Enjoy a permanent perspective of eternal hope in God's harbor of goodness and purpose for your life. Let the joy of the Lord be your strength, and you will live in victory on the path of life He's prepared for you! What do you say? What are you waiting for? You have everything to gain and nothing to loose. Let's get to it! The ship is about to leave the harbor for the greatest adventure of your life... All aboard! Char-Ching, another pearl!

Sing to the LORD, bless His name; Proclaim the good news of His salvation from day to day. —Psalm 96:2

BIBLIOGRAPHICAL NOTES

*Be joyful in hope, patient in
affliction, faithful in prayer.*

—Romans 12:12

Abbott, Elliot. Penny Marshall. (1992). *A League of Their Own.* United States: Columbia Pictures.

Alexander, Eric. (2003). *Farther Than the Eye Can See.* Serac Adventure Films Seewww.highersummits.com Vail, Colorado. For bookings-Ken Davis Productions, Brian Scheer, brian@highersummits.com 615-599-8955.

Caidin, Martin. *The Six Million Dollar Man.* (1974-1978). ABC, United States. A spin-off of the show was produced *http://en.wikipedia. org/wiki/The_Bionic_Woman" \o "The Bionic Woman" The Bionic Woman.*

Calvary Chapel San Bernardino. *Quotes about the Bible.* http://www. calvarysbd.com/quotes_bible.htm" http://www.calvarysbd.com/ quotes_bible.htm

Caras, Roger. (2007). *Welcome to the Quote Garden!* http://www.quote-garden.com/dogs.html" http://www.quotegarden.com/dogs.html accessed May 23, 2007.

Chapman, Steven Curtis. (1997). *I Will Be There.* Greatest Hits, Sparrow.

Crowe, Cameron. (1996). *Jerry Maguire.* United States: Gracie Films.

Chrichton, Michael. (1993-2007). *Quotes About Life.* Famous Quotes and Famous Sayings Network.http://quotations.home.worldnet. att.net/life.html. Accessed June 9, 2007.

Denver, John. Milt Okun. (1972). *Rocky Mountain High.* http://www.cdun-iverse.com/sresult.asp?style=music&HT_Search=xlabel&HT_ Search_Info=RCA+Records+%28USA%29" RCA Records (USA).

Elliot, Elisabeth. (2005). *Back to the Bible, Gateway To Joy.* Daily Christian Quote. http://dailychristianquote.com/dcqelliot.html June 3, 2007.

Flint, Annie Johnson (2001). *Wealth of Oath.* http://www.wellofoath.com/home.asp?pg=Bios&toc=Annie+Johnson+Flint Accessed June 2, 2007.

Finerman, Wendy; Robert Zemeckis. (1994). *Forest Gump.* USA. Paramount Pictures.

Fosdick, Harry Emerson. (2007). *Secrets of Success.* http://www.secretsof-success.com/article/quotes_success4.html Accessed June 11, 2007.

Gary Chapman (2004). *The Five Love Languages: How to Express Heartfelt Commitment to Your Mate* (new edition). Northfield Press.

Gaither, Gloria. *Quotes about Chance.* *Zaadz Newsletters.* http://quotes.zaadz.com/quotes/topics/chance?page=25 Accessed June 1, 2007.

Gandhi, Mahatma. 2005-2006. *The God Light.* http://www.thegodlight.co.uk/gandhi.htm Accessed June 10, 2007.

Gordon, Nancy. 2006. *Paws for Comfort.* http://pawsforcomfort.com/site/node/15. Accessed June 10, 2007.

Gordon, Nancy. 2002. *The Healing Power of Puppy Love. http://fmaware.org/patient/coping/puppylove.htm* Accessed June 10, 2007.

Graham, Billy. Word of Life Study Guide by John Paul Miller. Pg. 22. http://www.calvarysbd.com/pdf/phil03.pdf. Accessed June 1, 2007.

Hand, David, and Felix Salten and Larry Morey. 1942. *Bambi.* Walt Disney Productions.

Hooke, S.H. 1941. *Bible in Basic English.* (BBE) USA: Cambridge University Press Online address: http://www.o-bible.com/bbe.html.

Johnson, Kenneth. 1976-1978. *The Bionic Women.* United States: American Broadcasting Company, ABC.

Lewis, C.S. http://thinkexist.com/quotation/love-anything-and-your-heart-will-be-wrung-and/347988.html . Last accessed January, 24, 2008.

Lucado, Max. (2004). *God Came Near.* Thomas Nelson.

MacArthur, John F. 1997. The MacArthur Study Bible, *How We Got The Bible.* (Dallas: Word Publishing) - Public Domain.

Manchester, Melissa. "http://www.secondhandsongs.com/artist/1674" Peter Allen, Carole Bayer Sager (1978) *Don't Cry Out Loud.* Don't Cry Out Loud. "http://www.cduniverse.com/sresult. asp?style=music&HT_Search=xlabel&HT_Search_Info=Wounde d+Bird&cart=548566685" Arista.

Mayo Clinic Staff. 2007. Tools for healthier lives. Nervous System. Mayo Foundation for Medical Education and Research. http://www. mayoclinic.com/health/AboutThisSite/AM00057. Apr 13, 2006

Powell, Colin. 2007. *Secrets of Success.* http://www.secretsofsuccess.com/ article/quotes_success4.html Accessed June 11, 2007.

Reddy, Helen. (1974). *You and Me Against the World* Love Songs for Jeffrey. USA. Capital.

Roach, John. (2005). Journal Ranks Top 25 Unanswered Science Questions. http://news.nationalgeographic.com Accessed July 7, 2005.

Rogers, Kenny. (1994). *She Believes In Me.* Twenty Greatest Hits. Capital Records.

Scripture taken from The Message. (MSG) Copyright © 1993, 1994, 1995, 1996, 2000, 2001, 2002. Used by permission of NavPress Publishing Group.

Scripture quotations taken from the Amplified® Bible (AMP)Copyright © 1954, 1958, 1962, 1964, 1965, 1987 by The Lockman Foundation Used by permission. (www.Lockman.org)

Scripture taken from the New American Standard Bible®, (NASB) Copyright © 1960,1962,1963,1968,1971,1972,1973,1975,1977,199 5 by The Lockman Foundation. Used by permission.

Scripture taken from the New King James Version. (NKJV) Copyright © 1982 by Thomas Nelson, Inc. Used by permission. All rights reserved.

Silverstein, Shel (1964). *The Giving Tree.* Harper & Row Publishers, New York.

Smith, Michael W. (1990) *Place in This World.* Go West Young Man. Reunion Records.

Smith, Michael W., Debbie Smith. (1983). *Friends.* Michael W. Smith Project. Reunion Records.

Stott, Jeffrey and Steve Nicolaides. http://www.imdb.com/name/ nm0001661/ Rob Reiner. (1992). *A Few Good Men.* USA: http:// en.wikipedia.org/wiki/Castle_Rock_Entertainment \o Castle Rock Entertainment" Castle Rock Entertainment, http://en.wikipedia. org/wiki/Columbia_Pictures" \o Columbia Pictures

Take My Hand: Song by The Kry, From their album "YOU", Copyrighted 1994, Le Kri Music Inc/ BMI, Malaco Records/ BMI All rights reserved. Used by permission from Jean-Luc Lajoie.

The Modern Language Bible: (1969). The New Berkely Version in Modern English, Zondervan Publishing House.

Walsh, Sheila. (1999). *Life Is Tough But God Is Faithful.* Nashville, Tennessee, Thomas Nelson, Inc.

Warren, Rick. (2002). *The Purpose Driven Life.* Zondervan, Grand Rapids, Michigan.

Webster, John David. (2005). *Miracle.* Made to Shine. USA: BHT Records Blanton/Harrell Entertainment, Inc. Word Distribution.

Wikimedia Project. (2007). *Wikipedia, the Free Encyclopedia.* WikipediaÆ is a registered trademark of the http://www.wikimediafounda- tion.org Wikimedia Foundation, Inc.

Williams, Bern. (2007). Welcome to the Quote Garden! http://www. quotegarden.com/dogs.html accessed May 23, 2007.

Various quotes used in this book can be found on:
http://en.thinkexist.com/quotation

For Further Information:

The Invisible Disabilities Advocate®
www.InvisibleDisabilities.org
Helping People Understand Chronic Illness and Pain.

But You LOOK Good! - Booklet
A Guide to Understanding and Encouraging People Living with Chronic Illness and Pain. www.ButYouLookGood.org

Where Is God MinistriesSM
www.WhereIsGod.net
Finding God's Strength Amidst Chronic Illness and Pain.

Bibliographical Notes

Not By Sight - Booklet
A Guide to Ministering to
Believers Living with
Chronic Illness and Pain.
www.NotBySight.net

Again, Second Chance with Saving Gracie, Inc. and Dr. Diane Dike would like to honor all those who work to make the world a better place through random acts of kindness in soup kitchens, nursing homes, in adoption programs, those who teach, and work to help those in need or those who are less fortunate.

As well as those rescue groups who work tirelessly to rescue animals in need. You are a light in the darkness and we would like to send you our Gracie Glow-in-the-dark band as a thank you gift.

This is a picture of the Orlando Italian Greyhound meet up group. Many of the IGs were rescued and given the opportunity to live out happy lives with much love. If we can help support your efforts please contact us. Also, join Gracie's Challenge, our goal is for no person or dog to be left behind! We believe there is enough love in this world for ALL of us! We've developed fundraising programs to help you..

FINALE

Spread love everywhere you go.
Let no one ever come to you
without leaving happier.

—Mother Teresa

By Third Day

None of us in the band were aware of your conditions even after all that time out on tour. Needless to say, we were very moved after I clicked on the link and read your story and what is happening with you. I was taken aback by your amazing testimony.

We wanted to express our concern and let you know that we are inspired by your courage and your attitude. We lifted you, Paul and Gracie up tonight as we prayed before our show. We are currently out on tour supporting the album "Wherever You Are" which is a project about the struggles of life, the trials that bring us to our knees and the

heart of God in the midst of it all. So, your story was very humbling and reminded us of the message we are giving and the importance of remembering those who are living it!

Thank you for filling us in and we will continue to think of and pray for you all. I am honored that you would use my note in your book. I hope you are doing well today and your spirits are high. I still remember your lively personality and smile, even as we would pass in the hallways of all those arenas! You have a remarkable story to tell and one that I know will bring hope to many. May God truly bless you and Paul and may He continue to increase peace and joy in you both.

Peace,

David Carr and the rest of Third Day

Tai Anderson (Third Day) and me looking strong and courageous

Enjoy Other Books By This Author

Book one in, *The Adventures of Gracie and Diane* series:

✿ *Gracie Comes Home* also with audio of Gracie and Diane reading

✿ Soft cover Spanish and English version

✿ Book two in *The Adventures of Gracie and Diane* series: *Gracie Discovers Her Purpose*- Soon to be released!

✿ *God Made Only One of Me Devotional Journal*: Soon to be released!

✿ Dissertation available-UMI number 9840083 Copyright 1996. Order from UMI Services 1-800-521-0600. *A Study of Adolescent Depression, Suicide, Self-Esteem and Family Strength in Special Education Female Students Compared with Regular Education Female Students* by Diane Joan Provencher Harper. Doctor of Philosophy Dissertation Human Services Track with Specialization in Counseling Psychology. Walden University Minneapolis, Minnesota Institute for Advanced Studies May 1996.

Enjoy Other Merchandise

✿ Plush Gracie Beanie Babies
✿ Aviator Gracie & *Gracie Comes Home* Book Cover T-shirts
✿ *The Adventures of Gracie and Diane* tote bag

✿Join "Gracie's Challenge" Glow-in-the-dark wrist bands. Free with a donation of any amount. We are thankful for our supporters and we will gladly send a thank you band to all who would like one. Wearing this band is a symbol of your commitment to *be a light in the darkness!*

✿ A "Love Kit:" includes a Book w/ audio, Gracie Baby, T-shirt, and a personal note all in a handy tote bag.

❀ Thank you for your support. The funds raised by your purchase of Gracie merchandise enable us to deliver "Love Kits" to sick or hurting people across the globe. We also support animal rescue groups. Mother Teresa said, "If you can't feed a hundred people, then feed just one." Thank you for helping *Second Chance with Saving Grace* feed children, animals, and people with the message of hope and encouragement that is embodied in this book and Gracie's story.

Quantity discounts available

To order more copies of this book please go to: www.DianeDike.org

To Contact This Author

If this book has encouraged you, we would like to hear about it. To order additional books, to schedule Gracie and Diane to speak for your organization, become an "Ambassador of Love," or to find out more information, please contact:

DianeDike@aol.com

Diane Dike, Ph.D.
P.O. Box 673
Eagle, Colorado 81631

Be sure to keep up with us our web site, share it with your friends and come visit us if we are in your area:

www.DianeDike.org

Carpe Diem

♥ One final note friend (in case no one has ever told you) ♥

Promise me you'll always remember: You're braver than you believe, and stronger than you seem, and smarter than you think.

—Christopher Robin, to Pooh